Translation and

Subjectivity

PUBLIC WORLDS

Edited by Dilip Gaonkar and Benjamin Lee

N A O K I S A K A I

Translation and

Subjectivity

On "Japan" and

Cultural Nationalism

Foreword by Meaghan Morris

PUBLIC WORLDS, VOLUME 3

UNIVERSITY OF MINNESOTA PRESS

MINNEAPOLIS LONDON

Chapter 1 first appeared in Japanese translation in *Gendai Shisô*, no. 859 (January 1996): 250–78; reprinted with acknowledgment of Iwanami Shoten and by permission of the author. Chapter 2 first appeared in *Shakai Kagaku no Hôbô*, vol. 3 (Tokyo: Iwanami Shoten, 1993), pp. 1–37; reprinted with acknowledgment of Iwanami Shoten and by permission of the author. Chapter 3 first appeared in *boundary 2*, vol. 18, no. 3 (fall 1991): 157–90, and in Japanese translation in *Shisô*, no. 797 (November 1990): 102–36; reprinted by permission of Duke University Press and with acknowledgment of Iwanami Shoten and the author. Chapter 4 first appeared in *Discours social/Social Discourse*, vol. 6, nos. 1–2 (1994): 89–114, and in Japanese translation in *Jôkyô II*, vol. 3, no. 10 (December 1992): 82–117; reprinted with acknowledgment of Jôkyô Publishers, Tokyo, and by permission of the author. Chapter 5 first appeared in *South Atlantic Quarterly*, vol. 87, no. 3 (summer 1988): 475–504, and in Japanese translation in *Gendai Shisô*, vol. 15-15 (December 1987): 184–207; reprinted by permission of Duke University Press and with acknowledgment of Seito-sha, Tokyo, and by permission of the author. Chapter 6 first appeared in *Sengo Nihon no Seishin-shi* (Tokyo: Iwanami Shoten, 1988), pp. 310–34; reprinted with acknowledgment of Iwanami Shoten and by permission of the author.

Published by the University of Minnesota Press
111 Third Avenue South, Suite 290, Minneapolis, MN 55401–2520
Printed in the United States of America on acid-free paper
http://www.upress.umn.edu

Second Printing, 1999

Library of Congress Cataloging-in-Publication Data

Sakai, Naoki, 1946–
    Translation and subjectivity : on Japan and cultural nationalism /
Naoki Sakai ; Foreword by Meaghan Morris.
        p.   cm. — (Public worlds) : v. 3)
    Includes index.
    ISBN 0-8166-2862-9 (alk. paper). — ISBN 0-8166-2863-7 (pbk. : alk. paper)
    1. Japan—Intellectual life.   I. Title.   II. Series.
    DS821.S2413   1997
    952—dc21   97-11443
                                                                       CIP

≈

For Gail

Contents

Foreword

Meaghan Morris

In a previous book by Naoki Sakai, *Voices of the Past: The Status of Language in Eighteenth-Century Japanese Discourse*, there is a wonderful passage about a subject with which I am entirely unacquainted, the ethics of Itô Jinsai—a seventeenth-century Confucian scholar and critic of Song rationalism—that disconcerts and delights me with a sense of partial familiarity. Expounding the conception of sociality in the Song philosophy of mind, Sakai notes that the primordial agreement of Zhu Xi's ideal community assumed "a transparency of communication comparable to the face of a clear mirror" secured by subduing the "dust" of materiality, the "trace" (in Itô Jinsai's terms) of all the accidents, surprises, blockages, and sheer bodily energy of actual social encounters: "as though incommensurability ought not to have been there, as though it were somewhat outrageous and morbid to admit that one cannot actually know another's mind."[1]

More than the structuring contrast between idealist and materialist philosophies that guides me through the passage (I learn that Itô situated virtue outside the mind, in social relationships with others and in the "actual execution of social action"), the phrase "somewhat outrageous and morbid" jolts my imagination. Bypassing any timidity about extrapolating from a comparison of two modes of Confucianism equally new to me, it irresistibly sets me thinking about the prim dust-busters of the Anglo-

American academy today—those so outraged by any sort of "opacity" in a text, any "obscurity" clouding (from them) the point of an argument, any "dense" talk of textuality in relation to practical activities, that they can bear no serious discussion of the social grit of incomprehension as an intrinsic rather than an incidental factor in communication.

Certainly, few advocates today of "unruffled empathetic transference" (as Sakai calls it in this new book) might agree with Zhu Xi that the mind's interior is equivalent to the totality of the universe in its rationality; achieving conformity with corporate formats of thought is these days ambition enough. They simply prefer not to make a fuss about "incommensurability"; to get on with things *as though* contingency and otherness can be rendered immaterial to the conduct of social life, and *as though* transparency and reciprocity were possible between people of goodwill. So what strikes them as morbid about discursively reflexive work in the humanities ("theory") is its habit of emphasizing instead of ignoring the aporia of "another's mind" as the problem arises in diverse forms—often trailing clouds of discomfiting social and historical dust—in the everyday life of scholarship.

From this perspective, there is more to the famous opacity of theory than a convoluted syntax or a taste for tainting plain English prose with dense dollops of Latin. Theory's opacity is more incorrigibly a matter of foregrounding whatever smudges *in practice* transparency of communication and ruffles the smoothness of professional exchanges. Complicating activity with paralyzing talk of ambivalence and undecidability, querulously finding differences rumpling every situation, endlessly wondering "what are we doing?" and worrying "who is 'we'?" theory itself is a "dusty" practice: an irritant or, worse, a divisive agent in an academy streamlined for speedy information flow and efficient knowledge production. By making people think too much about the conditions of their practical agency—about the subject as *shutai*, in Sakai's philosophical vocabulary—theory obscures the clear objects of study required by responsible scholarly work.

Returning for a moment to *Voices of the Past*, I find that this detour has taken me no great distance from Sakai's account of how Song rationalism pathologized the very possibility of admitting heterogeneity and contingency as material facts of life; it may bring me closer to appreciating the otherness of Song rationalism. Zhu Xi's argument gained, Sakai says, rhetorical force by proceeding as though incommensurability "ought not to have been there" in its perfectly ordered world: "it persuaded readers to accept the image of what would happen if communality were not there and convinced them that such a situation would never ensue." Now, I well know the device of hinting that the stability of the world as we know it depends on sustaining in communities a *communal* sense of cohesion. However, no argument in the world known to me could carry conviction by rendering harmony primordial and cataclysm impossible. The hints I hear gain their force as threats from an already accepted image of chaos as cosmic in scale, and disaster as ever ready to ensue from the ordinary disorders of modernity.

Yet this is how jeremiads against theory are able to sound convincing when they pathologize the activity of taking seriously a heterogeneity and a power of contingency widely agreed to be "there"; volatile forces in an inherently dangerous world, they are best observed by an uninvolved epistemic subject (*shukan*) operating at immense distance, "as though" from another planet. In this mode of containment, otherness and incommensurability may be "there" but not in "this" enunciative practice, "this" discipline, "this" community. Hence the resonance of the hint, its threat: what might happen if communality were not *here*?

This is the sort of question that has prompted apparently sober scholars in recent years to credit assorted theoretical practices with nation-wrecking powers beyond the wildest dreams of theory's most unworldly proponents. Given the excesses of such polemics, it is easier now to ridicule the fear impelling this question than to begin to answer it—as Sakai does in *Translation and Subjectivity*—in a positive spirit. Ridiculing the fears of others, of course, can be a way of avoiding one's own. Anxiety about "what might happen" immediately seems less absurd if the question is rephrased as a demand for a practical image of non-"communal" sociality, for example: how is it possible to create a transnational space of debate that crosses linguistic as well as racial, ethnic, gender, sexual, and religious boundaries?

Such a space certainly seems desirable, as existing national modes of regulating community are reshaped by the very forces of economic and technological change that are rendering so *un*certain traditional ideals of distance and separation between a scholar and "his" objects of study, once there to be talked about, now here and talking back. Yet is it *possible*? A space, say, where people could confront from different contexts the legacy of the imperialisms that have given all the categories of "culture" so much of their diversely lived rigidity, while also engaging with the new geographies of capitalism transforming the very concept of "global" power along with the maps and material forms of its distribution, a space in which people *really* sharing no sense of communality could articulate their differences—without ignoring the new questions of class interest posed by the emergence of the space itself in the dreams of intellectuals dispersed around the world?

If this scenario, or something like it, seems desirable, even urgent if scholarship is to sustain any claim to a critical future, it can also seem hopelessly utopian. Formidable problems face any experiment in creating such a space, on however small a scale. Produced in actual places, intellectually transnational spaces can be exhausting, even dire—sizzling with acrimony, accusation, power plays less than candidly pursued, self-servingly tactical essentialisms, and an endless looping of the process of disclosing others' ethnocentrism that Sakai calls (recognizing its necessity) "retaliatory debunking." At the other extreme, such spaces can be transnational in name only, and dull: a product of the locally powerful metropolitan academy in which scholars from different university systems give papers formatted perfectly for international publication in a coherent volume and a single language, understanding each other fluently as they discourse about incommensurability and disjunction.

In between, where the real productivity of the pressures exerted from these extremes is negotiated with hope, patience, and a spirit of improvisation, people often talk about the exhausting nature of trying to work across several borders at once without many useful working models of how to go about it. A working model for dealing with a problem is not the same thing as a technical vocabulary describing it or a conceptual framework establishing its significance. Both are plentifully available in cultural theory, but in forms tending to multiply purely rhetorical prescriptions that are stirring as they build a peroration yet have an elusive pertinence to other kinds of activity: what other sort of social action, really, could "blast out of the continuum of the history" after Walter Benjamin, "wage war on totality" with Lyotard, or help Habermas to "reconcile a modernity at odds with itself"—for example?

A working model requires a less apocalyptic concept of historical practice. *Impurely* rhetorical, it should be able to connect with things that people do, or could conceivably do, in the ordinary course of their lives. A working model might be called "exemplary" in the sense that instead of presenting people with a heroic but unrealized project over which they must puzzle to find practical examples (unless, in a more sophisticated response, they quell all desire for examples), it is itself a "singular" practice out of which a project might be invented or devised.[2] This does not mean abandoning theoretical or cultural work for other sorts of activity. Poetry is often exemplary in just this inviting, challenging way, and so are essays written as singular *experiments* in learning, thinking, and communicating.

For me, the most exhilarating achievement of *Translation and Subjectivity* as an essay in this sense is that it does offer a working model of transnational cultural theory and history while also setting out a rigorous and, I find, powerfully convincing historical argument in defense of its method. As with any good essay, this method is immediately engaging but not especially easy to describe. Sakai has a formidable range of learning, and *Translation and Subjectivity* is a multilayered work in which different lines of inquiry cross over each other, densely woven at one point, diverging at another; each chapter has its own coherence, while connecting with all the others. As I found to my cost when I tried to begin this foreword unobliquely with a few paragraphs sketching the curve of the main line of argument (and drafted several articles on Australian topics I had never thought about before), this book has a way of *generating* ideas that is immensely productive for a reader.

This urge to extrapolate from Sakai's work is not, I think, a matter of free association on my part but an outcome of the *involving* mode of composition—in Deleuze and Guattari's sense of "composition" as a way in which multiplicities dynamically hold together[3]—achieved in the fine detail of his writing as well as formulated as a social practice by this book. There is no dodging the issue: it is this propensity of the text to send readings off in many directions unanticipated "in" the text—and, following Sakai's translation in *Voices of the Past* of a phrase used by Itô Jinsai, the propensity of this text to "extend and propagate" its principles "toward the outside"[4]—that gives *Translation and Subjectivity* a clear, practical force as a working model for transnational studies in culture. Making an eloquent case for a "practice of theory" across national and linguistic borders, tracing the terrible historical complicity of the logics of universalism and particularism as they have deemed such a practice impossible, Sakai's is a thoroughly *plausible* account of why and how it might be possible to work across boundaries of culture in a productive and sustainable way.

It achieves this by thinking through translation in a, well, thoroughly *practical* manner. In this respect, Sakai clearly shares with other theorists a conception of translation as a practice producing difference out of incommensurability (rather than equivalence out of difference) and of the "matter" of translation as heterogeneous all the way down; here the "body of enunciation" (*shutai*) is as irreducible to "*the* subject," split or whole, of most discourse grammars as it is to the immaterial "sender" of communication theories. This approach is practical in the sense that it asks what actually happens in an effort of translation, rather than beginning with a presupposed ideal or an already accepted story of what a world without need of translation—without the "dust" created by linguistic difference and textual materiality, without folds of incommensurability and the grit of incomprehension, in short, a world without language—would or should be like.

Clearly, too, *Translation and Subjectivity* shares with much postcolonial research a commitment to rethinking translation in its worldly uses for the exercise and legitimation of imperial power, the manufacture of national community, and as a site of survival and resistance for people dispossessed by empires and by nations. Beginning with a multilingual text by Theresa Hak Kyung Cha (a Korean-American immigrant whose mother was displaced from Korea to Manchuria by Japanese colonialism) and ending with a study of death in the language of the "Arechi" poets, survivors of the "Fifteen Year War" (1931–45), these essays on "the subject of 'Japan'" are concerned with what Sakai calls "the unexpected legacy of imperialism," present effects of past maneuvers that "never failed to generate more than they were designed to achieve." Thus the two extraordinary central chapters on Watsuji Tetsurô's anthropology, ethics, and theories of national character trace in sobering detail a trajectory along which the thought of an anti-imperialist critic of the West and a critical admirer of Heidegger became involved in shaping a culturalism that not only helped justify "more" imperialism (and racism) in mid-twentieth-century Japan, but continues to inflect debates about "East" and "West" today—debates that circulate in complex spirals of translation and theory examined by all four chapters in the middle of the book.

Given these commitments, the distinctive practicality of Sakai's approach derives, for me, from the way it brings them together in a wonderfully supple analysis of translation as a *social* relation, a practice always in some way carried out in the company of others and structuring the situation in which it is performed. Moving intricately between linguistic, philosophical, and historical modes of inquiry, drawing materials from television and the history of modern intellectual tourism persuasively together with studies of poetry and social theory, this analysis of translation's sociality seems particularly useful to me for at least three distinct levels or aspects of practice—broadly, rhetorical, institutional, and political—significant to most cultural "studies" projects and activities.

Fundamental to all three aspects is the way Sakai conceives of translation as a mode of address, and of address as preceding communication. Drawing on his own experience of writing these essays "in" translation simultaneously for English- and Japanese-speaking audiences—an approach remarkably different (if one stops to think) from positioning one as the primary audience of the "original" text, and the other as a secondary receiver of translation—he carefully distinguishes a "heterolingual" mode of address, one seeking to engage with *mixed* as well as differing audiences, from the "homolingual" address assumed to mediate two separate language communities modeled as "national" in identity ("a" collective subject) and treated as homogeneous.

Now, the difficulty of talking to an irreducibly or "wildly" mixed audience, and of participating as a member of one, is basic for any effort at transnational intellectual work—and often quietly called insuperable by scholars who have tried. Yet this same difficulty is also familiar to a great many people, scholars included, who do not necessarily think of themselves as knowing foreign languages but routinely negotiate "multiple tongues" in everyday social life, and in conditions that make attempting a homolingual address impossibly arrogant or useless. Of course, for some people "multiple tongues" has to mean discrete national languages, from which it would follow that the problem of addressing in Japanese a "mixed" audience of Japanese-speakers has nothing significant in common with transnationalism. However, Sakai shows clearly why this idea is not sustainable outside the homolingual mode, and how a heterolingual address works to produce community precisely by never assuming communality or taking comprehension for granted—across or within the borders of a nation-state.

Sakai's own way of doing this is not only to avoid the posture of a representative national speaker addressing other nationally representative speakers, but also to forgo using the "we" of cultural or civilizational communality; he writes for what he calls a "nonaggregate" community of foreigners. I think this protocol as it works through the text is largely responsible for what I call the "involving" quality of the composition of *Translation and Subjectivity*. It has an openness that has nothing to do with intellectual casualness or whimsy; this book makes serious demands on its readers. However, it is not insiderly in making its demands; the text does not nationally or culturally *characterize* its readers in moments of puzzlement or surprise. Instead of inviting readers "in" a discussion from which some would immediately find themselves excluded by, say, "not knowing" Japanese or "not doing" Asian Studies, it draws readers "out," soliciting an engagement that can take place as much in the reader's work of connecting to the text from fields outside Sakai's as in the ordinary activity of reading to understand.

At a second level of Sakai's analysis of translation as a mode of sociality, this questioning of what people actually do, and could conceivably do, in translation is extended to academic disciplines or fields that have specialized in inscribing cultural difference: the "history of Japanese thought" is discussed in chapter 2, while "Asian Studies" is the framework for Sakai's second study of Watsuji in chapter 4. Linked by a back-and-forth movement of translation and commentary, both these practices have a history of producing "the subject of 'Japan'" as a nexus of theories, debates, and desires about "East"/"West" relations: both have a capacity to shape *by* their practice "knowing" subjects of desire for cultural otherness or uniqueness in a matrix of comparative identities; both can produce expert enunciators of "characteristics" who may interpret for other audiences the flow of theories and debates about "Japan," "the East," and "the West."

Here, too, questions of address and reception are put to practices of cultural distinction. After asking what people actually *do* by studying "Japanese thought" or training in "Asian" Studies, Sakai goes on in each case to consider what they *could* do in a practice of theory that would question historically the operative categories ("Japanese"/"non-Japanese," "Western"/ "non-Western," for example) enabling and structuring each practice; and what might happen if the civilizational others posited by the very idea of a subject called "'Japanese' thought," and positioned as objects of "Asian" Studies, were openly *included* in the community potentially addressed by practitioners of each.

In this way, the question of how to speak to an essentially mixed audience and how to listen as a foreigner in a community of foreigners is transposed from the level of a social protocol as it informs rhetorical conduct (homolingual or heterolingual), to the level of a politics of theory as it transforms disciplinary practices. The continuity of this movement is doubly secured historically: on the one hand, by an account of the relatively recent development of the idea of "Japan" as a homogeneously "Japanese"-speaking nation that ought to have its own distinctive thought; on the other hand, by a reading of Watsuji's *Climate and Culture* (1928–34) that frames as Asian Studies his theories of Indian, Chinese, and Jewish "character"—subtly drawing out the supremacist as well as separatist implications of the way Watsuji excluded the colonized "natives" and the diasporic "stateless" he describes from his projected field of address.

Coming to the text (as I do) from a background more or less equally distant from Japanese thought and Asian Studies, it can be helpful for a while to read chapters 2 and 4 as a pair, making connections that significantly alter one's maps of modern intellectual history. I do Media Studies, and although there is no formal discipline of "Australian thought" (and many jokes about its absence), I might have studied it if there were; after reading *Translation and Subjectivity*, I am curious about its nonformation (and the jokes) in a new and more serious way. I also find this book as illuminating about all the history of all the anxious punditry on "Japan" traversing Australian media space—the breathless diagnoses of Japanese responses to American views of Japanese attitudes to trade and regional diplomacy, the ominous forecasts of a culture-scripted disaster lying in wait for "them" or (more commonly in Australia) for "us," the exoticizing, often comic pop ethnographies of Japanese "ways"—as it is invaluable to me as a history of the racist theories of national/ethnic character that were "common sense" to most Australians from the 1890s to the 1960s, and are still today recycled in journalism, political commentary, and popular legend.

At a certain point, however, it became more important to ask why this "pair" of chapters on academic practices is interrupted by a third, "Return to the West/Return to the East," on Watsuji's revision of Heidegger, sentimentality in cultural restorationist movements, and the postwar emperor system. Tracing *how* Watsuji's mimetic impulse toward European philosophy became, in reaction to its obsessions in the 1930s with recovering the distinctiveness of "the West," a desire for symmetry that produced in his thought an equally ethnocentric "return to the East," chapter 3 is in fact a powerful critique of the very impulse symmetrically to "pair" or polarize equivalent terms in a comparative cultural analysis. Showing how this logic of "cofiguration" can unfold toward corporatism and state assimilationism as well as cultural nationalism, it is also a practical demonstration of how and why a recognition that *asymmetrical* relations hold between *different* terms does not, as some critics suppose, foster an atomistic celebration of so-called opaque particulars,[5] but enables those terms to be articulated by a transnational history.

As a study in the sentimental economy of modern patriotic "fury," the third chapter shows unequivocally why this politics of theory matters. It explains *en abîme* why the rhetorical and disciplinary aspects of Sakai's theory of translation fold out of a third, *political* dimension of his analysis— a critique of the discourse of the modern nation-state and the idea of "national language" as these have, more or less violently, suppressed heterogeneity and pathologized otherness inside and outside the borders they enable. However, in connecting homolingualism's worldliness to the most aggressive and passionate outbursts of "communalism" orchestrated by modern imperial nationalism, Sakai does not slide by analogy from the denial of linguistic mixity to the oppression of minorities and migrants. Rather, *Translation and Subjectivity* builds directly on Sakai's historical work in *Voices of the Past* on how the emergence in the eighteenth century of a new regime of translation made it possible—in actual conditions of linguistic and social diversity—to conceive of a single "Japanese" language and ethnos capable of claiming a continuous history, and to *represent* translation as occurring between two autonomous entities susceptible to nationalization.

Many readers may be familiar with Sakai's analysis of this logic of "cofiguration"—a rivalrous mode of comparison organized by symmetry and equivalence—from his critique of the "West/non-West," "modern/premodern," and "universal/particular" pairs that have pervaded social theory through to recent debates about the political uncertainties of postmodernity. Developed here in chapter 5, this superb demonstration of the underlying complicity or *alliance* binding these virulently opposed terms in a "projective mutual accusation," to borrow a phrase from Eve Sedgwick,[6] is all the more persuasive read in close conjunction with Sakai's critique of the "national languages and literatures" problematic that so much avowedly postmodern cultural studies would like to have left behind.

Media culture studies, in particular, are often projected immediately into a time zone already "after" the nation and "beyond" modernism's ambivalent preoccupation with so-called natural language. However, the ease with which the concept of "natural" language is then casually referred to *national* language—"Japanese, French, English . . . ," a quick explanation goes—suggests the pertinence of Sakai's claim that we are still very much confined by the latter, and in fact have difficulty understanding our own practices of translation without recourse to the schema of cofiguration.

Consider how "translation" crops up today in a variety of public debates in the United States as in Australia. It has a warm, fuzzy use as a metaphor of mutually enriching social relations in a cosmopolitan future (Robert Hughes's vision of multiculturalism, for example).[7] It is sharply contested in institutions as a model for a more just and realistic approach to cultural difference in the unequal, divided societies that now exist (by, say, making multilingualism a premise as well as an aim of pedagogy in state schools). And it is demanded or denounced in disparate battles waged through the media about the impact of anything stigmatized as foreign from immigrants and tourists to political correctness and the Internet on the cohesiveness of nations, the integrity of languages, and the quality of cultures. The *concept* of translation is not the sole province of linguists and literary scholars, but one of the resources people commonly draw on to respond to the effects of economic, social, and cultural change in their lives.

Yet in all these debates, translation is also commonly understood to be a form of diplomacy carried out by special agents between discrete, homosocial, and potentially rivalrous "cultures" acting like nations—a tool of what Sakai calls "bilateral internationalism." This is what Hughes has in mind when, despite his own criticism of the transfiguration of social differences as national, he awards potential elite status to people "who can think and act with informed grace across ethnic, cultural, linguistic lines";[8] this is why the claim that more than one language is spoken in the name of "English" can be heard by *opponents* of "informed" line crossing as necessarily a declaration of separatism; and this is how any number of diverse issues and problems intrinsic to the societies in which debates about them arise are paranoiacally unified as a foreign body that can and should be expelled from "our" communal space.

However, to ascribe these responses simply to someone else's brand of politics would miss the point of Sakai's critique of cofiguration: namely, that it really is hard for anyone now to imagine translation outside it. Consider those experimental intellectual spaces in which "trans-," "multi-," "cross-," and "inter-" ways of thinking connectedness are heatedly debated, and borders are not conflated with national boundaries or treated as sacred. I think they are most exhausting not when riven by conflicts, which tend to be intelligible *as* "conflict" to participants to a greater or lesser degree, but in moments of relative calm when people wonder what to do next, how to communicate differently in the future—and the scary mirage of an *exhaustive* knowledge of the world reappears.

The ideal of total "pluralistic" internationalism is not, of course, a plausible one in today's academy, for individuals or collectives. Working conditions alone preclude most people from pursuing it past the odd dream of learning several languages and reading dozens of histories in one's spare time, although it does flash by in long lists of differences tailing off in "etc. . . ."; in global-systems analyses where the overwhelming spread of data deflects attention from the complexity of the world to the awesome athleticism of an author; and in the glazed eyes of people confronting a talk about an overly foreign place, as though the act of listening symmetrically imposes on the hearer an obligation equal to the speaker's to "know about" that place. It is easy to mock such impulses (personally, I am never free of them), but in this context pluralistic internationalism acts as a model *in default*—a "default" model that doesn't work—of other ways of coming to terms with the infinity of what one does not or cannot know of others, and with incomprehension as a factor intrinsic to the effort of communication.

Addressing these problems subtly and directly, *Translation and Subjectivity* makes it possible to imagine ways out of the logic of cofiguration. If translation loses in the process its special-agent status, the position of a formal translator is not effaced (as though, once again, there were no linguistic difference and no problem of intelligibility); rendered liminal rather than mediating, it brings out the *ordinary* instability, strenuously concealed by communalism, of the "we" produced in any communicative effort that is never sure of succeeding. Liminality as a threshold or in-between "place" is diversely interpreted now by cultural theorists; reading this book, I came to think of the translator's liminality not only in terms of the inside/outside paradox of the frame or boundary, but also as a movement oscillating between familiar and unfamiliar, actual and potential *exteriors*; in a heterolingual mode of address, the translator's position, I would guess, is that of one who accepts to have no choice but to "extend and propagate toward the outside" in a condition of chronic uncertainty about the outcome.

At the same time, Sakai's careful tracing of historical practices specific to different experiences of liminality is a reframing of "the subject of 'Japan'" that radically alters at least this reader's sense of what that phrase is open to meaning. Most immediately, the idea of a nation in its interiority is displaced in an outsiderly essay on the history of that idea: here is a "nonaggregate" Japan produced by reading *from* the oppressed or unlivable edges of national space (the multilingual unworking of "literature" by a Korean American, the refusal of returned Japanese soldiers to write as "living" in a new Japan continuous with the old) while also reading *for* the liminality enunciated but disavowed in the texts of a canonical national thinker such as Watsuji—reframed here as the writings of a foreigner and a tourist abroad.

Another movement, however, traces the outside circulation of certain European ideas of interiorized nationality, opening them up to theoretical and historical criticism. Watsuji is also a translator whose philosophical studies and solutions in Japanese of the problem of translating the senses that "subject" can have in European languages become, in Sakai's revision, the basis for a theory of subjectivity *as* an otherness, a foreignness, and an exteriority "in" any language or community. Most marvelous to me in this movement is the way it begins from a reading of Watsuji's interpretation of the distinction between practical and epistemic agency (*shutai/shukan*) active in so much controversy about theory today, then expands and transforms the distinction to organize in English a practical understanding of the project of "theory"; a plausible, limited, and very exact definition of that problematic term, "the West"; and a succinct way of naming and explaining one of theory's most elusive and useful concepts, the *practice* of enunciation.

It is always easier to sense what *shutai* means than to "put it into words," not least because it "means" what occurs as, and vanishes in, any process of putting into words; it is something we know about intimately by doing. Yet an exposition can take pages to draw together ideas of the fleeting and the material, the open and the historical, the involved and the productive in practice, and, after all that effort, there is still no word—just a series of words, like "practice" and "body," carrying baggage or traces of hybrid histories, that never quite resonate effectively. Perhaps we are dealing with a "nonaggregate" concept, or with the core of the concept of the nonaggregate. However, insofar as the opacity of theoretical discourse sometimes is a matter of overdoing the Latin in English, defining one's audience too exclusively as a closed society of experts bound by access to a special language, I suggest that *shutai* in Sakai's sense is capable of translating those pages of exposition in a way that not only makes the concept more accessible but opens it up to new uses.

At stake here is the serious problem of how a transnational scholarly practice directly essaying heterolingualism might actually work, and the status for such a practice of "examples"; in his study of Cha's *Dictée*, Sakai draws on an old working model of language learning and subject formation (*bungaku*, today translatable as "literature") used before the birth of Japanese as a national language. Academic theorists today, however, have their own specific reasons for facing this problem; increasingly, scholarly discourse can never be sure of circulating within one linguistic community, however unevenly circulation takes place. Yet this does not mean "we are all" constrained or incited equally to write for different audiences, anymore than "we all" have the same relationship to nationalism.

If Sakai's is for me an exemplary response to these issues, it is so in its singularity. *Translation and Subjectivity* is no more a general model of what a heterolingual cultural studies should henceforth "do" than it is an instance of an *exceptional* or personal bilingualism. Sakai does not propose a universally applicable norm of conduct, a strategy of repetition as return; to write for different audiences is necessarily to care about context, to respond to contingency, to admit limitation: in short, to be willing repeatedly to differ. This "will," however, is not a property of individuals with a "talent for translation" but a complex and *variable* condition of sociality; for many people, learning multiple languages is not a gift, a pleasure, or a tool of trade but a forced process scored by painful legacies of history—as Sakai emphasizes in his discussion of Cha's desire in *Dictée* for her dead mother's mother tongue.

What I would borrow from Sakai's reading of that text is his defense of the value of making connections "anachronically" as well as transnationally to other practices, other singularities. On first reading *Voices of the Past*, I puzzled for a long time over my desire to relate what I read appreciatively there about Itô Jinsai's critique of Song rationalism to controversies today: what does it mean to link two ways of stigmatizing talk about heterogeneity and contingency when those ways are so remote from each other, culturally and historically? It can simply mean, of course, that one is reading ("actively," as convention adds). However, to read is not necessarily to read well, and in moving outside one's own patch of expertise there are always questions and doubts, not only about what happens when one's capacity for misunderstanding becomes excessive, but also at the point where my "adventure" becomes "appropriation" for someone else.

After reading *Translation and Subjectivity*, however, I came to see the earlier book as itself a powerful work of translation that challenged my sense of cultural and historical propriety, leaving me far less sure of the intellectual remoteness from "my" concerns of a thinker living in "Japan" three hundred years ago. In Itô's world, incommensurability is very much "here" as well as "there," and difficulty in communication has to be accepted as an ordinary condition of social life. If sociality is produced by the participation of many different minds, among the unintended outcomes likely to follow any action there will be unanticipated, perhaps unwelcome or even "fraying," criticisms.

This can be frightening, as students of culture are well aware. When there is no communality or when borders are crossed, sometimes unknowingly, one is never sure of "what will happen." Sakai explains that "the core of Itô's ethics is the moment we are forced to face through this fear," since "one is capable of being ethical precisely because one is uncertain of the consequences of an intended ethical action."[9] However, because sociality is relational one is not alone in this uncertainty; others have a say in determining an action's value. In Itô's world, "the virtuous is . . . always a collective work."

A transnational practice of theory today could not be grounded in any agreement about ethics or the value of discussing virtue (for some people, an outrageous and morbid topic). What I learn from this anachronic reading is rather a way to think about noncommunal communication as a *project* requiring both practical involvement—one attempts it without knowing what will happen—and what *Translation and Subjectivity* calls "trust," an adventurous, unsentimental approach to sociality that accepts its aleatory nature. The academic community that can evaluate efforts in this spirit may be more potential than actual (a "coming community," as Giorgio Agamben puts it), but with this book Sakai has given us a history, a theory, and a language that will richly contribute to the process of its formation.

Acknowledgments

The Chinese character on the front cover means "trace" and by its use I would like to suggest that each of the essays contained in this volume not only addresses the problematic concerning the trace of the other in translation and the subject as a subject matter of translation but also indicates traces of friendship. When the chapters in this volume were written and delivered over the last twelve years, they were read and commented on by many of my friends prior to publication. Their encouragement and support have left indelible traces on each chapter. Among those friends are the late Maeda Ai, Iyotani Toshio, Brett deBary, William Haver, Chen Kuanhsing, Harry Harootunian, Karatani Kôjin, J. Victor Koschmann, Marilyn Ivy, Yamaguchi Jirô, Meaghan Morris, Narita Ryûichi, Benjamin Lee, Timothy Murray, Yamanouchi Yasushi, Christopher Fynsk, Hirota Masaki, Susan Buck-Morss, Tomiyama Ichirô, Pheng Cheah, Wakita Haruko, Liao Pinghui, Masao Miyoshi, Dilip Gaonkar, Matsuzawa Hiroaki, Dominick LaCapra, Sakiyama Masaki, and Thomas Lamarre. Needless to say, there are many others, including graduate students who participated in my seminars and reading sessions, and whose enthusiastic endorsement as well as critiques of my arguments are appreciated very much. I would also like to thank David Thorstad for his painstaking copyediting and Lewis Harrington for his help in proofreading. Finally, although I wrote these essays, I repeatedly consulted about the intelligibility of my presentation and the appropriateness of my expression with Gail Sakai, to whom this book is dedicated.

Introduction: Writing for Multiple Audiences

and the Heterolingual Address

The essays in this volume were written over about a decade with the earliest being "Death and Poetic Language in Postwar Japan" in 1985 and the latest "The Problem of 'Japanese Thought'" in 1993, and each of them addresses either the problems of translation or of subjectivity, or of both translation and subjectivity. Some were first delivered orally at conferences. Others were prepared for publication in journals and anthologies. All have been translated either from English into Japanese or from Japanese into English at one stage or another, so that they have all been presented to both English- and Japanese-speaking audiences; which is to say, none of these essays was prepared with a view to the completion of its writing-reading circulation within the interior of one language, within the putative homogeneity of one linguistic community. Translation is not only the subject matter I undertook to discuss as the theme in the essays, but it was also a necessary condition for the emergence of these essays. From the outset they were marked or, if one prefers, stigmatized by their heterolinguality of addressing themselves to the *other* language speakers as well. Initially I did not have a keen awareness of what writing simultaneously for these two different audiences might entail, but by the time the translation of chapter 3, "Return to the West/Return to the East: Watsuji Tetsurô's Anthropology and Discussions of Authenticity," appeared in Japan in 1990, there was no doubt in my mind that the practice of writing for two different audiences could not be dissociated from the problematic of translation that I had pursued in my previous study of eighteenth-century Japanese discourse.

What the practice of the heterolingual address evoked in me was not the sense of the peculiarity of writing for two linguistically different readerships; rather, it made me aware of other social and even political issues involved in translation, and it illuminated what I had long suspected about the assumptions of the nonheterolingual address, namely, the homolingual address. In this respect, the practice of writing these essays confirmed what I had expected when I analyzed the conceptions and regimes of translation in eighteenth-century discourse in what is referred to as Japan today. Strictly speaking, it is not because two different language unities are given that we have to translate (or interpret) one text into another; it is because translation *articulates* languages so that we may postulate the two unities of the translating and the translated languages as if they were autonomous and closed entities through *a certain representation of translation*. In my previous book, I claimed that the schema of what Roman Jakobson called "interlingual translation" became possible as a consequence of a new discursive transformation in the eighteenth century, and that an introduction of a certain regime of translation, perhaps for the first time, gave rise to the possibility of conceiving of a spoken ordinary language, of people living in some vague area designated by the name Japan, as distinguished from and contrasted to the language(s) of the Middle Kingdom, that is, China.[1] But, of course, as the country was divided into many domains and social groups with vast dialectical and stylistic variety, nowhere could the Japanese language as universally spoken by the "Japanese people" be found in the eighteenth century. The Japanese language could only be conceived of as a lost and dead language whose restoration was earnestly called for. I argued that the Japanese language and the Japanese ethnos were *stillborn*, then, as the phonocentric notion of language became dominant in certain discourses. Thus the emergence of Japanese language and Japanese ethnicity was irreparably associated with the problematic of translation.

It is nearly a century since the stillborn language and ethnos were resurrected, although their revival, or restoration, did not take place in one stroke but in temporal and spatial dispersion. And these unities have regulated the ways in which social and cultural formations associated with people in Japan have been represented. Today, whether in Japan or elsewhere, there are not many who do not take the unities of the Japanese and their language for granted. The status change of these unities from that of the "stillborn" to that of the "positively present," or the resurrection of the Japanese language and the Japanese ethnos/nation, is, of course, indicative of the emergence of the modern Japanese nation-state. Needless to say, it is extremely difficult to comprehend what we perform in translation outside the discourse of the modern nation-state, and this difficulty only teaches us how massively we are confined within the discourse regulated by the idea of the national language and what I called the schema of cofiguration.

Writing for two different audiences, however, provided me with an opportunity to glimpse a possibility of comprehending translation without relying on the discourse of the nation-state and the schema of cofiguration, and to further develop a set of tropes that allow me to understand what I perform in translation without resorting to the schema of interlingual translation. As I endeavor to articulate translation differently, in due course I will have to be even more attentive to the ambiguity of some of the expressions without which it would be almost impossible to talk about translation. Can the multiplicity of languages without which translation seems unnecessary be measured numerically, so that one can assume that languages are countable? What constitutes the unitary unit of a language that is not implicated in another language or other languages? Under what conditions can we regard English or Japanese, for example, as a language, and not as languages? And what does one expect in referring to a family of languages, as in the denomination "European languages" or even "Western languages"? I will return to these questions. What must first of all be responded to seems to be the question of how translation structures the situation in which it is performed: what sort of social relation is translation in the first place?

To write for two different audiences is nothing new. A great many writers have done it. Yet, its ethicopolitical significance has been noted by very few, such as Walter Benjamin. I believe this is because the problematization of the stance characterized as "writing for two different audiences" could require an overall reconsideration of the basic terms in which we represent to ourselves how our translational enunciation is a practice of erecting or modifying social relations. Unless the terms in which we represent to ourselves what we do in translation are fundamentally reorganized, we will continue to figure it as a somewhat tritely heroic and exceptional act of some arbitrator bridging two separate communities, instead of drawing attention to the aspects of translation in which translation is an essentially hybridizing instance.

What must be evaded in writing for different audiences is what I want to call homolingual address, that is, a regime of someone relating herself or himself to others in enunciation whereby the addresser adopts the position representative of a putatively homogeneous language society and relates to the general addressees, who are also representative of an equally homogeneous language community. Let me note that by the homolingual address I do not imply the social condition of conversation in which both the addresser and the addressee supposedly belong to the same language community; they believe themselves to belong to different languages yet could still address themselves homolingually. Accordingly, I had to be attentive to my uses of the pronominal "we" and other markers of collective invocation, and had to try to nominate my possible audience by designating a linguistically heterogeneous ensemble. In other words, I tried to speak and listen, write and read among the "us" for whom neither reciprocal apprehension nor transparent communication was guaranteed. The putative collectivity of the "we" that I wished to invoke by addressing myself to them did not have to coincide with a linguistic community whose commonness is built around the assumed assurance of immediate and reciprocal apprehension in conversation. Among "us," on the contrary, "we" ought constantly to encounter not only misunderstanding and misapprehension but also lack of comprehension. Thus, "we" comprise an essentially mixed audience among whom the addresser's relation to the addressee could hardly be imagined to be one of unruffled empathetic transference, and to address myself to such an audience by saying "we" was to reach out to the addressees without either an assurance of immediate apprehension or an expectation of uniform response from them. "We" are rather a nonaggregate community;[2] for the addressees would respond to my delivery with varying degrees of comprehension, including cases of the zero degree at which they would miss its signification completely. I want to call this manner of relating the addresser to the addressees the heterolingual *address*.

The two verbal designations "to address" and "to communicate" can be distinguished from one another precisely because the former precludes the description of what it accomplishes, as a performative, whereas the latter anticipates its accomplishment, just as "aiming" and "striking" can be distinguished in the contrasting phrases "aiming at a target" and "striking a target." In order to "strike a target" one first has to "aim at it." Unless one aims first, one cannot even "fail to strike it." In this sense, just as "aiming" is prior to "striking," so "addressing" is anterior to "communicating." And "addressing" is distinguished from "communicating" because an addressing does not guarantee the message's arrival at the destination.[3] Thus, "we" as a pronominal invocation in *address* designates a relation, which is performative in nature, independent of whether or not "we" actually communicate the same information. And the relation thus designated appears to be what Jean-Luc Nancy would refer to as a nonrelational relation,"[4] a relation that probably becomes most intelligible at the demise of all the "communication theories." Or, to put it more rigorously, "we" as a case of the vocative designation cannot be confused with a group of those who are capable of communicating the same information with each other, for such a group can be posited only imaginarily and *in representation*. Furthermore, translation is required in order to determine the sameness of the information: what remains the same in information cannot be identified unless it is translated. What is translated and transferred can be recognized as such only after translation. The translatable and the untranslatable are both posterior to translation as *repetition*. Untranslatablity does not exist before translation: translation is the a priori of the untranslatable.

In the heterolingual address, the disparity between addressing and communicating is most conspicuously perceived, while the regime of homolingual address serves to repress the awareness of this disparity between the invocation of "we" and its representation and thereby reinforces the assumption of immediate and reciprocal apprehension. As Benjamin clearly saw it, the end of translation is not the communication of information, since translation is an instance where communication of and as an inscription ineluctably ensues.[5]

In most cases of homolingual address in publication, the writer's language is also the reader's so that the writer and the readers are both presumably embraced within the putatively unitary community of a single language. This kind of regime of address entails the insider dialogue of a member of an English- or Japanese-speaking society addressing other members of the same society. But this is not the only type of homolingual address: there are, if not many, cases in which the writer's language is distinctively not the readers'. The writer as representative of one language community could address herself to readers whose language is definitively not hers. And, in this situation, translation should be absolutely essential because the writer would either have to speak the language of the addressee or have to deliver a message in her own language that is subsequently translated into that of the addressee. So, can we say that this type of address is not definitively homolingual because the speaker addresses herself to a linguistically heterogeneous group of readers?

Here consideration of the position occupied by the translator is crucial. As long as the position of the translator is set aside and viewed to be secondary, this type of address is still homolingual in the sense that two different language communities are posited as separate from one another in the *representation of translation*, and that translation is understood to be a transfer of a message from one clearly circumscribed language community into another distinctively enclosed language community. It goes without saying that the image of translator as a somewhat heroic prestigious agent derives from these assumptions of the homolingual address. And all the assumptions that I have so far problematized would disavowedly persist as if they had never been called into question.

What is kept out of this regime of homolingual address is the mingling and cohabitation of plural language heritage in the audience, and subsequent to this address, speech addressed by or to a foreign language speaker is put aside as secondary to the authentic form of delivery or as an exceptional case outside normalcy. The scene where one speaks without assuming that everybody among the addressees will understand what is delivered by the speaker is premeditatedly excluded. In other words, the fact that one must first "address" is confused with the assumption that supposedly "we" should be able to "communicate" among ourselves if "we" are a linguistic community. In other words, communication is not associated with writing, inscription, or even "exscription" but with communion in the homolingual address.[6] The regime of homolingual address unwittingly postulates even more assumptions: since speech by or to a foreigner is secondary, the normal delivery must accomplish itself within the same medium, and translation, insofar as it requires the postulation of differing media, cannot be either primordial or originary. Under this regime, an utterance must be delivered first; it is translated secondarily. It postulates a sphere of linguistic homogeneity where "communication" is guaranteed and taken to be anterior to "address." This is done by establishing a certain economy of failure in communication.

This is to say that, in the homolingual address, the experience of not comprehending an other's enunciation or of the other miscomprehending your verbal delivery is grasped immediately as *an experience of understanding the experience of not comprehending*. For instance, when you were spoken to by an unknown man and could not figure out what he tried to convey, you describe this incident in the following manner: "A man spoke to me in Russian, so I could not understand him" (provided, of course, that you do not speak Russian). In the first place, it is very dubious as to whether an experience of noncomprehension can be called an experience at all. Furthermore, this manner of conceptualizing the failure of communication by the representation of an experience that contains the explanation of its own putative cause should necessarily entail an implicit tautology that merges its description and the putative explanation of it indistinguishably. Consequently, it is assumed that the experience of noncomprehension comes simultaneously equipped with an explanation as to why you fail to comprehend. It is assumed, in other words, that you necessarily experience an incident of discommunication while knowing why you happen to fail in communication. Here, we may as well draw attention to the mundane insight that communication fails all the time, not necessarily because of the gap between linguistic communities, but also because of the fact that communication takes place only as "exscription":[7] to try to communicate is to expose oneself to exteriority, to a certain exteriority that cannot be reduced to the externality of a referent to a signification. When we fail to communicate, we cannot attribute the failure to its possible cause—whether it is excessive noise in the medium or the addressee's refusal to respond—precisely because we fail to communicate. In our case, failure in communication means that each of us stands exposed to, but *distant* from, the other without grasping the cause for "our" separation.[8] It is only retrospectively, and, in the final analysis, subsequent to the representation of translation, that we begin to figure out an experience of noncomprehension of an other's utterance according to the international schematism.

As Jacques Rancière argues in regard to the tenets of *equality*, what gathers us together is not commonness among us but a will to communicate despite an acute awareness of how difficult it is. "All words, written or spoken, are a translation that only takes on meaning in the counter-translation, in the invention of the possible causes of the sound heard or of the written trace: the will to figure out that applies itself to all indices, in order to know what one reasonable animal has to say to what it considers the soul of another reasonable animal."[9] Only where it is impossible to assume that one should automatically be able to say what one oneself means and an other able to incept what one wants to say—that is, only where an enunciation and its inception are, respectively, a translation and a countertranslation—can we claim to participate in a nonaggregate community where what I want to call the heterolingual address is the rule, where it is imperative to evade the homolingual address.

In a nonaggregate community, therefore, we are together and can address ourselves as "we" because we are distant from one another and because our togetherness is not grounded on any common homogeneity.

In my deliberate efforts to avoid the regime of homolingual address and to articulate a relation of a nonaggregate community with the readers, I had to learn how to never designate the collective alliance of the narrator and the readers by either the "we" of national affiliation or the "we" of cultural or civilizational communality. Yet, to evade the regime of homolingual address is also to give up a clear hierarchical marking of initial enunciation and subsequent translation. (Without annulling the intelligibility of the word "translation," it should be possible to detect the *oscillation or indeterminacy of personality* with regard to the situation of translation/interpretation in which a translator speaks as she translates. This is one of the reasons why the place for the translator cannot be indicated in the "communication model." I will come back to this problem.) I wrote these essays in search of an address that establishes the "we" of a community without taking national, ethnic, or linguistic affiliation for granted. Therefore, it is perhaps misleading to say that the essays were first enunciated and, then and separately, translated. Not only because of my delayed acquisition of the English language but also because of the essays' heterolingual address to the readers, they may as well be said to be translated as they were written, and written as they were translated. As I became aware that I had ineluctably come to occupy the position of the translator as I was writing within a so-called bilingual address, the writing of an essay could no longer be comprehended without regard to translation. It seemed that, particularly in my case, translation and enunciation could not manageably be distinguished from one another unless vigilant efforts were undertaken to prepare a conceptual sensitivity so as to detect the particular traits of translation and isolate the act of translation from the other forms of enunciative performatives.

A tentative distinction between heterolingual and homolingual addresses is thus called for in order to mark a difference in the attitude of the addresser to the addressee, which in fact derives from two conflicting modes of alterity. The homolingual address assumes the normalcy of reciprocal and transparent communication in a homogeneous medium so that the idea of translation does not make sense unless a positively heterogeneous medium is involved. In contrast, the heterolingual address does not abide by the normalcy of reciprocal and transparent communication, but instead assumes that every utterance can fail to communicate because heterogeneity is inherent in any medium, linguistic or otherwise. Every translation calls for a countertranslation, and in this sort of address it is clearly evident that within the framework of communication, translation must be endless. Thus, in the heterolingual address, the addressee must translate any delivery, whether in speech or writing, in order for that delivery to actually be received. Also in the heterolingual address, addressing in enunciation is not supposed to coincide with eventual communication, so that it is demanded of the addressee to *act* to incept or receive what is offered by the addresser. This is to say, what is addressed to the addressee is not automatically delivered precisely because of the disparity between addressing and communicating, of a disparity that also expresses the essential *distance* not only of the addressee from the addresser but also of the addressee or addresser from himself or herself. In the heterolingual address, therefore, the act of inception or reception occurs as the act of translation, and translation takes place at every listening or reading. Whereas translation is necessary only between the interior of a homogeneous medium and its outside in the case of the homolingual address, it is upheld in the heterolingual address that, in principle, translation occurs whenever the addressee accepts a delivery from the addresser.

Thus differentiated, the two addresses respectively suggest the two alternative attitudes with regard to the otherness of the addressee. Although you would presume that the addressee who is incapable of comprehending your delivery should appear marked and anticipated as such to you when you adopt the attitude of the homolingual address, such a precaution or anterior knowledge is not guaranteed in the attitude of the heterolingual address. In the latter attitude, you would probably have to address yourself to the addressee, no matter whether the addressee is singular or plural, without assuming that the addressee would necessarily and automatically comprehend what you were about to say: you would, of course, wish the addressee to comprehend what you say—for, without this wish, the act of addressing would not constitute itself—but you would not take it for granted. In this respect, you are always confronted, so to speak, with foreigners in your enunciation when your attitude is that of the heterolingual address. Precisely because you wish to communicate with her, him, or them, so the first, and perhaps most fundamental, determination of your addressee is that of the one who might not comprehend your language, that is, of the foreigner. The idea of a nonaggregate community of foreigners is unintelligible unless we are able to conceive of a community where we relate to ourselves through the attitude of the heterolingual address.

Precisely because of her positionality, the translator has to enunciate for an essentially mixed and linguistically heterogeneous audience. In order to function as a translator, she must listen, read, speak, or write in the multiplicity of languages, so that the representation of translation as a transfer from one language to another is possible only as long as the translator acts as a heterolingual agent and addresses herself from a position of linguistic multiplicity: she necessarily occupies a position in which multiple languages are implicated within one another.[10] The translator who is present to both the writer and the readers regulates communicative transactions, but her mediation must be erased in the representation of translation according to which the message issued by the writer in one language is transferred into an equivalent message in another language, which is then received by the readers. In these cases as well, the writer addresses the readers with the presumption of a homolingual communion. The assumption that one can make oneself understood without perceptible hindrance, as long as one belongs in the same linguistic community, survives intact here. Translation is believed to be necessary because incommensurability exists not necessarily between the addresser and the addressee but essentially between one linguistic community and another.

It is well known that Roman Jakobson classified translation into three classes: "1) Intralingual translation or *rewording* is an interpretation of verbal signs by means of other signs of the same language. 2) Interlingual translation or *translation proper* is an interpretation of verbal signs by means of some other language. 3) Intersemiotic translation or *transmutation* is an interpretation of verbal signs by means of signs of nonverbal sign systems."[11]

I do not think that the propriety of Jakobson's "translation proper" can be maintained outside the attitude of the homolingual address. And we would have to call into question the supposed discernibility of interlingual from intralingual translation, of translation between separate languages from rewording within the same language unity, as soon as we adopt the attitude of the heterolingual address. In other words, viewed from the position of the translator, neither the unitary unity of a language nor the plurality of language unities can be taken for granted. Moreover, not only the professionally assigned translator, but the rest of us as well, would have to be responsible for the task of the translator. At the same time, we would be obliged to call into question other discursive positivities similar to the unity of a particular ethnic or national language, such as the unities of ethnic and national cultures, when we take the attitude of the heterolingual address. So far I have talked as if those unities, English, Japanese, and other language unities, and the name "translator" itself were self-evident, but as soon as we are in the heterolingual address, we will find that these putative unities and names have to be put in brackets.

In addition, how could we possibly define what Jakobson calls intersemiotic transmutation, when we cannot easily separate verbal signs from nonverbal signs in such texts as the *calligraphic* one. Is a calligraphic text verbal or nonverbal? Is it a text to see or a text to read? Is it possible to translate a calligraphic text? If it is, in what sense is it so? What are the conditions under which the verbal is immediately equated to the linguistic? A series of questions like these will gradually suggest to us that there could be discursive formations in which the propriety of "translation proper" can hardly be taken for granted. Today, no matter whether you reside around the Pacific Basin or along the Atlantic, the idea of translation is almost always self-evident and very few would insist otherwise. However, by imposing on ourselves the attitude of the heterolingual address, we are able to call into question that self-evidence, and thereby explore those ethicopolitical assumptions and habituated regimes that serve to sustain this position.

Let me point to two sites where the problematic of translation seems to manifest itself most intensely, so as to delimit that self-evidence and mark its historicity. The first concerns itself with subjectivity, and the second with schematism in translation.

The Subject of Translation/the Subject in Transit

Can the translator make a promise in translation? Can she then be responsible for what she says while translating? The answer must always be double as long as the name "translator" signifies neither a professional specialty nor a social status but instead designates an agent or a human being who is engaged in the act of translation. Yes, the translator can make a promise, but always on behalf of somebody else. In that respect, no, she "herself" cannot really make a promise. Likewise, the translator must be responsible for her translation, for every word of it, but she cannot be held responsible for what is pledged in what she says. For she is not allowed to say what she means in what she says in translation; she is supposed to say what she says without meaning. At the same time that the translator must be absolutely responsible for what she says, her task begins with her pledge to say what the original addresser means to say. Her responsibility consists in her commitment to withdraw her wish to express herself from what she says even though she has to seek and interpret what the addresser means in the first place. Therefore the translator is also the interpreter.

A cursory reflection like this on the relations between the original addresser and his translator, or the translator and her addressee, amply illustrates the extremely ambiguous and unstable positionality the translator has to occupy with regard to the original addresser and the addressee. The translator listens to or reads what the original addresser enunciates. In this respect, there is no doubt that she is an addressee. But it is not supposed that the addresser speaks or writes to her. The addressee for the enunciation of the addresser must not be located at the site where the translator is, so that the addressee is always located elsewhere in translation. The translator is both an addressee and not an addressee at the same time. This is to say that, even though the translator is spoken or written to, she cannot be addressed as "you" by the addresser. Or, if she can be addressed as "you," then the putative audience for whom the translator interprets cannot be the direct addressee in the enunciation of the addresser; that audience will be redesignated as a third party, as "them." A similar disjunction can be observed in the translational enunciation of the translator. The translator speaks or writes to the audience, so in this respect she is undoubtedly an addresser. But, supposedly it is not the translator who in translation is speaking or writing for the addressee. "I" uttered by the translator does not designate the translator herself but the original addresser as the subject of the original enunciation. And if by "I" the translator indicates the subject of the secondary and translational enunciation, she will then have to designate the original addresser as "he" or "she."

Let me reformulate this pronominal disjunction slightly differently. It is always possible for what is translated to be conveyed as a quotation, either in direct or indirect mode. Suppose the original addresser says "Kyô wa ii tenki da." Then a translation of what the original addresser says can, for example, be accommodated as a subordinate clause in the statement of either "He/she (= the original addresser) said, 'It is fine today,'" or "He/she said that it was fine that day." Yet, when explicitly formatted as a subordinate clause, a translational utterance as a whole is rendered as the translator's—that is, the utterance would present itself as being addressed to the audience not by the original addresser but by the translator. In order to avoid the dislocation of the original addresser, the translator chooses to drop the phrase indicating the subject of the enunciation, and just say: "It is fine today." In translational utterance, however, we cannot assume that the translator can immediately make manifest her rapport to the subject of the enunciation by restating this utterance in the following manner: "I say 'It is fine today'" or "I say that it is fine today." Rather, it must be restated as follows: "I say 'he said "It is fine today"'" or "I say that he said that it was fine that day." In translational enunciation, every utterance must be able to be accompanied by the designation through a double framing "I say, 'the addresser says, ". . . ."'" In this respect, the translator must speak in a forked tongue, and her enunciation must necessarily be one of mimicry. Furthermore, the translator renders conspicuous the operation of framing in the process of the constitution of subjectivity in enunciation.[12]

In the enunciation of translation, the subject of the enunciation and the subject of the enunciated are not expected to coincide with one another. The translator's desire must be at least displaced, if not entirely dissipated, in translational enunciation. Thus, the translator cannot be designated either as "I" or as "you" straightforwardly: she disrupts the attempt to appropriate the relation of the addresser and the addressee into the *personal* relation of first person vis-à-vis second person. To follow the determination of a "person" as espoused by Émile Benveniste—that is, that only those directly addressing and addressed in what he calls "discourse" as distinct from "story" or "history" can be called persons, and that those who are referred to or talked about in the capacity of "he," "she," or "they" in "story" or "history" cannot be "persons"[13]—the addresser, the translator, and the addressee cannot be persons simultaneously; the translator cannot be either the first or second or even third "person" undisruptively. Although the translator can be so in Foucauldian "discourse"—whose formulation I understand to be explicitly antipersonalist—she can only have a transitory and temporary position in the personalist notion of "discourse" such as Benveniste's. Thanks to this formulation of "discourse" in which every enunciative position is depersonalized from the outset, we dispense with the hermeneutic problematics of the horizon of understanding. Ineluctably, translation introduces a disjunctive instability into the putatively *personal* relations among the agents of speech, writing, listening, and reading. In respect to personal relationality as well as to the addresser/addressee structure, the translator must be internally split and multiple, and devoid of a stable positionality. At best, she can be *a subject in transit*, first because the translator cannot be an "individual" in the sense of *individuum* in order to perform translation, and second because she is a *singular* that marks an elusive point of discontinuity in the social, whereas translation is the practice of creating continuity at that singular point of discontinuity. Translation is an instance of *continuity in discontinuity* [14] and a poietic social practice that institutes a relation at the site of incommensurability. This is why the aspect of discontinuity inherent in translation would be completely repressed if we were to determine translation to be a form of communication. And this is what I have referred to as the *oscillation or indeterminacy of personality in translation*.

Thus, by considering the position of the translator, we are introduced into the problematic of subjectivity in an illuminating manner. The internal split within the translator, which reflects in a certain way the split between the addresser—or the addressee, and furthermore the split within the addresser and the addressee themselves[15]—and the translator demonstrates the way in which the subject constitutes itself. In a sense, this internal split within the translator is homologous to what is referred to as the fractured I, the temporality of "I speak," which necessarily introduces an irreparable distance between the speaking I and the I that is signified, between the subject of the enunciation and the subject of the enunciated.

Yet, in the case of translation, the oscillation or indeterminacy of the personality of the translator marks the instability of the we as the subject rather than the I. Particularly in the regime of homolingual address, the translator is supposed to assume the role of the arbitrator not only between the addresser and the addressee but also between the linguistic communities of the addresser and the addressee. Thus, translation ceases to be a *repetition* and is rendered representable. And, in the regime of homolingual address, translation as repetition is often exhaustibly replaced by the representation of translation.

Let me elaborate on the process in which translation is displaced by its representation, and the constitution of collective subjectivity such as national and ethnic subjectivity in the representation of translation. Through the labor of the translator, the incommensurability as difference that calls for the service of the translator in the first place is negotiated and worked on. In other words, the work of translation is a practice by which the initial discontinuity between the addresser and the addressee is made continuous and recognizable. In this respect, translation is just like other social

[handwritten margin note: Schema of Configuration]

... the points of discontinuity in social formation con ...tively and after translation, therefore, can we ...mmensurability as a gap, crevice, or border be ...ntities, spheres, or domains.[17] But, when repre sented as a gap, ...r border, it is no longer incommensurate. As I dis cuss in chapter 4, incommensurability or difference is more like "feeling" that is prior to the explanation of how incommensurability is given rise to and cannot be determined as a represented difference (or species differ ence in the arborescent schemata of the species and the genus) between two subjects or entities.[18] What makes it possible to represent the initial difference as an already determined difference between one language unity and another is the work of translation itself. This is why we always have to remind ourselves that the untranslatable, or what can never be appropri ated by the economy of translational communication, cannot exist prior to the enunciation of translation. It is translation that gives birth to the un translatable. Thus, the untranslatable is as much a testimony to the social ity of the translator, whose figure exposes the presence of a nonaggregate community between the addresser and the addressee, as to the translat able itself. However, the essential sociality of the untranslatable is ignored in the homolingual address, and with the repression of this insight, the homolingual address ends up equating translation to communication.

By erasing the temporality of translation with which the *oscillation or indeterminacy of personality in translation* is closely associated and which can be thought in an analogy to the aporetic temporality of "I think," we displace translation with the representation of translation. Only in the representation of translation can we construe the process of translation as a transfer of some message from "this" side to "that" side, as a dialogue between one person and another, between one group and another, as if dialogue should necessarily take place according to the model of communication. Thus the representation of translation also enables the representation of ethnic or national subjects, and, in spite of the presence of the translator who is always in between, translation, no longer as difference or repetition but as representation, is made to discriminatorily posit one language unity against another (and one "cultural" unity against another). In this sense, the representation of translation transforms *difference in repetition* into *species difference* (diaphora) between two specific identities, and helps constitute the putative unities of national languages, and thereby reinscribes the initial difference and incommensurability as a specific, that is, commensurate and conceptual, difference between two particular languages within the continuity of the generality of Language.[19] As a result of this displacement, translation is represented as a form of communication between two fully formed, different but *comparable*, language communities.

Following Kantian schematism, I have called the discursive apparatus that makes it possible to represent translation "the schema of cofiguration." As the practice of translation remains radically heterogeneous to the representation of translation, translation need not be represented as a communication between two clearly delineated linguistic communities. There should be many different ways to apprehend translation in which the subjectivity of a community does not necessarily constitute itself in terms of language unity or the homogeneous sphere of ethnic or national culture. The particular representation of translation in which translation is understood to be communication between two particular languages is, no doubt, a historical construct. And it is this particular representation of translation that gave rise to the possibility of figuring out the unity of ethnic or national language together with another language unity. Indeed, this is one of the reasons for which I have claimed that the Japanese language was born, or stillborn, in the eighteenth century among a very small portion of literary people, when the schema of cofiguration came into being. This is to say that the schema of cofiguration is a means by which a national community represents itself to itself, thereby constituting itself as a subject. But it seemed to me that this autoconstitution of the national subject would not proceed unitarily; on the contrary, it would constitute itself only by making visible the figure of an other with which it engages in a translational relationship. Hence, the figure of the Japanese language was given rise to cofiguratively, only when some Japanese intellectuals began to determine the predominant inscriptive styles of the times as pertaining to the figure of the specifically Chinese, or as being contaminated by the Chinese language. It is important to note that, through the representation of translation, the two unities are represented as two equivalents resembling one another. Precisely because they are represented in equivalence and resemblance, however, it is possible to determine them as conceptually different. The relationship of the two terms in equivalence and resemblance gives rise to a possibility of extracting an infinite number of distinctions between the two. Just as in the cofiguration of "the West and the Rest" in which the West represents itself, thereby constituting itself configuratively by representing the exemplary figure of the Rest, conceptual difference allows for the evaluative determination of the one term as superior over the other. This is how the desire for "Japanese language" was invoked through the schema of cofiguration in the regime of translation.

Finally, I must deal with one formative principle without which the national subject would fail to gather together a wide variety of conceptual differences around the unitary figure of an ethnos or nation; for, even processed through the schema of cofiguration, the regime of translation could multiply conceptual differences in many disparate registers. In particular there is no guarantee that Jakobson's intralingual translations can be organized with the interlingual translation or *translation proper* as the overall guiding rule of translation. Conceptual differences can be posited between one style and another—*Kanbun* or literary Chinese and *Sôrôbun* or a distinct epistolary style mixing the syntax of literary Chinese and *Kana* characters, for example, in the case of Tokugawa Japan—one regional dialect and another, so-called ideographic and phonetic inscriptive systems, and so on. These differences can be marked between genres, but what characterizes the emergence of the national language is that generic differences that can be represented cofiguratively in the regime of translation are all subsumed under the generality of the national language; these genres have to be perceived as the species within the genus of the Japanese language. This time, although our terminology may be confusing since the term "genre" itself derives from the genus, the generic difference must be allocated at the level of the species while the unity of national language transcends the species and is conceived of as an overarching genus. What Jakobson implies by the differentiation between intralingual and interlingual translations is nothing but the hierarchization of these translational registers. It goes without saying that this differentiation itself is a historical construct. I believe that, in historical contexts prior to the eighteenth century in the geographic regions designated as Japan today, we cannot assume such a generic taxonomy, and that the lack of historicity would only sanction the continuous regimes of National History and National Literature. At the same time, we now can understand why the regime of translation with the schema of cofiguration plays such an important role in the formation of the Japanese as a national subject.

By now it should be evident that, given my analysis of the regime of translation and the homolingual address, culturalism in which Japanese culture and nation are obstinately reified and essentialized is, as a matter of fact, not particular to Japanese journalism and academia at all. Culturalism that endorses nationalism in terms of national language and ethnic culture is as persistently endemic in Japanese Studies in the United States, Europe, and elsewhere as in Japan today. For, as I will show in some of the following chapters, behind Westerners' as well as Japanese insistence on Japanese cultural uniqueness looms an equally obstinate essentialization of the West.

East Asian names throughout this book, except those of Asians who are resident outside East Asia, are written in the East Asian order—surname first—after the style Asian Studies specialists have adopted in their studies in English.

1

Distinguishing Literature and the Work of Translation: Theresa Hak Kyung Cha's *Dictée* and Repetition without Return[1]

The temptation to regard 'language' or 'literature' as the guarantor of a nation's 'pedigree' (remember that *natio* has in Latin an almost eugenic connotation) recalls the similar (and frequently more destructive) employment of the concept of 'color'. In both cases an apparently exclusionary process is meant somehow to isolate the pure 'pedigree' of a race, a language, or a literature, even as that process ends up in a compensating search for some emblem of universality.

> James Snead, in *Nation and Dissemination*

To be a foreigner, but in one's own language, not only when speaking a language other than one's own. To be bilingual, multilingual, but in one and the same language, without even a dialect or patois.

> Gilles Deleuze and Félix Guattari, *A Thousand Plateaus*

It is impossible to undo the consequences of the history of imperialisms no matter how desperately one wishes that imperialisms had never been effectuated. We live in the effects of the imperialist maneuvers of the past and the progressive present, in their pervasive effects in which everyone in today's world is inevitably implicated. From those effects some may be able to extract almost inexhaustible privileges; because of the same effects, others may be condemned to what appears to be unending adversities. Yet, one should also be reminded that those maneuvers have never failed to generate more than they were designed to achieve, and that imperialisms have been judged, criticized, and threatened by what they unwillingly or unwittingly brought into being in the process of their self-realization. By forging an anachronistic connection that retrospectively links the design of an imperialist discourse in a past historical moment with the unexpected legacy of it in a present moment, therefore, I believe it is possible to disclose sites and special angles from which the imperialist discourse can be critically construed. And what I have in mind by "the unexpected legacy of imperialism" in this chapter is, above all else, what is pointed to by the mass of displaced or oppressed people, including those refugees in diaspora, whose existence one would not be able to comprehend but for the imperialist manuevers that destroyed their previous habitats.

The global use of the English language has often been criticized for its suppression of other languages and its monopoly of information in the world. Undoubtedly the universal acceptance of English cannot be dissociated either from the history of Anglo-American imperialism, which the Japanese have earnestly attempted to reproduce in their own versions for a century or so, or from the ubiquity of transnational capitalism, whose effects are increasingly manifest all over the world. Yet, more often than not, the critique of English-language imperialism has been conducted on the basis of a particularism premised on the identity of national language and national culture. In this particularism, it is taken to be a norm that each people should express itself in its own "natural" language, and the world is construed as the configuration of particular languages, a set of schemata that projects the image of a pluralistic international world—perhaps the best example of this vision can be found in prewar Japanese "philosophy of World History"[2]—as a composite of particular peoples and their corresponding national languages. And a homogeneous cultural and linguistic space is assumed to prevail within each of those "natural" national communities where linguistic hybridity and "polyglots" are often suppressed as traits indicating the absence of authenticity. According to this view, to recognize a people's "authentic" linguistic and cultural identity immediately equates to paying respect to them, and to fail to do so means to insult them. In order to have some idea of an international dialogue, therefore, one is urged to figure out a symmetrical scheme by means of which one nationality is authorized in relation to another. The occasion of such a dialogue is supposed to serve as a means of mutual authorization and recognition that operates as a form of transference. Although such a scheme is not only inevitable but also necessary at certain stages of international encounter, its persistence and the obsessive insistence on it can hinder the possibility of working through differences to create new relations between the parties involved.

Besides the fact that such a nationalist particularism may well be an accomplice to and even essential for the universalism of transnational capitalism, it neglects one aspect of the global use of the English language, namely, English as an element for heterogeneity where a nation and a language do not correspond to each other at all. It also fails to recognize the history of both collective and personal experiences in which the figure of a national language is constituted in accordance with the figure of another. It seems that the formation of the identity of a national language and its political implications cannot be understood unless in this history of cofiguring or configuration; for it is only as a figure that the identity of a language unity or *langue* can be perceived.

The formation of national literature also seems to coincide with the severance of literacy and multilingualism as well as the emergence of vernacular phonocentrism in the conception of writing. I must hasten to add, however, that the terms "literacy," "unilingualism," "multilingualism," and "vernacularism" are conventional categories loaded with all sorts of hitches, and that multilingualism cannot be generalized because of its historical and regional heterogeneity in contrast to the relative homogeneity of the unilingualism brought forth by the modern nationalistic cofiguring. Nevertheless, in the meantime, let me yield to those "suspect" categories.

For instance, to be able to read and write was to be able to operate in more than one linguistic medium in some parts of Japan at least until the eighteenth century. Literacy was comprehended within the context of multiple tongues, multilingualism, as Leonard Forster vividly described the Europe of the late-medieval and Renaissance periods, or as we know from Chinua Achebe's work.[3] Moreover, literacy was not regulated by the demand that the primary function of writing should be to transcribe what is suggested by "mother tongue." Therefore, it often meant a capacity to read and write in a rather "macaronic" medium that was rather different from the language of familiarity (cf. literary Chinese in premodern East Asia, Latin in Europe, etc.). Yet, I would hesitate to portray this situation by equating literacy with the capacity to read and write in an explicitly foreign language because, I suspect, the figuration of a foreign language, in clear contrast to the language of familiarity or "mother tongue," had yet to be inaugurated. And, I want to stress, it is not easy to talk about the mother tongue without first equating with its figure.

The mother tongue is amorphous, as is testified to by the fact that the child, for example, does not or need not know its mother tongue as a systematicity of rules, as a grammar. And although, in the final analysis, I do not believe it possible to conceive of any language, including the mother tongue, in which presumably one is exhaustively at home, usually the first determination of the mother tongue comes from this absence of the need to know its grammar; the mother tongue precedes the thematization of its existence in terms of its grammatical features; in principle, it is that on the ground of which any linguistic articulation is made possible, so that its existence itself cannot be linguistically thematized. Therefore, just the same as Plato's "khora," which has often been associated with "mother" or "wet nurse," it seems to elude ontological determination. For the speaker, her or his mother tongue is given neither as a set of explicit regularities nor as a subject of which properties are predicated, because the mother tongue precedes all those predicative determinations (hence, the mother tongue is not a subject), without which it is doomed to remain indeterminate, that is, nonbeing. This is to say that the thematization of the mother tongue requires figures or schemata that form and give a form to the amorphous "mother tongue."

In order to preserve the theoretical ambiguity inherent in the designation "the mother tongue," allow me to link the mother tongue to what one might call "khoraic place."[4] (The mother tongue should be linked to, not subsumed under, "khoraic place" because "khoraic place" is not a concept.) The alliance of literacy and multilingualism before their severance may be formulated as follows: the mother tongue, which the speaker lived by speaking in its putative immediacy, had not been captured in a singular relationship to the figure of one's national language, so that it was impossible to thematize and let stand, within the framework of nationalistic self-representation and subjectivity, the "khoraic place" that is said to elude the principles of identity and noncontradiction.

In Japan until the eighteenth century, for instance, the mother tongue was not yet one's natural national language: nature and the nation had yet to be communicated. Thus the formation of modern literary culture, it seems, is marked by a new conception of literacy that dissociates literacy from multilingualism and macaronics, and redefines it primarily as a "regime," or a set of practical and lived relations to the text, to transcribe what is putatively lived in the immediacy of ordinary everyday speech into some preservable form. Concurrently, the figure of the mother tongue as the natural national language was brought into being through a cofiguring schematism. The disciplines of national literature as well as comparative literature presuppose and depend on the operation of this cofiguring, and in turn reinforce it. It seems to me that the construction of "literature" in the modern nation-state has been irreparably tied to the history of this cofiguring, and also of another new "regime" of translation based on this cofiguring, a history that, as I will show, has consisted of the simultaneous invocations of the desire for one nation to imitate the figure of another and the desire to distinguish itself by asserting its own uniqueness. From the outset, therefore, the construction of national "literature" has always already been haunted by that of "comparative literature": national literature has inherently been comparative literature.

As is most evident in modern Japanese history, literature from the regions outside Europe and North America, with the exception of China, was not included in these cofiguring schemata of the international configuration. Unlike French, English (later Anglo-American), German, Russian, and Japanese—national, white (excluding Japan), and imperialist (including Japan)—literatures, cultural and linguistic formations in areas such as Africa, the Middle East, Latin America, South Asia, and so on are not included in this international world as far as the modern institution of literature is concerned. In other words, Japanese literature has not been placed in the cofigurative mimetic relationship with another national literature that is not the literature of the imperialist nation-state. Because of this institutional setting, the identity of Japanese literature as a national literature has never been figured out in relation to the peoples who were colonized or subordinated by those imperialist nations. Subsequently, within the institution of comparative literature, or, more specifically, of comparative national literatures whose membership was originally predicated on the nation's imperialist success, Japanese literature had not been compared with the literature of those peoples who were not backed up by strong imperialist states until recently.[5] Needless to say, one might as well wonder about the political significance of this present event, the thirteenth congress of the International Comparative Literature Association in Tokyo, when one learns that this is the first congress to be held outside the so-called West.

When contrasting the institution of "literature" with previous discourses on social texts, what has been repressed in "literature" is rendered explicit. Here, I employ the Japanese word *bungaku* as a guiding thread, although by no means can one assume a genealogical continuity between the pre-Meiji *bungaku* and "literature," which was translated into *bun-gaku*, a compound consisting of two characters, *bun* and *gaku*. *Bungaku* in the sense of "literature" was certainly a neologism, then, but it does not follow that the same compound had not been used prior to the Meiji period. Unlike such neologisms as *shakai*, one of the few translations for English "society" or French "société," *bungaku* by some historical accidence happened to coincide with the old term, which had already been available but which followed a quite different semantic economy in pre-Meiji discourse. Furthermore, the use of this term was far from unitary with regard to doctrinal implications, the degree of its dispersion among the population at large, and the mode of its dependency on the classics. For instance, during the Tokugawa period, one cannot ignore the absence of modern national education as exemplified in the hierarchical system of schools and universities in which the institution of "literature" has been installed, together with its particular pedagogic protocols, and a specific enunciative modality for the "literature" experts.

An early nineteenth-century thinker, Suzuki Akira, who followed the eighteenth-century philosopher Ogyû Sorai's theses on ancient texts and the method of their interpretation, attempted an explication of this *bungaku* thematically, and addressed the issues concerning the procedure of learning in which the work of learning a foreign language was taken to be the process wherein the speaking subject was constructed. Unlike their contemporaries, both Ogyû and Suzuki assumed the severence of literacy and multilingualism, so that an explicitly foreign language was already posited in contrast to the language of familiarity. However, they argued that they discovered the language of familiarity not in their contemporary world but in antiquity—classical Chinese in the case of Ogyû, classical Japanese in the case of Suzuki.[6] As it is most clearly shown in Ogyû Sorai's theses, the process of learning that required a lengthy and repetitive exercise constituted the core of *bungaku*. What was aimed at in this process of learning could not be limited to the acquisition of an ability to speak the language either of ancient China or of ancient Japan. The character *bun* was read in a much broader sense: it was not the narrow concept of the literary text, as is the case in modern "literature."[7] According to the old definition of *bungaku*, *bun* encompassed "the reign of the country through means other than direct verbal orders and ordinances." Thus, it meant the texture of a certain social reality that is "lived" by people and whereby the people are ruled: etymologically, *bun* can mean figure (*aya*), pattern, grain, tattoo, and so on. Primarily, it was neither a set of abstract doctrines nor imperative statements that were determined in conceptual terms. Its distinctive feature lay in its concreteness and its immediacy to those who abided by it. Conceptualized thus, *bun* was in fact akin to what we today understand by ideology. People were supposed to internalize the *bun* of behavior patterns, and it was by "living" this texture that they were successfully ruled. From the outset, *bun* was a political concept that also concerned itself with texts of nonverbal kinds.[8]

Nevertheless, *bungaku* was not merely a given, a gift, since the compound contained another character, *gaku*, which meant work, labor, the laborious process of learning. *Bun* was something that had to be learned through repetitive practice. It had to be mastered to the extent that one could perceive it as one's second nature, and "live" it and "live" by it. *Gaku* was not only the process of acquiring knowledge, but also a process in which a speaking and acting subject was formed. The subject was formed by acquiring an ability to "live" this texture, only within which a certain subjectivity was believed viable. It goes without saying that the formation of a certain subjectivity within this texture was also called "virtue."[9] And, in relation to the whole of *bun*, which was also called the Way, the Way of the present community could be illuminated as distinct from the Way of the other community. In this sense, the Way of the present whole could be cofigured together with the Way of another whole. And this cofiguring is a means by which to distinguish one communal whole from another in representation. Needless to say, the Way of ancient Japan (*jôko no michi*) held the ultimate authority and served as the primal principle or *archê* for Suzuki's learning. Through *bungaku* the learner was expected to become fully assimilated into the whole of *bun*: he or she was transformed into a subject that was constituted in that particular textuality. The learning of *bungaku* was the process of a return to the original wholeness in which the subject was in perfect conformity with the Way, although return in this case did not necessarily imply the restoration of the origin in a chronology.

Whereas "literature" seems blind to the very process of manufacturing subjects, Suzuki's *bungaku* illustrated its awareness of the politicality of *bungaku* as what I call subjective—*shutai-teki*—technology unrelentingly. I like to modify this "technology" with a Japanese adjectival, *shutai-teki*, which is derived from the noun *shutai*, one possible translation for the word "subject" from European languages, because the *shutai-teki* or subjective technology whereby the subject (*shutai*) constitutes and manufactures itself can possibly be contrasted to the ordinary and conventional comprehension of technology—*shukan-teki* technology, one might call it—by means of which the subject (*shukan*, a different translation for the same word "subject") manipulates and transforms the object for a predetermined objective. In the *shukan-teki* technology, the object of technological manipulation always remains other than the subject who applies technology as a means to the object, whereas such a stable division cannot exist between subject and object in the case of the *shutai-teki* technology precisely because its objective is a self-fashioning for, of, and by the subject.[10] The subjective technology concerns itself with the poiesis of the subject by itself.

In this connection, let me consider Theresa Hak Kyung Cha's *Dictée*, a poetic text that problematizes much of what has been assumed in "literature." In this multilingual text, the stable configuration of natural languages and the national identity of the literary text are not presupposed. The poet speaks in multiple tongues. Perhaps because it was written from the perspective of a Korean-American immigrant, it addresses itself to the problematic of language learning, which is closely related to the issues of the heterogeneity of the English language and its multinationalism. Hence, it shows an unexpected affinity with *bungaku*, which originated before the birth of Japanese as a national language and its people as a nation.

In spite of, or precisely because of, the overwhelming presence in *Dictée* of what one might call a death wish beyond the pleasure principle, a wish for compassion and reunion with the loss through one's own death, I feel I must confront this text and undertake this *work* because the text forces me to *work* on those assumed schemes according to which the reading of literature is usually conducted. This text is a work not primarily because it is a product or an accomplishment of the author's labor, but rather in the sense that the reading of it requires a different kind of labor. Rather than constructing itself in conformity with an assembly of conventional schemes or the regime that is time and time again called "literature," the text engages in the intervention of this regime. Accordingly, my reading of *Dictée* has to take the form of a series of inquiries intervening in the operation of the regime, and it seems that the "working through" of this text could bring about the transformation of that regime, thereby disclosing the historicity of "literature" as an assembly of the operative regularities that have been routinized in the formation of academic disciplines and general social formation.

In *Dictée*, we find many quotations from other sources. In a sense, *Dictée* can be portrayed as a montage of quotations, including those from *other* languages. So, first of all, the text disturbs the anticipated homogeneity of a single "natural" language. Yet, it is not merely the purity of the language that foreign quotations seem to disrupt. Here, let me draw attention to the specific mode of the allocation of quotations in *Dictée*'s montage: particularly significant in this respect are both the quantitative proportion of different languages in the whole of this text and the manner in which those quotations are framed and foregrounded. Aside from the fact that each of the nine chapters has a title that consists of a Greek name and an English phrase or word—in an equal distribution of two languages, Greek and English—the first page or page one, which is actually preceded by a total of nine pages, including a page in which a blurred photograph of a Hangul inscription is reproduced,[11] is devoted to two languages, French and English, in equal proportion. This symmetrical equation between two languages is sustained by the fact that paragraphs are made to correspond to each other through translation. Because one is a translation of another, the reader is asked to assume the relationship of equivalence between these paragraphs. This use of two languages in equal proportion is repeated in parts of the chapters "Urania Astronomy," and "Elitere Lyric Poetry." Also printed in some pages are Chinese characters whose nationality is indeterminate not only because historically they have been an integral part of many different "national languages" in East Asia, such as Korean and Japanese, but also because they are registered in their graphic visuality rather than as a substitute for orality. One of the most striking effects of this compositional practice is that it destabilizes the assumed hierarchy of the main language and other subordinate languages that are quoted; the reader is made unsure of which language *Dictée* as a whole is written in. The reader would expect that, in spite of the inclusion in the text of phrases, words, and characters from foreign languages, *Dictée* as a whole is essentially in English, and it is this very expectation that is put in jeopardy by this compositional tactic; it problematizes the location of this text within the configuration of the English language and its other languages. The text is composed in such a way that it cannot be situated within the essentially separatist international world that is constituted by the cofiguring of languages; it refuses to simply side with the "us" of the readers; it feigns to speak the readers' language, but it does not hide its pretense and thereby shows the irrevocable presence of the history of political coercion in the very choice of a language.

What stands out in this text, therefore, is not the distinctive and distinguishing identities of language unities such as English and French, but rather the movement from one language to another. *Dictée* presents itself not as a work that is produced and completed within one language unity but as a work of passage from one language to another. Thus it deals thematically with the problem of translation, not in its putative symmetrical equivalence of the signification between two languages, but as the work of labor that is required to move from one language to another. Translation is not comprehended in terms of its accurate correspondence between two sentences in two languages.

Traduire en francais:
1 I want you to speak.
2 I wanted him to speak.
3 I shall want you to speak.
4 Are you afraid he will speak?
5 Were you afraid they would speak?
6 It will be better for him to speak to us.
7 Was it necessary for you to write?
8 Wait till I write.
9 Why didn't you wait so that I could write you?[12]

The deliberate listing of these sentences succinctly delineates a power relationship inherent in the translation of a language into another, as well as in the situation of foreign-language instruction. Besides, the juxtaposition of two languages within the regime of a translation exercise discloses how the relationship of languages is formed, utilized, and confirmed as part of the cofiguring of languages.

In *Dictée*, the problem of translation is never divorced from that of dictation, of a form of practice in which the learner imitates and attempts to reproduce utterances not so much in order to say what she means as to say what she is expected to say *without meaning it*. She speaks, but she does not mean what she says, or she cannot mean what she says. "She mimicks the speaking. That might resemble speech. (Anything at all.)"[13] Therefore, for the very reason that the learner requires such a discipline, utterances in a translation exercise fail in principle to constitute themselves first as locution and generally as speech acts. According to J. L. Austin, speech can be a locution only insofar as the speaker says something and means it. Consequently, utterances in a translation exercise can be seen as what Austin calls "phatic acts" ("the uttering of certain vocables or words, i.e., noises of certain types, belonging to and as belonging to, a certain vocabulary, conforming to and as conforming to a certain grammar"),[14] but never as "rhetic acts" ("the performance of an act of using those vocables with a certain more-or-less definite sense and reference").[15]

Nevertheless, those utterances that do not even qualify as speech acts do things: they perform and achieve certain perlocutionary effects, so to speak. By saying things in these nonlocutionary speech acts, the speaker does something and brings about some transformation in the world; through these nonrhetic acts, she not only acts in a mimetic and dramatic performance but also exercises and, therefore, works. But, at first sight, what the utterances of these nonlocutionary speech acts accomplish is not found in the speech situation. By uttering words in a translation exercise, the speaker cannot solicit the listener, for instance, to shoot someone (illocution); neither can she make the listener shoot someone (perlocution). Precisely because the speech situation is marked as a translation/dictation exercise, utterances in it are supposed to be taken frivolously. Consequently, they are not supposed to be addressed to any human agent in the speech situation at all. In other words, these are acts that are somewhat detached from the situation, and they seem devoid of a "performative" function.

Yet these utterances undoubtedly serve to transform the speaker herself and, in this respect, they should bring about fundamental changes to the "lived" relations that she lives. The way in which those nonlocutionary speech acts change her lived relations to the world is drastic and, sometimes, even traumatic. Those speech acts change the world systematically through the transformation of her relations to it; slowly but irreparably they inscribe a regime (which, according to Ogyû Sorai, ancient Chinese once called *wen*, signified by an ideogram that meant tattoo and inscription at the same time) on the speaker's body. In this respect, translation is a *subjective* or *shutai-teki* technology that transforms the world by transforming the speaker. By highlighting the aspect of "saying something without meaning it," the exemplary quotations of a translation/dictation exercise in *Dictée* reveal the work of translation as a subjective technology that transforms the speaker and prepares the constitution of a speaking subject.

But, when we are in the ordinary and natural situation, can we say what we mean at all? Is it possible to say what we mean once we are outside the context of a translation exercise? Or do we fail to say what we mean because we have to operate in the medium of a foreign language? Let me put the question in reverse. In contrast to the deprived state to which we tend to ascribe our experience with foreign languages, is it possible to postulate the sphere where one is securely at home in language?

Theresa Hak Kyung Cha repeatedly incites the reader to ask these questions in her text.

One can hardly dissociate the text's deliberate compositional arrangement concerning the allocation of spaces for different languages from an obsessive concern for her mother tongue, her dead mother's *langue*, and her deprivation thereof. Perhaps what is most acrimoniously put in question is the possibility of construing one's experience of learning another language simply in terms of the one-way journey from one's own language to its other, from a mother tongue to a foreign one. But, in this text, she does not give the putative position of her original language, where what she says supposedly coincides with what she means: the language from which the speaker begins her journey and to which she returns to conclude her journey is deprived. Therefore, the point of departure for her is the absence of both a starting point and a point of return. By emphasizing disparity between what she says and what she means, Theresa Hak Kyung Cha problematizes the scheme whereby the points of departure and destination are determined in this laborious work of languages. "Our destination is fixed on the perpetual motion of search. Fixed its perpetual exile."[16]

Disparity between what is said and what is meant manifests itself most forcefully in the sense of the inadequacy that marks each of her enunciations. As a result, she always utters statements "in parenthesis," as it were, with an air of not fully committing herself to their signification. Because of this sense of inadequacy, the words and other notational conventions do not recede into the preconscious, and instead remain thematized. "Open paragraph It was the first day period She had come from a far period tonight at dinner comma the families would ask comma open quotation marks . . ."[17] This is the sort of situation that profoundly disturbed John R. Searle, another theorist of speech acts. Searle argues:

> It is generally claimed by philosophers and logicians that in a case like 2
> [= "Socrates" has eight letters] the word "Socrates" does not occur at all,
> rather a completely new word occurs, the proper name of the word. Proper
> names of words or other expressions, they claim, are formed by putting
> quotation marks around the expression, or rather, around what would
> be the expression if it were a use of the expression and not just a part of a
> new proper name. On this account, the word which begins 2 is not, as
> you might think, "Socrates", it is ""Socrates"". And the word I just wrote,
> elusively enough, is not ""Socrates"", but is """Socrates""" which com-
> pletely new word is yet another proper name of a proper name, namely,
> """"Socrates"""". And so on up in a hierarchy of names of names of
> names. . . . I find this account absurd. And I believe it is not harmlessly so
> but rests on a profound miscomprehension of how proper names, quotation
> marks, and other elements of language really work."[18]

Searle seems to postulate the existence of some substratum on which one can say exactly what one means definitively and without surplus, and is able to say no more or no less than one means and where an enunciation is not framed at all. Insofar as one speaks within this substratum, Socrates is, simply and straightforwardly, not "Socrates" but Socrates, and Cha is neither a three-letter word nor a one-character name (車), but Cha. Within the sphere defined by the substratum that is proper to the speaker, she should be able to say what she means; she would not need to frame up her subjectivity in relation to her enunciation.

Without doubt it is in the element of what Searle characterizes as absurdity that Cha's narration proceeds. Yet, this does not serve as an acknowledgment that *Dictée's* language is exceptional and abnormal; for one would have to assume that there can be a sphere of nonexceptional and normal language uses where his version of absurdity could completely be annihilated, and that the substratum of one's linguistic property and propriety could be circumscribed and identified as the English language. But would that end up abolishing heterogeneity in the English language? In the final analysis, would that necessarily harbor an oppressive attempt at assimilationism? Rather, the text helps disclose a relentless ethnocentricity without which Searle's argument would not be able to sustain itself,[19] and it seems that the text also indicates the direction of getting out of such a pitfall.

In *Dictée*, an endless regression of quotation marks occurs, and accordingly the organs, including notational conventions, which serve as a framework for enunciation, remain stubbornly visible. And these organs do encompass physiological organs such as the oral passage, larynx, vocal folds, and, of course, tongue (*langue*).[20] "To bite the tongue. / Swallow. Deep. Deeper. / Swallow. Again even more. / Just until there would be no more of organ. / Organ no more. / Cries."[21] The speaker's body, which makes it possible for her to speak at all and which also functions as a frame and frames up the utterance of the statement, refuses to disappear and be forgotten. Therefore, every utterance that she makes is "in parenthesis," surrounded by quotation marks, and framed by the body. Theresa Hak Kyung Cha attributes this impossibility of discarding corporeality in her enunciation to the fact that she is deprived of her mother tongue, her dead mother's *langue* (tongue). Her lack of a mother tongue presents itself as an obstacle, opacity to the desired transparency of communication in which the body is supposed to disappear completely. In this instance, the body is neither the specularity of the self nor the anchorage of our incarnation in this world: above all, corporeality is unidentifiable noise, and material resistance to the formation of the imagined harmonious symbiosis of the mother and the child, of mother's language and the speaker. It is precisely in this instance that the body is most manifestly revealed to be *shutai*, "the body of enunciation," which makes it impossible for the speaker's body to be fully framed up as a subject and because of which no body can be exhaustively at home in any language, even in one's mother tongue.[22]

Here, one cannot stress too much the importance of avoiding certain reductionisms that explain away this difficult text, a text that demands a great deal from the readers, as an exemplary instance of a stereotype that is ascribed to a particularized social group.[23] We cannot read it merely as an index of a national character—in this case, the Korean national character; neither can we sentimentalize it as the expression of an immigrant who has failed to adapt herself to so-called mainstream society, and who, consequently, has to be treated kindly or patronized almost a decade after her death. Apart from the fact that the stereotype always serves to erase what history achieves in generating differences that are irreducible to differences between identities, the text in fact questions and radically undermines those reductionist readings and is directly engaged in the task of refuting them. To say that the text has to be read as a typical reaction to a foreign environment by the Korean is to insulate the reader from the questioning power of the text and thereby to distance the reader from the text by means of the imagined and somewhat invisible screen that warrants the eternalized and, therefore, separatist *distinction* between "us" and "them." It is, consequently, to refuse to read the text itself insofar as the text is a work or a working.

In *Dictée* the deprivation of her mother tongue is reproduced and repeated, and, before moving on to the issue of reproduction and doubling, one might count at least three probable reasons for this loss: first, under Japanese colonial rule, the Korean people with whom the speaker maintained a strong affinity were brutally deprived of their mother language; second, as her mother had to leave Korea because of Japanese colonial rule and had to live and teach in another Japanese colony, Manchuria, under Japanese supervision (where she taught foreign languages, including the colonizer's language to Korean immigrants there), the speaker's fate in the United States could be construed as parallel with her mother's; and third, as a consequence of the Korean-American political relation, she had to leave Korea: she has to live in a foreign medium, which also marks the state of deprivation of her mother's mother tongue. This recognition could lead to an intense search for her mother's mother tongue, and an absolute identification with it. But, at the same time, I find myself drawn to a reading that discerns in *Dictée* the trace of an effort to sustain a certain ironical distance from the mother tongue as well as from the colonizer's language. For her, every language is a foreign language. But is it only for her that every language is a foreign language?

What is a foreign language? What is foreign about a foreign language? And how do we know the foreignness of a foreign language, which establishes the difference between one's own language and other languages that are alien? One might say, "Although I know my own language, I do not know foreign languages." Thereby one asserts that one at least knows one does not know foreign languages. I, for instance, do not know Russian or Swahili. Therefore, I assert that I do not know the languages called Russian and Swahili, which I do not know. But how can I know the languages that I do not know to exist? How can I make any assertion about what I declare I have no knowledge of, but which I nevertheless want to know? Hence, my statement that I do not know Swahili must be open to the probability that Swahili does not exist. We can hardly ascribe any empirical validity to any statement about one's ignorance of foreign languages. Nonetheless, we must acknowledge our ignorance of a foreign language in order to want to know it.

An inquiry, as a kind of seeking, is mostly guided beforehand by what is sought; for otherwise we would not even begin to seek. But, in this case, although we seek a foreign language in the passage toward it, our seeking is not guided by what is sought. In the question "What is a foreign language?" the meaning of what is asked about is *not* already available to us in an implicit understanding of it—not as in a hermeneutic inquiry in which even if we do not know the horizon in terms of which the meaning of what is sought is to be grasped and fixed, some vague understanding of it is an irrefutable fact, our ignorance as to what we seek is absolute. What is sought is not in proximity to us; it is far away from us and beyond our reach. Thus it is the configuration of languages that enables me to relate myself to what Kant calls an "object in the idea," and, in this respect, it can be regarded as a sort of schema, even as something like a schema-world.[24] Through the configuration I perceive an unthinkable foreign language as a certain figure, but it is not as an object of empirical knowledge that I perceive it.

Since, at least at the initial stage, I am deprived of any means at all by which to verify a judgment about the figure of a foreign language, the language cannot be given to me as an object of experience: its initial appearance simply does not take place in the realm of empirical knowledge. Nevertheless, the figure of a foreign language is indispensable in my practical orientation toward it. So the figure makes it possible for me to wish to know what it represents; it directs me toward the unthinkable that it figures; it solicits me to venture into a project toward the unknown. Instead of serving as a rule for positive knowledge, the figure concerns itself with the creation of the possibility of a particular knowledge.

I cannot lay my hands on this unknown in order to grasp it unless I work to approach it. To get near it, my seeking requires me to work; in order to work to get near it, my seeking would satisfy itself not with what is disclosed by it but with the transformation of me that will be brought about by my act of seeking. Essentially, it is not destined for a manifestation, but rather it is a laboring that bears, and that at the same time changes, me in a fundamental manner. It is, therefore, an ecstatic project, a project of moving away from and getting out of the selfsame that the figure of a foreign language solicits me to venture into. It is a project of transforming me into that which is not familiar rather than a project of returning to the authentic self. Or at least, at the outset, it appears so.

When one learns a language one does not know, one tries to approach this unknown and unthinkable language only through the configuration of languages. The configuration is given to me through language instructors, or else essentially as a hearsay devoid of original evidence. And the lack of my knowledge of foreign languages means that I am unable to reach the evidence in order to ascertain that hearsay. For how can I know the language I do not know? The evidence is inscribed in the language that is unknown to me and, by definition, it should be illegible. My inability to ascertain it is not accidental: foreign languages that I do not know must be given to me through this configuration that is an absolute hearsay. I am simply told that there is a certain language and that certain people speak it and live in it. I am also told that my language is different from theirs, while languages, including my own, are usually located on the geocultural map of the world. Although I do not know those languages whose names and locations are given to me, that is the only knowledge I can rely on in classifying and identifying peoples whose languages and lives I do not know. Needless to say, the classification and imagined locations of languages are institutionalized in the disciplinary taxonomy by which foreign-language learning is facilitated.

But the configuration as a gift is essential in order to make one desire to and begin to know a language one does not know. I need some indication, some guideline or figure that points to the direction of what I seek unwittingly. At the very least, the unity of a language I do not know has to be given as a figure that incites my desire to know it.

Let us note that, however inconsequential a risk it may be in one's life or career, it is nonetheless a venture, an aleatory one, to decide to undertake a work or labor in order to approach this unknown Other for which there is no adequate concept, but only a figure; for, to do so requires a sort of bet, commitment to that hearsay without any guarantee. Furthermore, by deciding to subject oneself to the hearsay, one takes up a position of subordination in relation to language instructors and other positions of authority that are determined in the given institutional formation. In order to work to approach the unthinkable, one has to enter various power relations based on knowledge. Thus, the figure of a foreign language can force one to traverse those layers of social and political formation that one would otherwise never need to confront. This travel to the unthinkable, which may be not only laborious but also painful, disjoints the subjective position putatively proper to the learner and could invite her or him into unexpected social contexts. And, in an unequivocal manner, reaching out toward the unknown Other demands, first of all, a work and labor by which one transforms oneself.

At first, the figure of an unknown language is abstract and vague. But, as one learns it, it gradually becomes concrete, and, at the same time, one's own language emerges as a contrasting figure. Against the background of the newly acquired and partial knowledge of a foreign language I am learning, I also learn that what I have already known and retained in hermeneutic proximity is being articulated. In contrast to the unknown, the already familiar is figured out. As the difference between my language and a foreign language is articulated, I am informed of the figure of my language that I have lived but that I have not *known*. Here, we must note a certain anteriority of the unknown to the familiar: although I have, so to speak, lived my language, I do no know it in the sense that I come to know a foreign language. Only through the configuration of languages can I get to know my own lived language.

Just as foreign-language learning almost always involves translation of one sort or another, the figure of one's own language is further articulated as the figure of the foreign language is articulated. Therefore, the concretization of the figure of a foreign language is always accompanied by an articulation of the figure of one's own language. And, more often than not, it is also a process of both negotiating, on the one hand, and reifying, on the other, the difference between the familiar language and the unknown one, which can never be perceived in symmetrical terms by any means; for it is the absence of the terms for comparison that characterizes the initial relation of my language to an unknown language. And the concretization of the figure necessarily entails the availability of the terms for comparison in which both the familiar and the unknown are rendered representable and come to be represented by their respective figures. Hence, the process of learning a language we do not know is in fact a process of cofiguring that takes place within the framework of the *initial configuration*.

The desire to know a foreign language is then formed according to the configuration of languages, and this desire is repeatedly invested through the repetition of exercises that is required in order to master that language, as if the desire would eventually be satisfied while the investment is returned. The process of cofiguring might well advance as though each figure, either of the familiar language or of the unknown language, directly corresponded to the closed unity of a systematicity; the process would be understood as a set trajectory that is programmed at its initial conception or *archê* and that is destined to reach the finality of complete saturation or purity. Then, the familiar and the unknown languages would both be presented as objects that could be juxtaposed on a homogeneous and ahistorical plane and gazed at from some transcendental viewpoint. They would become comparable objects. Consequently, the very unidentifiable and indeterminate difference between my language and a foreign language would be reified, fixed, and eternalized, while we would cease to view that difference as something negotiable, as an ambiguous sociality that is essentially open to many different articulations.[25] In this case, language learning serves as a typical subjective technology that produces a speaking subject according to a preconceived plan. What is suggested brilliantly by *Dictée* is exactly the undoing of the work of subjective technology, the abortion of the manufacturing of the speaking subject according to such a preconceived plan as the vision of the international world put forth by the essentially assimilationist "pluralistic World History." On two different but parallel historical fronts—the prewar Japanese colonial rule and the postwar American domination in Korea—which the speaker's desire for her mother's mother tongue happens to designate and outline, *Dictée* puts in jeopardy the subjective technology for assimilationism.[26]

What is often overlooked, *Dictée* illustrates, is that the process of learning does not necessarily lead to the inauguration of the initial project. The learning does not actually take us to the destination that was indicated at the moment of departure, of the initial investment of our desire to know. In the process, therefore, the configuration does not remain identical; for the work of learning an unknown language also works on the cofiguring of languages and thereby transforms the conditions for the anticipated trajectory of one's advancement in language learning. Instead of edging toward the promised goal, we may be overwhelmed and made erratic by the sight of many different social relations that have been made available through the work and labor of languages. We may begin to lose ourselves and the sight of our destination.

As one works toward the mastery of a language, the entire picture on which the points of departure and destination are projected also changes.

The network of imagined relations through which one relates oneself to oneself, to language unities, and to social groups, including nations, begins to undergo a drastic mutation. Yet the work of language learning cannot be thought of as a procedure in which what is conceived in the mode of potentiality is brought into being in actuality. In that sense, it does not produce a "work." It resembles the "work" of making a product according to a preconceived plan much less than a failure in the execution of such a plan. Therefore, what this "unwork"[27] accomplishes is the dispersion, displacement, and fragmentation of the core of desire itself. Desire to arrive at the destination is displaced by many different desires for different relations; the desire to know an unknown language decomposes and multiplies into many heterogeneous desires.

Dictée, skillfully and aggressively, mimicks the learning of foreign languages and portrays the process of learning in which what one says differs irreparably from what one means. In an allegorical fashion, Theresa Hak Kyung Cha discloses the experience of being in a country of immigrants where, in principle, what one says is not identical to what one means. And let me draw attention to the fact that this irreducible distance between what one says and what one means is linked to the speaker's corporeality, and that this sense of mimicry prevents her from plunging into excessive identification, often accompanied by scapegoating violence, with the host nation, the United States in her case; here, mimicry is not only a form of critique but also a paean to the social.[28] As long as the distance between the said and the meaning is not reduced to zero, the body as opacity would not cease to announce itself; neither would it be reduced to transparency. The body intervenes in the transformation and constitution of the speaking subject in language learning. It is presented as a disruptive force that holds the speaker back from advancing toward the destination pointed at by the figure of a language she learns; it emerges precisely as that which prevents her from imagining herself being able to completely internalize a foreign language, thereby rendering it transparent. And it is precisely because of this opacity that the speaker discloses the space of "in-between," a space for "community" for subjects in transit, a community that cannot be contained in or by a nation.

Here we have to be cautious in the determination of the body we are talking about. It is only in reaction to the speaker reaching out to the unknown that the body resists. In other words, the body as resistance is always contingent upon the speaker's social relation to the Other, so it is neither a substance nor an identity upon which the subjectivity of the speaker is constituted. This is to say that corporeality as resistance should not be understood merely as the inertia deriving from its pre-given cultural or linguistic constitution: it is what is called desistance rather than oppositional resistance.[29] Therefore, the deprivation of the speaker's mother tongue is not something that can be compensated for by returning her body to the original state.

In *Dictée*, the speaker seeks her mother's mother tongue. But what she reproduces in this yearning is, ironically enough, the condition in which her mother was put. "Your father left and your mother left as the others. You suffer the knowledge of having to leave. Of having left."[30] Her mother was born deprived of her immediate access to the land of her mother tongue. Thus, the particular condition under which her mother was put was given to the speaker as being already repeated. By having to leave the land of their mother tongue because of Japanese imperialist policies, the speaker's mother's parents in fact put her mother in a situation similar to the one the Korean population at large was subjected to. "Still, you speak the tongue the mandatory language like the others. It is not your own."[31] The mother was born under this condition, among "Refugees. Immigrants. Exiles." Just like the speaker who is a refugee, immigrant, exile in the United States, her mother was "bilingual," and "trilingual." "The tongue that is forbidden is your own mother tongue."[32]

An almost unbearable tension or ambivalence is created by the two diametrically opposite readings of the text. (Needless to say, just as the poet speaks in multiple tongues, the text of *Dictée* is open to many different readings.) Since the mother's tongue was already multilingual, to seek the mother's tongue would reproduce this multilinguality of her mother's tongue as well as the deprivation of the mother tongue in her mother's tongue. Therefore, what she in fact ends up seeking in her mother's tongue should be precisely the loss of the mother tongue in general, a loss that finds its best expression in the obstinate desistance of the body to the mastery of the mandatory language. It should be quite possible or even plausible to imagine that, through this loss, the speaker could find some solidarity with Korean people and those peoples who are deprived of their choice of languages. And this loss can be made to mean desistance to the smooth working of the subjective technology. That is to say that, insofar as the body disrupts the programmed trajectory of an imposed project and lends itself to other different and accidental possibilities of sociality, it should be understood as a bricolage that is infinitely open to different social articulations or as "undecidability at the frontiers of cultural hybridity."[33] Corporeality can be seen as one of the possibilities by means of which to *work on* the schemata of cofiguring and change them.

But, as if counteracting some awareness of sociality in the body, *Dictée* also projects a completely different comprehension of the body[34] and manifests an inclination toward the imagined dissolution of the obstinate corporeal desistance by "The eternity of one act. In the completion of one existence. One martyrdom. For the history of one nation. Of one people."[35] What is at issue here is, of course, the consolidation of the nation as the subject of resistance to imperialist oppression and violence. And we are urged to face the fact that the construction of the social imaginary of the nation is tied to the issue of the imaginary treatment of one's own death, of the erasure of one's own body that resists.

Exactly at this point, therefore, *Dictée* refuses to capture the work of unworking in the learning of languages. As in Suzuki's *bungaku*, Cha seems to adhere to the idea that learning is essentially a transitory process toward a final destination, in spite of all her indications to the contrary. It goes without saying that the finality of the destination is essential, in the last analysis, for the construction of the nation. And the sense of finality is given as follows:

> Some will not know age. Some not age. Time stops. Time will stop for some.
> For them especially. Eternal time. No age. Time fixes for some. Their image,
> the memory of them is not given to deterioration, unlike the captured image
> that extracts from the soul precisely by reproducing, multiplying itself. Their
> countenance evokes not the hallowed beauty, beauty from seasonal decay,
> evokes not the inevitable, not death, but the dy-ing.[36]

Thus, the desire to know a foreign language is constantly translated into its polar opposite: desire for one's own *national* language. Against the force of unworking toward the dispersion of such a desire, she has to sustain the desire for this very desire itself, the desire for her *national* mother tongue that is irreparably lost, and for the absolute identification with its figure. To the extent that the nation as a social imaginary is formed as a result of the metonymic linkage between the whole and the individual through the imagined anticipation of one's own death in the struggle against imperialism, *Dictée* too seems to affirm the thesis that the nation-state essentially is a reaction to imperialism or its historical effect.

Strangely enough, the initial configuration of languages through which desire is invested does not seem to dissipate throughout *Dictée*. Just as in the institutions of national literature and comparative literature, desire is ordained to remain intact in this text. Hence, Theresa Hak Kyung Cha ends up manufacturing the identity of her mother's tongue with *national* language as a recuperative or restorative loss to which she wishes to return.

It goes without saying that she imagines the possibility of satisfying her desire in risking her own death for the whole. In this respect too, *Dictée* invites us to see the operation of poetics in the poiesis or manufacture of the identity of national language.

At the same time, *Dictée* harbors a most radical attempt to work on the configuration of languages. It disrupts the symmetrical boundary of the inside and the outside of a national language, and puts the process of cofiguring in jeopardy.

Dictée is one of the best examples of textual performance which cannot be contained in either the ready-made category of national literature or comparative literature; rather, it demonstrates the politicality of literature in the most evocative manner.

I believe that the ambivalence inherent in this text is irreducible. This is because, on the one hand, the need to fight against imperialist oppression—which may well require manufacture in the future of the national community as the subject of resistance—is far from diminished in the world today, and, on the other hand, the homogenization of that national community could too often lead to the tremendous victimization of those who are culturally and linguistically heterogeneous.

However unbearable it may be, the text seems to say, we have to live with this ambivalence.

2

The Problem of "Japanese Thought": The Formation

of "Japan" and the Schema of Cofiguration[1]

The Positing of an Inquiry

Why do we have to call into question "Japanese" thought or Japanese "thought"? Why do we have to regard the being of Japanese thought as questionable? Also, what sort of knowledge are we to pursue in the name of "Japanese thought"? And what should "Japanese thought" designate in the first place?

It is important to keep in mind that we cannot respond to these questions by first collecting concrete examples of "Japanese thought" and then abstracting the common features that all share; for, unless we have already assumed what is comprehended by "Japanese thought," we can neither collect its examples nor distinguish what falls under the class of "Japanese thought" from what does not.

The same may be said about those discursive positivities that have been sustained in pedagogic and research institutions, that is, about disciplines such as "Japanese literature" and "Japanese history." It is not the putative objects for knowing but the existence of academic disciplines that allow us to seek to know about "Japanese literature," "Japanese history," and, of course, "Japanese thought." We might remind ourselves of a Foucauldian insight. It is not because the objects of knowledge are preparatorily given that certain disciplines are formed to investigate them; on the contrary, the objects are engendered because the disciplines are in place. Thus we might argue that, as the discourse of *kokubungaku* or "the national literature" was formed, "Japanese literature" came into being; that the "Japanese language" emerged at the time when a discipline was instituted to investigate that presumptive object or when some preliminary form of Japanese linguistics was constructed. Accordingly, the most concise, if not the most satisfactory, definition of "Japanese thought" could be given as the presumptive object that the discipline of "the history of Japanese thought" thematically investigates. That is to say, ours is not a perspective from which the history of Japanese thought as a discipline is determined by the existence of its object, Japanese thought, but rather one from which the object is made possible by the existence of the discipline. Of course, this is not to say that "Japanese thought" is never discussed outside the confines of this field of academic specialization. Rather, it seems plausible that the most reliable answer to the initial questions asked here is to be found in the field whose expertise consists in the investigation of Japanese thought.

In this field, nonetheless, hardly any work can be found that manifestly offers the essence of Japanese thought, whereas the question "What is Japanese thought?" has so frequently been asked. Furthermore, one should take note of the fragility and immaturity of this field as a pedagogic and research institutional arrangement in comparison to Japanese literature and Japanese history, which are more solidly established in the systems of national education. Undoubtedly, as a field of specialized knowledge the history of Japanese thought finds its own legitimacy in a certain comprehension of what "Japanese thought" is, but the explicit definition of Japanese thought on which that expertise is supposedly built is nowhere in sight. On this account, for example, Kaji Nobuyuki wrote the following: "We cannot presume that Japanese thought is already existent somewhere. Nor can we assume that Japanese thought has already been formed. It exists only in our continual questioning and investigation as to what it is and what the history of it can be."[2] Thus the history of Japanese thought is an academic field that is continually motivated by the question "What is Japanese thought?" In this context, being guided by some vague apprehension of their objective, students engage themselves in the task of the decipherment of Japanese thought in pursuit of a clearer definition of it. It should appear to be a hermeneutic inquiry, as an ekstatic or self-transcending project toward the meaning of its own inquiry. To put it in more formal terms, therefore, the history of Japanese thought is a field of knowledge that is sustained and reproduced by a desire for the meaning of Japanese thought, a desire that is made possible by the positing of "Japanese thought" as its ultimate objective. But, let me note, the field exists only as long as the desire remains frustrated. Should the desire be satiable, "the history of Japanese thought" as a domain of discourse would naturally dissolve once its desire had been gratified. It is in existence so long as the desire for the meaning of Japanese thought is repeatedly aroused by the inquiry about what it is. In this domain of discourse, the being of Japanese thought is assumed but never disclosed, and its esoteric essence is projected into the past, while this institution of knowledge is sustained by the insatiable desire for it. ⌉

⌈ Consequently, we must develop the problem of Japanese thought from perspectives that are not entirely in accord with the desire conjured up by the question "What is Japanese thought?"; instead of submitting ourselves to that desire to want to know "what Japanese thought is," we must rather analyze the apparatus whereby the desire itself is reproduced, by always shifting our focus away from it. In short, we must "deduce" the components of the desire such as "Japan" and "thought," and stop "taking these seriously." Yet, this does not mean that we must take the position of transcendental consciousness by putting empirical judgments in brackets.⌉ What is in demand in order to prevent the desire from focusing onto its putative object and, instead, to let it disperse, is a certain art by means of which we prepare a series of interruptions so that the question "What is Japanese thought?" may not result in the consolidation of the history of Japanese thought as a discipline. And I would still like to call this art a history or historiography that historicizes the conditions of possibility for the history of Japanese thought.⌉

⌈On the one hand, "Japanese thought" is neither immediately given nor known to the students, yet we believe that it is possible for them to study it. On the other hand, although "Martian thought," for example, is equally neither immediately given nor known, we do not believe that it is plausible to study it, nor that its history could constitute a field of knowledge. Indeed, this is because, whereas the being of Japanese thought is assumed ascribable to the presence of "the Japanese" or of "the Japanese culture" as an environment for it, there cannot be any equivalent to which "Martian thought" may be ascribed. We presume that there has been the mode of thinking particular or proper to the unified group of people called "the Japanese" who inhabit the geographic territory called "Japan" today. We would feel justified to continue to ask "what Japanese thought is" as long as we fail to call into question the presence of "the Japanese," "the Japanese culture," or some vague notion of "Japan."⌉

[However, it is one thing to demonstrate that a name has always been there indicating some notion of unified geographic area, and quite another to assert that it necessarily presumes the existence of the unity of people living in an area designated by that name. From the historical genealogy of the name "Japan"—or *Na* or *Wa* in antiquity—we cannot infer the past existence of the unified social group called "Japan," since the concept signified by the name does not immediately entail that the populace unified under that name was there. Of course, no human grouping gains an enduring presence unless it is named, but the presence of a name in a certain historical period does not necessarily guarantee the presence of a social unity organized in that name. Discursive formation of a much higher complexity than a geographic proper name is required in order that the unity of a group thus named be a social reality, that is, that the members of the populace identify themselves with that unity through the medium of the name. The geographic proper name "America," for instance, exists, but this does not imply that there is a community called "America." A variety of people inhabit the area designated by America, from Alaska in the north to Tierra del Fuego in the south, but—unless America is confused with the United States of America—they do not form a single community.

What has been accepted unproblematically in the history of Japanese thought is that, by openly acknowledging the esoteric inaccessibility of Japanese thought, we have evaded doubts and obvious incongruities about the assumptions of "the Japanese" and "Japan," as if the existence of "the Japanese" in the past had been rather a matter of negligible triviality compared with the gravity of the problematic nature of Japanese thought itself. For instance, Watsuji Tetsurô, discussing "the Japanese spirit" (a substitute for Japanese thought), argued as follows:

> When we are not specifically interrogated as to what the Japanese spirit is, we think we all know what it is. But once the question is raised, we gradually become unsure about it. In the end, we will find that none of us knows what it is. In fact, having been obliged to write about the Japanese spirit, I must at least admit this much—that I am not clear what I am to write about.[3]

But, right after this, Watsuji's argument meanders and slides on to a different topic, namely, that the Japanese spirit is not necessarily reactionary but could serve a progressive function; although admitting the historicity of the idea of "self-awareness as a nation" without which "neither the modern state based on self-awareness as a nation nor nationalism would be possible," Watsuji abruptly and without reasoning begins to narrate the history of the Japanese spirit as "the self-awareness of the ethnic community as a nation"[4] starting with antiquity. In other words, he first admits that "nationalism" is a historically limited notion, but, in spite of all the inconsistencies, he ventures to presume that "the ethnic community as the Japanese nation" had potentially existed even in antiquity, and launches the task of describing the history of the Japanese spirit. It is noteworthy that Watsuji treats the term, "Japan," "Japanese ethnos," and "national subject" as interchangeable. In his argument, "Japan" as a geographic unity repeatedly becomes "Japan" as "the national subject."[5] Underlying his argument is this rather simplistic reasoning: "the Japanese" must have been because the geographic area "Japan" was there. What we have to note in this instance is that the thought of "the Japanese" as "the national subject" had already been given as unknown and unknowable. This is to say that, although "we," the students of the history of Japanese thought in general, do not know what "Japanese thought" is, "we" at least know that it existed.

This inquisitive operation about the understanding of *our* history, to bring into the open what has already been comprehended, has been repeated not only by Watsuji but also by a great number of the students of Japanese intellectual and cultural history, thereby reproducing the desire for "Japanese thought that had been created by the Japanese people themselves."[6] By positing in the past "the Japanese as an ethnos" or "the national subject," we would then be solicited to assume not "the quiddity" but "the essence or being" of Japanese thought, while this assumption of Japanese thought helps constitute the horizon of understanding against which past historical documents would be read in pursuit of what it is. You do not know what Japanese thought is, but you at least know that it has long existed, so that you can continue to inquire into it.

Thus, the questioning of Japanese thought engenders the channels of tautological inquiries and responses within which, in principle, one is not expected to call into question the existence of Japanese thought; there, one is prohibited from asking whether or not "the Japanese" or "the national subject" existed in the past at all. To engage in the history of Japanese thought without a critical assessment of the formation of the discipline would, therefore, result in the reproduction of what Tosaka Jun once called "the cognition of national history." It is "the most convenient argument in which the conclusion is the premise from the outset."[7]

The Student of the History of Japanese Thought and the Enunciative Positionality

It is necessary to point out that "the Japanese" and "the Japanese ethnos as national subject," but for the assumptions of which "Japanese thought" would be meaningless, have been taken for granted without due process of argumentation. But, to point this out is not sufficient; for we have to pursue not only the constative problematic as to how to accurately represent the past in historiography but also the performative problematic as to what the student *does* by inquiring into "Japanese thought." Insofar as our concerns are confined to what happened and what was thought in the past, the positing of "the Japanese" and "the ethnic community" should be no more than a matter of hypothesis. The other, hitherto neglected, aspect of the history of Japanese thought would be in our sight as soon as we extend the scope of our questioning to include what the students of the history of Japanese thought *would do* by studying it. It is invariably related to the modes of identification for the students. At the same time, it is a problem of the discursive formation in which the enunciative positions for students are constructed.

ENUNCIATION FROM WITHIN OR WITHOUT "JAPANESE THOUGHT"

Whether or not the student of the history of Japanese thought perceives an excessively emotive charge in the modifier "Japanese" depends to a great extent on which enunciative position he or she adopts: the student speaks from either the position that is continuous with Japanese thought or the position that is discontinuous. Identifying with the continuous or the discontinuous position, the student would discuss Japanese thought inherently as his or her own or as somebody else's problem, respectively. Hence, even if the student admits that the Japanese as a "nation" is essentially a modern invention, the student who is "Japanese" would still approach historical documents of the past with a certain expectation of familiarity and intimacy since those documents are classified under the heading of "*Japanese* thought." Indeed, what is presumed in this tacit expectation is that, since the student and the authors of those documents both belong to the "same" Japan, there must be some common ground that foreigners could never share. It is, let us note, in the performative aspect of academic disciplines such as Japanese history and Japanese literature that "the nation" (*kokumin*) and "the ethnos" (*minzoku*) are distinguished from each other *and* merged together as if they were synonymous. In these disciplines, one is often forgetful of such an elementary historical sense as the fact that, "paradoxical as it may appear, the old ideas that existed in Japan in the past should sound very foreign from the viewpoint of present-day Japanese life."[8] A fairly well known scholar once made a pathetic confession: he had struggled with works by European philosophers such as Plato and Hegel for a long time in his youth until he encountered *Sankyô Giryû* by Prince Shôtoku (a seventh-century Buddhist treatise written in literary Chinese), when he finally realized that he could understand Prince Shô-toku's work much more intimately than Westerners' because he and the Prince were both "the same" as Japanese. Whether or not we are allowed to take his words seriously without risking our own seriousness, such a senti-ment as the one expressed in this confession is surely an effect of the iden-tification with the continuous position.

Most of the pre-twentieth-century historical documents are in lan-guages that are foreign by today's standard, and the linguistic diversity of early modern and premodern documents is just striking in comparison to the relative similarity of medieval English and modern English. As a result, they are illegible for the majority of the present-day Japanese population. In other words, as far as those documents are concerned, most Japanese who are alive today are foreigners to them; the notions and sentiments ex-pressed in the documents are, in turn, undeniably alien to the contempo-rary Japanese. Nonetheless, the presumptive continuity of "the Japanese" does not allow contemporary Japanese to view Japanese thought of the past essentially as "foreigners'" thought.

By reading the historical documents and arguing about Japanese thought of the past, students utilize the historical past as an excuse to reproduce *in the present* the distinction between "the Japanese" and "foreigners," a distinc-tion whose relevance should be nil outside the contexts of the modern and present time. Depending on whether the student identifies with or "su-tures" the position continuous with "Japanese thought," he or she is likely to take an opposite attitude toward it. Whereas the student speaking from the continuous position might approach the subject matter sympatheti-cally, the other students who suture the discontinuous position would in all likelihood do so antipathetically.

Let me call those who suture the discontinuous position "anti-Japanese," not for their resultant attitude or hostility toward the putative object called "Japan" but for their mode of identification. It is noteworthy that the students of the "anti-Japanese" position could in principle take—and some actually did take—an extremely pro-Japanese attitude. Yet, in the majority of cases, the choice of enunciative positionality seems to predetermine what they will eventually read in the historical documents. This is espe-cially evident among those students who have lived in Japan and witnessed the exclusionary sides of contemporary Japanese society; too often they end up discovering in the documents of the past the same traits they have observed in the present, "because they were written by the same Japanese!"

Antithetical though their position may be, they subject themselves to the parallel modes of enunciation in which both the "Japanese" and "anti-Japanese" enunciative positions are constructed in their transferential supplementarity. [It is important to keep in mind that the choice of "suturing" between "the Japanese" and "the anti-Japanese" positions is entirely within the purview of the dialectic of the addresser and the addressee, a dialectic of the transference and countertransference of the other's desire.]

In the history of Japanese thought as an ensemble of institutionalized utterances, one could instantly depict the rule according to which the addresser and the addressee are made to suture their respective positions. Of course, an individual addresser may well occupy many different subjective positions, such as university teacher, housewife, local politician, and so forth, but, as far as utterances in the history of Japanese thought are concerned, the student has to adopt a caesural position either of "the Japanese"/"non-Japanese" or of "the anti-Japanese"/"non-Japanese" and enunciates as "the Japanese" or "the anti-Japanese" because he or she has adopted that ambiguous and split positionality; for, for the choice of "suturing" to be offered, there must be a possibility of metaleptic nonidentification, of being neither Japanese nor anti-Japanese but non-Japanese, distant from either position. The possibility of being non-Japanese is the possibility of engendering a metaleptic distance, or getting out of the previous narrative level, without which a subsequent "suturing" or identification would be impossible. The student simultaneously belongs to the register in which "Japan" can be objectified, and another register in which the opposition of the Japanese and the anti-Japanese is significant. In order for the student to address himself or herself either as "the Japanese" or as "the anti-Japanese," the caesura of the enunciative positionality and the duality of its registration seem inevitable.

Two theses can be drawn from this observation. [First, as long as one addresses oneself by "suturing" the position continuous with "Japanese thought," one can speak as a Japanese no matter where one is from.] In the history of Japanese thought, as in any academic discipline, one may speak as a Japanese even if one is brought up in Africa, North America, or China; for, even though such an enunciative position might coincide with one's national identity in the majority of cases, these must be clearly differentiated. "Japanese" is not a natural attribute to an individual but an identity constituted relationally within a specific discourse in each instance. Second, the essentially modern character of this discipline consists in a historical accident due to which the binary oppositions not only of "the Japanese" and "the anti-Japanese" but also of "the Japanese" or "the anti-Japanese" and "the non-Japanese" have been appropriated by the opposition of the non-West and the West. Thus, in this case, "Japan" was destined to play the role of a particular, exemplifying the non-West in contrast to the West. This is most evident in the fact that, in the field of Japanese intellectual history since the Meiji period, few works have been written that have no explicit or implicit reference to the history of Western thought. The history of Japanese thought was created as a symmetrical equivalent to the history of Western thought or of Western philosophy, so that this field has been dominated from the outset by demands for symmetry and equality.[9] The entire discipline has been built on the premise that, if there is thought in the West, there ought to be its equivalent in Japan. But these demands necessarily gave rise to the sense of a lack, as is best testified to by the often professed bitter realization that there was nothing worth calling philosophy in Japan, although there should be an equivalent to it. Because of this mimetic desire, intellectuals since Nishi Amane (1829–97) have repeatedly deplored the absence of a systematic reasoning or of philosophical thinking in Japan. As I will reiterate later, the self-referential character was inscribed on the history of Japanese thought by way of this mimetic desire.

THE WEST AS AN IDEALIZED READERSHIP

Among the specialists of the history of Japanese thought, who indeed include figures like Inoue Tetsujirô (1855–1944), very few have not immersed themselves in the study of Western philosophy at one time or another in their career. Although the overwhelming majority of works in Japanese intellectual history have been written in the Japanese language and are highly unlikely to find readership outside Japan, this field seems dictated by a concern to make "Japanese thought" intelligible to Western readership. Except for most of those who do not possess Japanese nationality, the students of the history of Japanese thought, generally speaking, address themselves as "the Japanese" either in anticipation of or in contradiction to what is presumptively expected of them by "Western readers" who in this respect primarily are not Japanese. And, "Western readers" thus posited, who are by definition "the anti-Japanese" (in the sense of one particularity as opposed to another particularity equals the Japanese), would inevitably occupy the position of "the non-Japanese" (as a result of a certain metalepsis in the sense of belonging to a different taxonomic dimension, not opposed to the Japanese as a particularity) as well, because the differences not only of the Japanese and the anti-Japanese but also of the Japanese and the non-Japanese have been appropriated by the opposition of the non-West and the West; that is, the student's choice to speak as Japanese and to "suture" the position continuous with "Japanese thought" is already a form of subjection whereby he or she is made to desire to meet the putative expectation of "the readers" in anticipation of what is expected by "the West." Of course, "Western readership" anticipated here is an ideal postulate and has in fact very little to do with the readers who happen to be from Western Europe or North America. Yet, within this schema of configuration or cofiguration, the history of Japanese thought has been possible only as a transferential equivalent to the history of Western thought. But, since the West as one of many plausible "anti-Japanese" positions has consistently been confused with the West as the generality of "the non-Japanese" positionality, the readers of "Western thought" have too often been taken to be "Western readers" of universal thought in general.

In addition, "Western readers" are posited as an equivalent to the readers who identify with the position continuous with "Japanese thought," so they are supposed to be capable of comprehending "from within" "the entirety of Western thought" from Heracleitus to Erigena, from Leibniz to Poincaré, down to Sartre and Habermas. Thus, "Western readers" were posited as "the subject" subsistent throughout the continuous history of the West.

However, it is important to keep in mind that the subjection of the Japanese to the putative West through desire for their own cultural and national authenticity cannot directly be understood as an interpersonal subjugation to the so-called Western individual. The history of Japanese thought as a discipline in fact includes those who would not "suture" the position continuous with "Japanese thought," and some of them regard themselves as ones "from the West." But, we should not forget that the students who address themselves as Westerners are equally subjected to the West through the schema of cofiguration. Only too frequently have we encountered those who happen to be from the so-called West (whose geographic, if not racial, identity is extremely obscure) and who, by "suturing" the position of "Western thought," delude themselves into believing that the entirety of "Western thought" is in fact subsistent in them. But, as goes without saying, their insistence on their Western identity as opposed to the Japanese one, and on "our" perspective distinct from "theirs," is a gesture symptomatic of the narcissistic form of double subjection whereby they submit themselves to the desire to perform the putative role of "the Westerners" in anticipation of what is expected of them by "the Japanese."

This destiny in which the history of Japanese thought seems to remain captive must not be understood in terms of its backwardness, nor of its lack of authenticity. These unavoidable consequences of the cofiguration indicate the historicity, or the essential modernity, of the history of Japanese thought as a discipline. As its presumed readers are the idealized Western readers, so Western thought that has been posited in the history of Japanese thought is an idea. And "Japanese thought" and Japan are ideas whose ideality must be sustained symmetrically by the ideas of "Western thought" and of the putative West. Thus an epistemic arrangement has come into being, according to which to insist on the particularity and autonomy of Japan is paradoxically to worship the putative ubiquity of the idealized West. Not only could "Japanese thought" not overcome the framework of modernity, but it also meant to continue to think within such a framework, thanks to this arrangement.

The attempt to posit the identity of one's own ethnicity or nationality in terms of the gap between it and the putative West, that is, to create the history of one's own nation through the dynamics of attraction to and repulsion from the West, has, almost without exception, been adopted as a historical mission by non-Western intellectuals. Eurocentrism, characteristic of modernity, is most powerfully manifest in narratives by non-Western intellectuals, and it is in this respect that the history of Japanese thought carries with it the seal of modernity. Accordingly, the supposed subjects of "Japanese thought," such as "a nation" or "an ethnos as the national community," must be reconsidered in reference to this dynamics.

As long as students identify with the subjective position of "the Japanese," "Japanese thought" reveals itself as "my" thought or "our" thought. But the obsession with one's own ethnicity or nationality would not make much sense except in relation to its opposite. The term of contrasting opposition may well be China or India, but invariably what has been presumed as "anti-Japanese" as well as "non-Japanese" remains "the West" or "Euro-American" civilization; for India or China could be regarded as possible "anti-Japanese" positions but never as a "non-Japanese" positionality, even in comparative studies. The attempts by a Tsuda Sôkichi or a Watsuji Tetsurô to read the ancient documents of Japan as expressing "our national thought" (waga kokumin shisô)[10] or "Japanese national self-awareness" (nihonjin no kokumin-teki jikaku), in which Japan is consistently compared with its inferior opponents such as India and China, received its legitimacy from the hierarchical order of the modern world and the dynamics of attraction to and repulsion from the West, of which those authors could not be free.

Therefore, "Japanese thought" was, from the outset, posited as the subject for comparative investigation. The history of Japanese thought has been a field of self-referential knowledge for Japanese students precisely because, in this field, they enunciate in comparative modalities. Comparison has been operative at the level not only of the propositional subject (*shugo*), where the subject matter is thematically discussed, but also of the institutionalized predication, which Michel Foucault called "enunciative modalities." The students have not had any other choices but to enunciate in a comparative setting, so the field could be the history neither of thought nor of philosophy; but it had to be the history of *Japanese* thought. They might be free in their choice of subject matter, but in the modern world they could never freely select enunciative modalities other than those of comparison.

The Regime of Translation and the Schema of Cofiguration

JAPANESE THOUGHT AS A SUBJECT OF COMPARISON

The relation to the self cannot be determined unless the relation to the other has already been determined. Not to mention Hegel on self-consciousness, it is a rudimentary premise, when dealing with the problem of identity in cultural and social contexts, that the relation to the other logically precedes that to the self. What is at issue here, indeed, is not a dialectic of the self and the other for individual consciousnesses, but a process in which the comparative framework of Japan (the self) and the West (the other) is installed. This framework is not merely epistemological in that it offers a means of comparative mapping. As I have repeatedly stressed, its function is also practical, since it fashions the shape of desire for the students of Japanese thought.

Therefore, let me tentatively advance the following formula: desire for "Japanese thought" is invoked through the schema of cofiguration in the regime of translation.

The regime of translation is an ideology that makes translators imagine their relationship to what they do in translation as the symmetrical exchange between two languages. The operation of translation as it is understood by common sense today is motivated by this ideology. The conventional notion of translation from English into Japanese, for instance, presumes that both English and Japanese are systematic wholes, and that translation is to establish a bridge for the exchange of equal values between the two wholes. A translation is believed to become more accurate as it approximates the rule of equal value exchange. In this regime of translation, it is required that one language be clearly and without ambiguity distinguishable from the other and that, in principle, two languages never overlap or mix like Siamese twins. It is through this regime that, in the eighteenth century, the idea of the original Japanese language was introduced into the multilingual social environment of the Japanese archipelago, where heterogeneous and creole languages were accepted.

By the schema of cofiguration, I want to point out the essentially "imaginary" nature of the comparative framework of Japan and the West, since the figure in cofiguration is imaginary in the sense that it is a sensible image on the one hand, and practical in its ability to evoke one to act toward the future on the other. Thus, the figure invokes imagination by which desire for identity is produced, and is the central issue for the logic of imagination. We would remain ignorant of how the desire for identity precipitates in the history of Japanese thought unless the issue of the figure is taken into consideration. I would like to underline, however, that desire does not develop unilinearly toward a figure but deploys itself spatially in contrast with an other figure.[11] In the desire to want to know "Japanese thought," not only Japan but also the West has to be figured out: Japan and the West have to be cofigured. The desire to identify either with Japan or the West is, therefore, invariably a mimetic one, so that the insistence on Japan's originality, for instance, would have to be mediated by the mimetic desire for the West. It goes without saying that, for the same reason, within the discipline of the history of Japanese thought—and, by extension, Japanese studies—the insistence on the West's uniqueness would, in turn, be a testimony to the students' disavowed desire to imitate what is expected of the West by the Japanese.

The regime of translation and the schema of cofiguration thus facilitate one another. Yet, the regime of translation as an ideology conceals within itself some inversions or perversions. To analyze these inversions is to understand the desire called "Japanese thought" in the formation of the discipline.

TRANSLATION AND AN UNKNOWN LANGUAGE

To define translation is a hard task. To take translation as broadly as possible, every reading and every interpretation would be one version or another of translation. I must, then, first delimit the scope of my investigation by excluding cases of translation that do not conform to bilingual translation from Korean to German, from Chinese to French, for example, where the unities of the two languages involved serve to define national or ethnic identities. Furthermore, I must put aside the problem, already touched on, that the unities of those languages have been predetermined as closed totalities. Let me note a few traits in this conventional and abstract notion of bilateral and bilingual international translation.

It is obvious that translation normally takes place between a known language and an unknown one, for translation would be unnecessary where everyone involved knows both languages. Generally, translation takes place when in the presence of two kinds of people—those who know both languages and those who only know one; that is, only when the language to be translated from is both known and unknown is translation an issue. Translation, therefore, is called upon on the condition that people must take two differing attitudes, different stances, in relation to what is being translated in translation. In other words, what characterizes translation from ordinary speech is that it gives rise to an attitude or stance that is neither that of the addresser nor the addressee. If what is being translated is addressed to those who do not know the language to be translated from, the translator (or the one who knows the language and who can understand what is being translated in that original language) would then be unable to take the stance of the addressee, for he or she would then have to dislodge from the stance of the addressee those for whom translation is necessary. The translator would have to take the attitude of a bystander who presides over the event in which the message is addressed to the addressee. The translator cannot take the pronominal position of either the first or the second person in the putatively personal address of this communication, yet has to participate in this situation, or what Émile Benveniste would call an "instance of discourse," as a bystander, as an indifferent observer who denies immediate involvement but nonetheless is present at the scene. Translation takes its place where the gap in the knowledge of languages results in the difference of attitudes and stances.

In short, translation is necessary because there is an unknown language for some people. Let us think through this almost self-evident and tautological statement.

Translation is done for those who do not know the language to be translated from. Therefore, because they do not know the language from which the message is translated, they are unable to tell whether or not the translation done for them is correct. Furthermore, so long as the translator believes he or she is translating correctly, there is no other means but the translation by which to judge whether or not it is correct. Unless the translator tries an incorrect translation or mistranslates on purpose, he or she cannot know if the translation is incorrect, for it is the translator who legislates the standard of translation, and only through the act of translation is the channel of equal exchange created. Following Wittgenstein, we then assert that the rules for correct translation are instituted by translationary practices. One can mistranslate precisely because one does know that one is mistranslating. Hence, we cannot think of an a priori rule whereby to judge the correctness or incorrectness of a given translation: all we can do to judge a translation is offer a new translation from the viewpoint of which an old translation can be corrected. Strictly speaking, there is no metatranslation that is not merely another translation. Only retrospectively, therefore, we can postulate a set of rules by which translational operation in general is conducted. As Heidegger clearly understood with regard to Kantian schematism, the representing of the rule is the schema.[12] And, as far as the regime of translation is concerned, the rule thus represented is an inversion in retrospection. Therefore, the notion of translation in which the same message is transferred from one linguistic medium to another is feasible only after the enunciation of translation has taken place, and the symmetrical equivalence implied in the correctness of translation between the original and its translation is necessarily a retrospective construction. This is why a judgment on a translation is inevitably an enunciation of another translation, and every judgment of its correctness must be preceded by an enunciation of translation.

The familiar sorts of problems that have repeatedly been debated with regard to translatability—"Is there any equivalent in Japanese to the word 'love' in English?" "Has a poem ever been truly translated into another language?"—have too often been represented as though they had been about the guiding rules for translation. As a matter of fact, they are nothing but derivatives of that retrospective inversion because of which the relationship of equivalence between the original and its translation and the enunciation of translation can be represented anachronistically. What is perceived as untranslatable and incommensurable in translational transaction, therefore, is possible only ex post facto and does not precede the enunciation of translation. It is because the enunciation of translation opens up the space of communication and commensurability that that which does not lend itself to translation becomes possible and manifest. But, it is necessary to keep in mind that the enunciation of translation is unrepresentable; the enunciation of translation (a practice that is essentially temporal) and the representation of translation (a representation that is essentially spatial) are in a disjunctive and mutually negative relation with one another;[13] the practice of translation remains radically heterogeneous to the representation of translation that is facilitated through the schema of cofiguration.

The analysis of the way in which translation is *represented* thus indicates the essentially imaginary nature of the notion of bilateral and bilingual international translation. Furthermore, such a representation of translation as a transfer of a message from one language into another is an ascertainable matter only for those who know both languages. For those for whom translation is called upon, it is not a matter about which they can dispute because the language to translate from is, in principle, outside their experience; that is, the representation of translation as such is given to them as a fable beyond their capacity of empirical validation. Here, we come back to another version of the same statement: for those for whom translation is an absolute necessity, the language to translate from is unknowable.

Take the case of translation from Swahili into Japanese. Most of the Japanese audience probably does not read Swahili; many of them, perhaps, do not even know of it. Hence, they would be dependent on the Japanese translation of an article or speech in Swahili. Here we come across a peculiar state of affairs. The readers who need translation do not know the language to translate from; it follows that, in principle, they should not be able to know how to identify that language which they do not know. If I were to give them a piece of translation from the original in Hattari and tell them it is from Swahili, therefore, they would never be able to tell if I were lying. Because the readers who need translation do not know the original language, they cannot identify that language; that is, those who cannot but be dependent on translation not only do not know that language, but they do not know whether or not it exists either. Nevertheless, the readers would not dare to doubt that it was from Swahili. This is simply because they do not know how to doubt it, just as we do not doubt that many unknown languages—for me, they happen to include Arabic, Spanish, and Swahili—exist in this world.

Everyone is familiar with entertainment shows in which comedians mimic the sounds of foreign languages such as Chinese and French without making the slightest sense in these languages. Probably, the majority of the audience who laugh at such abuses of foreign languages do not know these languages themselves and, therefore, cannot tell the fake from the authentic. What is most amusing about these shows is, in actuality, those laughing folks, that is, those of us who cannot tell how to recognize those languages, yet who still delude ourselves into believing that we can tell the fake from the authentic. In the end, of course, it is we who are laughed at.

Besides the fact that the mechanism of xenophobia is clearly delineated in such entertainment shows (try to substitute abhorrence for laughter and consider how this sort of joke turns into an ethnic joke that isolates an ethnic group as an object of laughter against which "we" are consolidated in a certain homosocial fashion), to reflect upon what I am doing by laughing then would make me aware that the only guarantee I have about an unknown language to translate from is hearsay. Such a language is given to me, in the first place, as a phantasmatic figure; for, by definition, I cannot have any means to validate the existence of a language unknown to me, and every testimony to its being is inscribed in the very language I cannot decipher. That I do not know a language means that I do not know how to recognize it, so my ignorance of a language must necessarily be my ignorance of the fact that I do not know it.

Accordingly, Swahili as an unknown language is given to me, in the first place, through hearsay as *an imaginary being*. Similarly to an unknown language to translate from, an unknown foreign language I want to learn is given to me only through hearsay as an imaginary being. This imaginary being, nevertheless, means the absolute and contingent command for the learner in the sense that, in Kafka's *Castle*, an order from the Castle is such an absolute but utterly contingent command for Surveyor K. Just as in the case of an unknown language in translation, this imaginary being of the language I am to learn regulates and guides my desire to want to know that language. The being of a foreign language unknown to me thus serves the role of an idea that directs me in the long and laborious process of learning it. It is not merely for being an image but also for its poietic function that the being of a foreign language is essentially imaginary.

A FOREIGN LANGUAGE AS A REGULATIVE IDEA

Consequently, a foreign language might be represented as a figure. But it is also what Kant called the Regulative Idea, in its poietic function. The language to translate from or foreign language is not given as "an object absolutely" but as "an object in the idea": in the case that an object is given absolutely, "our concepts are employed to determine the object," but in the latter case "there is in fact only a schema for which no object, not even a hypothetical one, is directly given and which only enables us to represent to ourselves other objects in an indirect manner, namely in their systematic unity, by means of their relation to this idea."[14] Accordingly, this idea has no claim to be a constitutive principle, a principle according to which our experience, that is, our empirical knowledge, is constituted. By assuming such an idea, "we do not really extend our knowledge beyond the objects of possible experience; we extend only the empirical unity of such experience, by means of the systematic unity for which the schema is provided by the idea."[15]

Let us turn our attention to the process of foreign language learning. If I begin to attend a Chinese-language class, I realize that many languages, including the one the Confucian classics are written in, *Beijing-hua*, the so-called standard language, and languages used in different regions in the People's Republic of China and the Republic of China (one of which might, to my astonishment, be *Kambun*, which could also be classified under "Japanese language"), have been subsumed under the name Chinese language. At this stage, I would not be able to answer if I am asked whether or not there is a language that corresponds to the name "Chinese language." However, this simply implies that, when I do not know Chinese—that is, before I begin to learn it—I cannot know that the name Chinese language may as well correspond to no single empirical object or contain a multiplicity. When I do not know Chinese, I have no other way but to accept what I am told is the Chinese language. So, in order for me to start learning Chinese, I have to believe in the idea of the Chinese language submissively and blindly, just as Surveyor K had to believe in the command from the Castle.

This is not limited to the case of beginners in foreign language learning: in essence, this should apply to all the empirical studies of languages; for, since academic linguistics is invariably based upon the assumption that the language is an institution that is systematically organized, linguistic study cannot begin to study a language until it posits that object as a systematic unity. Linguists do not come to discover the systematicity of a langue through and as a result of empirical research. On the contrary, the positing of such a systematic unity as a langue is the condition of possibility for linguistic research. As a corollary, the systematicity of a langue has to be given as a synchronic unity. It goes without saying that the synchronicity of a langue cannot be understood as a cross section of some concrete language at one historical moment: it is the idea of systematicity that we posit as a requirement of a language's internal organization, irrespective of the object language we may study, and that we disclose by a certain transcendental reduction. Systematicity as the synchronic unity of a langue logically—or, more precisely, transcendentally—precedes the precipitation of empirical data about the putative object of study. In this respect, the langue is a regulative idea that produces the possibility of systematic study about it. For instance, a regulative idea of Japanese language must first be posited for there to be the figure of Japanese around which linguistic knowledge about Japanese can precipitate.

Consequently, the unity called "Japanese" is an idea that "enables us to represent to ourselves other objects in an indirect manner, namely in their systematic unity, by means of their relation to this idea of 'the Japanese language.'"[16] It follows that the unity of Japanese language itself cannot be an object of experience in the Kantian sense; that is, we can neither experience "Japanese" nor validate its existence empirically.

As I advance in the learning of Chinese and begin to understand its diversity, I may possibly change the status of the foreign language I want to learn from the Chinese language to a more specific langue, *Beijing-hua*. Yet, the being of the langue *Beijing-hua* would give rise to the same set of problems. Again, we cannot experience the unity of that language. But the regulative idea of *Beijing-hua* would give me "its schema," according to which I would be able to synthesize a variety of experiences systematically and continue to learn the language of *Beijing*.

Except for cases of bilingualism and multilingualism where one learns a foreign language as one's native language, however, we usually learn a foreign language through a more familiar language (which is not always, but often is, the native language of the learner). In other words, the learning of a foreign language cannot do away with translation, and the comprehension of utterances in a foreign language most frequently occurs through the regime of translation. This is best illustrated by the fact that a foreign language dictionary is organized by the format of bilateral and bilingual translation. It is in the schema of cofiguration that a foreign language as an object in the regulative idea is represented.

To take examples most familiar to the readers of this series,[17] dictionaries used in foreign language education are organized according to a symmetrical format, as in English-Japanese, German-Japanese, and Chinese-Japanese or Japanese-English, Japanese-German, and Japanese-Chinese dictionaries, so that they would be of little use outside the regime of bilateral translation. In the modern discourses of education in which we have been disciplined, the regulative idea of the foreign language should most often be appropriated in the schema of cofiguration with a twin symmetrical format. I want to emphasize the historicity of these discourses concerning foreign languages. We should not forget that the regulative idea of the foreign language itself is not free from historical contingency and that, in the end, it is also a positivity in those discourses that comes into being at a certain moment and will probably disappear at another. Such a regulative idea does not direct our relation to a foreign language transhistorically. Insofar as the regions on the Japanese archipelago are concerned, it is only for the last two centuries or so that some people have begun to represent to themselves their relations to foreign languages according to the schema of cofiguration. Furthermore, until about a century ago, those who relied on this twin schema in their thinking of languages were definitely in the minority.[18]

The schema of cofiguration serves as a schema for the idea of foreign language, indeed. But, let us keep in mind that, because of its twin and symmetrical composition, it also serves as the schema for the idea of one's own language. As I have already discussed with regard to Japanese language, one can never *experience* either a foreign language or one's own (national language) as a systematic unity. It is, instead, in the schema of cofiguration that one's own language is represented as the object of a regulative idea. And this is not to claim, as in hermeneutics, that, through the encounter with foreign language or historical distance, one is made aware of one's own language or the tradition to which one has already and inherently pertained. One's own language as a regulative idea does not have its object in experience, so there should not be either our own language or tradition that inheres in ourselves. It is for this reason that one must construe the representation of one's own and foreign languages in terms not of the problematic of hermeneutic understanding but of the formation of a specific discourse.

Consequently, the figure of one's own language as a systematic unity is a correlate in this schema of cofiguration to its twin partner, the figure of a foreign language. One's own language neither precedes nor succeeds a foreign language; both come into being at the same time—that is, one's own language is always a foreign language for a foreign language, and the self-referential relationship to one's own language always assumes the schema of cofiguration. This is why the self-referentiality to one's own language necessarily comprises the desire to be seen from the viewpoint of a foreign language. The reason for which self-referentiality in fact can never free itself from the transferential desire to see from another's position is, thus, already outlined in the schema of cofiguration. Our desire to know what we have supposedly known in our own language thus arrives by way of our desire for the figure of a foreign language.

JAPANESE THOUGHT AND THE SCHEMA OF COFIGURATION

Needless to say, Japanese thought cannot be discussed in the same manner as we have discussed the Japanese language. For one thing, it is almost pointless to define Japanese thought as the sort of thought whose medium of expression is Japanese. On the one hand, what should be taken as the Japanese language, as we have seen, is variable from one historical period to another. On the other hand, many documents and verbal works that were published or publicized prior to the modern period in the Japanese archipelago were in what are judged to be foreign languages today. They are not materials written in the "Japanese language"; or, to put it more precisely, they belong to historical periods prior to the emergence of the Japanese language.

Nonetheless, Japanese thought as thematized in the history of Japanese thought is not unrelated to the regime of translation and the schema of cofiguration. This is because a regulative idea has to be posited by means of a schema similar to that of cofiguration, so as to postulate Japanese thought as the subject matter for that discipline.

Once more we must draw attention to the historical feature of the history of Japanese thought as a discipline, a feature that is, as it were, doubly modern. It is inevitably so, first, for the modernity of its embedded desire to distinguish Japanese thought by excluding foreign thought, and, second, for the modernity of historical constraints under which an idea of Japanese thought could come into being only in contrast to its opposite Western thought.

Should we take "Japan" to refer to the geographic area under the jurisdiction of the Japanese government today, we might as well give up any attempt to construct the history of Japanese thought as a coherent historical genealogy. We would find that there are fragmented and discontinuous utterances by many different peoples: the Kumaso and the Ezo in antiquity, heterogeneous masses outside the aristocracy during the so-called Middle Ages, the Ainu, the Okinawan, the Korean in the modern period, and so forth. In addition, we would discover documents in Sanskrit, literary Chinese, and even European languages. While admitting the diversity and multilayeredness of Japanese thought, historians have had to presuppose the Japanese ethnos (*minzoku*) as the subject of expression behind the manifest diversity of thought in the Japanese archipelago, and construct the genealogical coherence of the history of Japanese thought by presuming that the subject of its expression has been in existence continually. In this respect, the history of Japanese thought has adopted the same strategy whereby Japanese history as a discipline has devised the continuity of historical time on the basis of the putatively enduring presence of "the Japanese" since antiquity.

Since it is generally accepted that the nation (*kokumin*) is a *Gesellschaft*, an associative community mediated by the rationality of the state, whereas the ethnos (*minzoku*) is a *Gemeinschaft*, a natural community prior to state mediation, few historians have taken into serious consideration the view that such a natural community as the ethnos is also manufactured in modern discourse. Thus, historians have continually failed to call into question how the subject as an ethnos was constructed, and have rarely tried to construct a history of the Japanese archipelago as a patchwork of fragmented and discontinuous histories, as a history of simultaneous and successive rises and falls of polities in the social environment that should be best characterized in terms of multilingualism and hybrid cultural formation. To this extent, we now can see why the history of Japanese thought is possible only in the discourses of modernity that abide by the schema of cofiguration and necessarily repress the possibilities for the multilingual and multicultural social formation of hybridity. The history of Japanese thought would, then, be impossible unless it is joined with the bilateral opposition of the Japanese language and a foreign language, of the inside and the outside, with all those discursive regularities that make the modern institution of the nation (kokumin) and the ethnos (minzoku) appear as if they were transhistorical entities.

Indeed, the thought that is referred to as the symmetrical opposite to Japanese thought cannot be that of the Middle Kingdom or Tenjiku (India) but of "the West." There have been many attempts to compare Japanese thought with Chinese thought, Korean thought, and so forth. Particularly in recent years, as the motto "Datsua Nyûô" (Fleeing Asia and Entering the West)[19] has been increasingly unpopular, many have switched their orientation to "Datsuô Nyûa" (Fleeing the West and Entering Asia). Yet, such a reversal does not fundamentally change the way in which Japanese thought is comparatively identified, since the West in this case is not merely a geographic particular: it is an ambiguous and ubiquitous presence of a certain global domination whose subject can hardly be identifiable. What is at issue here is "the West" insofar as peoples in the so-called non-West have to refer to and rely on it so as to construct their own cultural and historical identity. Also indicated by the West is the organization of the modern world through which information is selected and transmitted globally. What sorts of global communication can we possibly propose with intellectuals in Asia, Africa, and Latin America without relying on the presence of the West as the common referential point? The means of transcontinental communication, ranging from the uses of colonizers' languages such as Spanish, French, and English to the current world networks of CNN and the BBC, has been monopolized by the West, although the West has incessantly expanded, shifted, and transformed itself at any point in modern history. Intellectuals in the non-West have invariably been implicated in this form of domination and have had to construct their identities in the dynamics of assimilation to and repulsion against this Occidental ethnocentrism. The history of Japanese thought was no exception. It could construct itself only in the midst of a sympathy and antipathy to the West, that is, in what I have depicted as the regime of translation.

Regardless of the extent that students of the history of Japanese thought are actually knowledgeable about Western thought—of course, the idea of "Western thought" itself is rife with obscurities and contradictions—they have to address themselves from a position equivalent to that of the translator to the readers who are equivalent to those for whom translation is in demand. Only on the condition that they supposedly know both sides could they possibly be qualified to talk about Japanese thought as particular to the Japanese. The students acquire a passage into Japanese thought through Western thought. The desire for Japanese thought comes to them by way of their desire for Western thought.

In translation, symmetry is usually between two national languages, as in the formats of French-Japanese and Japanese-German. If we are to pursue the parallelism between translation and the history of Japanese thought, we should expect to find French thought or German thought as a symmetrical opposite to Japanese thought. As a matter of fact, many comparative studies projects have been organized according to the formats of bilateral internationalism. And one would expect that, at universities, the discipline of the history of Japanese thought would be instituted and juxtaposed with that of the history of French thought or German thought. However, more often than not, Japanese thought slides into a different kind of symmetry, into a symmetry with the West or Euro-America, and is treated as representative of the East. Is this confusion prevalent because, in Europe, there has been a holistic tradition of cosmopolitanism beyond particularistic national histories since the medieval period? Perhaps this has less to do with the objective characteristics of the term of comparison than with the fact that symmetry is maintained not between putative objects but between the ideas that are independent of these objects. As a matter of fact, such confusion frequently occurs when the intellectuals of the non-West try to discuss the cultures and intellectual heritage of their own countries. We know of innumerable instances, such as one in which Oriental thought is, in the final analysis, nothing but Iranian thought or another in which Oriental tradition simply refers to the customs of China. And such a tendency is understandable when we consider that the intellectuals of the non-West cannot find ways to self-referentially discuss their own cultures and traditions as particular to their societies without positing "the West" as the general point of reference.

Likewise, in order for Japanese thought to be possible, it has to be dependent on Western thought. The West in this sense is an idea, not an empirical object. The modernity of the history of Japanese thought consists in this historical inevitability. Thus the modern is doomed to appear to be

Western in this discipline as long as we continue to think of the thought of the Japanese archipelago according to the schema of cofiguration. In order to articulate the particularity of Japan, the generality or universality of the West has to be taken for granted. And students who want to conceptualize the particularity of Japan would address themselves as the translators of thought, as bystanders in the encounter of civilizations, who would then enunciate from some transcendent stance overlooking both of the symmetrical opposites, the West and Japan, that have been figured out according to the schema of cofiguration.

Provided that the history of Japanese thought is an organization of institutionalized practices in such a regime, what does the student *do* in it? I am not asking what one understands and describes; my question is, "What does the student of the history of Japanese thought do in performing in accordance with this discipline?"

The History of Japanese Thought as a Subjective Technology [20]

JAPANESE THOUGHT AS AN EXISTENTIAL CONSTRAINT

Students engage themselves in the framework of the history of Japanese thought while suturing the position continuous with Japanese thought, primarily in order to objectify and problematize the existential constraints to which they have unwittingly been subjected. Whereas they can become conscious of the thinking habits and tradition that have been transmitted from the past by viewing them from the "non-Japanese" position, they would nonetheless have to accept these as their own destiny, as inescapable constraints for their thinking since they are also supposed to identify with the position continuous with Japanese thought. Thereupon, they would obtain two possibilities.

The first is to celebrate the existential constraints thus objectified as their good fortune, and even to be grateful for such a past ("Be proud of being Japanese!"). It goes without saying that this is a mirror opposite of what is referred to as the "narcissism of the West,"[21] to an attitude in which one is forever grateful for being a Westerner. (Yet—as we perhaps know too well—such a declaration of one's confidence in being what one is always carries with it the disavowal of anxiety for one's identity, and may well result in exclusionist violence, as the histories of colonialism and imperialism have amply illustrated.) It is not difficult to see that, as is the case with Watsuji Tetsurô's culturalism, the first choice would more often than not lead to the narcissistic celebration of the national culture.

The second is to regard the cultural heritage thus objectified as an obstacle that must be overcome from within. It is imperative to keep in mind that the history of Japanese thought has played an important role in criticizing politics and culture "from within" Japan in this fashion. But we must also keep in mind that, in order to continue to serve a critical function, the history of Japanese thought has to conserve the schema of cofiguration whereby to posit Japanese thought as an object for mimetic desire.

In this respect, Maruyama Masao's work in the history of Japanese thought is monumental in that it clearly displays the conditions of the production of the desire for Japanese thought: it also embodies penetrating insights into the conditions of possibility for the history of Japanese thought.

In *Studies in the Intellectual History of Tokugawa Japan*, Maruyama Masao brought up the central problem of historical transformation from the Japanese ethnos (*minzoku*) to the Japanese nation (*kokumin*), and his argument in this anthology is guided by an inquiry into how to establish the political technologies necessary to manufacture the nation equipped with "political national consciousness," which would identify with a national community spontaneously from within, out of the awareness of their common characteristics (*bunka-teki ittaisei*).[22] "Before a people can become a nation, they must actively desire to belong to a common community and participate in common institutions, or at least consider such a situation to be desirable."[23] Here Maruyama poses the main theme of his inquiry, which incidentally is also an analysis of the mechanism in which the desire for Japanese thought is produced in the history of Japanese thought. It is worth noting, furthermore, that the nation that is to come into being through identification with a national community is already given its unity as a community of national culture, as a community whose cultural identity has been achieved. And the being of the nation is defined as follows: "In other words, we can say that a nation exists only if the members of a given group of men are aware of the common characteristics that they share with each other and that distinguish them from other nations as a special nation and possess some desire to preserve and foster this unity."[24] As a consequence, the history of Japanese thought is narrated as the development of the thought of the Japanese ethnos (whose mode of being, to use Tanabe Hajime's terminology, is that of a *substratum, kitai*) into that of the Japanese nation (whose mode of being is that of *subject, shutai*), while the Japanese as the subject of thought has to be assumed to have been enduring throughout the development. And Maruyama argues that national consciousness emerges simultaneously as the comparative consciousness emerges that contrasts the Japanese with other nations. In the end, his critical attention focuses both on how they have failed to accomplish the "decisionistic" gathering of the national consciousness, of the consciousness of political communality, and on what the historical conditions for this failure are. Even in a review as cursory as this, it is evident that Maruyama's analysis follows an itinerary of the desire for Japanese thought according to the schema of cofiguration.

The essay in which Maruyama announced the overall comprehension of the ethnic unity turning into the national unity, the development of the Japanese ethnos into the Japanese nation, was originally published in 1942, yet *Studies in the Intellectual History of Tokugawa Japan* contains essays written earlier. Whether or not his narrative about the emergence of the Japanese national consciousness assumed the substantial identity of the Japanese ethnos and modern Japanese nation in the parts of this book devoted to the earlier essays as well is certainly a matter of debate: I am doubtful that Maruyama conceived of the Japanese nation in terms of the transhistorical existence of Japanese ethnos, even prior to 1942, when the defeat of Japanese Empire was not as yet a foreseeable certainty, and hopefully I will elucidate this question elsewhere.[25] In the meantime, however, let me read Maruyama's argument in this book as a whole on the premise of the continual development of an ethnos into a nation; for, regardless of whether or not the schema of cofiguration as inherent in it was by design to endorse the identity of the Japanese nation as a monoethnic entity in the prewar period when the Japanese nation was clearly a multiethnic formation, as in Tanabe Hajime's *Logic of Species*—sporadically published from the early 1930s until the early 1940s—amply demonstrates, Maruyama's argument in this book seems to predeterminedly anticipate the cultural nationalism of the postwar period of which Maruyama himself would become one of the most conspicuous proponents.

After asserting the separation of the social from the natural orders as a condition of emergence for the modern Japanese "nation" as the subject of invention in *Studies in the Intellectual History of Tokugawa Japan*, Maruyama equates the Way of the Sages within Ogyû Sorai's system with the Way's transcendence over human understanding. "For Sorai, the Way of the Sages is absolute, and therefore, far from being opposed to other modes of thought, it includes them all within it."[26] Yet, the Sages never cease to be personal beings. In other words, the Sages are not abstract ideas but personae with whom one can have a dialogic relation, so that the Sages are designed from the outset to be capable of participating in the *personal* relationship of the addresser and the addressee. Yet, the Way of the Sages cannot be compared with the existing particular institutions. It is beyond the partiality of any controvertible position; instead, it is the reality of the social totality for any community. It is the totality in which parts are synthesized into an organic whole and in which parts are proper to themselves ("A part is a part of the whole only if it retains its *particularity*").[27] However, the content of the Way of the Sages is not an idea that serves as a norm for individuals' deeds: it is a concrete reality of "rites and music, law enforcement and political administration."

Thus, the Sages should be envisaged as something like idealized readers. Yet, Maruyama claims that the Way of the Sages is at once "historically and geographically restricted,"[28] and absolute and universally valid beyond time and space. With astonishing accuracy, he outlines the position of "the West" and its idealized readers that is at the same time "anti-Japanese" and "non-Japanese," a particular and a universal, by giving a specific account of the Sages and ancient China in Sorai's system.[29] As if following "the predominance of the political factor" "in Sorai's conception of the sages,"[30] Maruyama makes a political decision to admit to the West a status that corresponds to that of ancient China in Sorai's. And, as Sorai supposedly did with Tokugawa polity and China in his "Learning of Ancient Text and Words" (*Kobunji-gaku*), he has *politically and absolutely* decided to obtain the possibility to objectify and for him to suture Japan by postulating the universality of "the West" as "the non-Japanese position." And I would like to add that, although this point has not been touched on by Maruyama, Ogyû's "Learning of Ancient Text and Words" and "Learning of Nagasaki Translators" (*Kiyô no gaku*) both rejected the multilinguistic coexistence of languages, and were formed on the premises that hybrid languages such as the "Japanese way of reading Chinese" (*wakun*), or the Japanese methods of annotating literary Chinese, be completely excluded. Ogyû had to separate the two contrasting figures of languages to translate from and into in order to introduce the regime of translation and the schema of cofiguration. And, of course, he could not have done so unless the hybrid mixture of heterogeneous linguistic media was excluded at first.[31] At least in theory, the introduction of the schema of cofiguration prompted the possibility of negatively evaluating an individual belonging to many different linguistic communities and of moving around among them: the norm that the truly authentic language for an individual should be neither hybrid nor multiple was then inaugurated. Yet, as is obvious from the position of the translator, which makes it impossible to adhere to either the exclusively personal relation of the addresser and the addressee or the utterly indifferent stance of the observer, the recognition of the truly authentic language has to be facilitated by the incessant oscillation between the inside and the outside of the scene of translation, the metaleptic stepping out and stepping in of the personal relation with the addresser and the addressee in the process of translation. It is by the essential linguistic hybridity inherent in the position of the translator that one comes to know the authenticity of one's own language. In spite of all these, the schema of cofiguration serves to negate the essential heterogeneity of a language.

Besides the problem as to what is meant by the unity of a linguistic community, the schema of cofiguration was incompatible with those regimes that allowed for hybridity, and thereby could be instrumental in giving rise to the idea of the internal unity of a language. This assessment should imply that, prior to the introduction of the schema of cofiguration, such a state as is suggested by the following should have been prevalent: "Generally speaking, in societies where an individual belongs to a plurality of groups of different kinds simultaneously, with his loyalty accordingly being diversely fragmented, it is difficult for a political authority to monopolize the nation's loyalty and to concentrate the nation's loyalty at the time of emergency, such as in war."[32] The awareness of the authentic language for the Japanese was supposed to be gained through the schema of cofiguration by learning ancient Chinese, the foreign language of the "non-Japanese" Sages.

The political philosophy of Ogyû Sorai is, for Maruyama Masao, a most brilliant forerunner of the modern that accurately portrayed the configuration of the enunciative positionality characteristic of modernity. In addition to the fact that Sorai's thought shared much in common with modern political consciousness, there can be found in it the outline of a useful regime in which the student disciplines himself by desiring "Japanese thought" in the history of Japanese thought. Granted that "a nation is something that wants to be a nation,"[33] one cannot evade the problems concerning political (or subjective) *techné* as to how to manufacture and effectively institute the desire to "want to be a nation" in pursuing the issue of how to manufacture "the nation." And, the nation cannot be unless the populace is endowed with a rather irrational mentality which bears with it "the active spontaneity of the ego." As Maruyama saw in Fukuzawa Yukichi ("How could you possibly expect true loyalty to the nation from the people who are too inert and passive to be rebellious?"),[34] the nation has to be an active subject. And, I must stress, the subject as such is the subject of invention, a subject that produces itself by representing itself. So, just as the Sages were presented by Sorai ("the Way they [the Sages] invented had to be placed beyond rational comprehension and value judgment"),[35] the "absolute other" has to be postulated; the subject produces itself through an imitative identification—which one might perceive to be more like aspiration—with "the absolute other," while acknowledging the unsurpassable distance between that other and itself; that is, the subject constitutes itself in the very desire to want to "learn from" and "imitate" that other. And, in order for the desire to be of an imitative nature, that from which the subject wants to learn must be not "an Idea" but "a Person."[36] Therefore, it is through the imitative relation to "the West" that the student of the history of Japanese thought acquires the possibility of representing "Japan," and Japan as an object of *personal* identification, at the same time. Put differently, it is through the imitative relation to "the West" that the Japanese ethnos that is merely a cultural identity produces itself as the Japanese nation as a political community.

What Maruyama wants the history of Japanese thought to *do* is to manufacture (or *poiein*) the subject as a nation. His work is nothing but an investigation into the subjective technology whereby "the Japanese nation" is manufactured.

THE MODERN WORLD AND THE NARCISSISM OF THE WEST

In *Thought and Behaviour in Modern Japanese Politics*, Maruyama's analysis of Japan's ultranationalism does not contradict the comparative framework dictated by the schema of cofiguration.[37] He carefully distinguishes the West as "the non-Japanese" position and the West as "the anti-Japanese" position, and expresses his almost existential commitment to the essence of the modern West. He refuses to reduce the modern "West" insofar as it is grasped in its absolute essence to "the West" as its accidental manifestation. Yet, the West is not taken to be merely a universal and ubiquitous "idea": it must be understood in its historical singularity, which should not be equated with a generality. Hence, his commitment to the modern West, which might be depicted as something like the Way invented by "the Person," does not exclude an awareness of the possible danger inherent in the West. Unlike many mediocre and opportunistic conceptions of modernity, his understanding of it is acutely conscious of the groundlessness of the nation as the modern subject that produces itself without a metaphysical safety net, as the subject that legislates its own existence "as the *abyss* of this self-legislation."[38] In due course, he cannot think of Nazism as a mere deviation from modernity or as unrelated to the essence of modern subjectivity.

As is known, Maruyama's view of "the West" as "a Person" contains a fundamental critique of theological universalism according to which the world is constituted by emanating from a single center. It is widely acknowledged that such a theological universalism has been upheld by missionaries and colonizers, and has served to reinforce the faith in the universality of Western civilization and to justify and empower colonialism (and postcolonialism) ever since "the Conquest of America." It is a universalism of self-indulgence that lacks a sense of the primordial split between "the self" and "the other." His view of "the West" as "a Person" might appear to enable us to envision a modern international order that is free from theological universalism, which has almost always been accompanied by the centrism of the civilized center versus the savage periphery and the sense of a civilizing mission.

> Nationalism, the guiding principle for the modern nation-state, and its essential moment, the concept of "sovereignty" are based on the *premises* that sovereign nation-states *coexist on the same plane as equals*, even if they might on occasion endorse the state's unconstrained adventurism: by no means are they compatible with the centrism of the civilized center versus the savage periphery [*chûka iteki-kan*], which would never admit the true center of the world but for itself.[39]

The image of the modern international world put forth here may well be the reason Maruyama's view of modernity is unpopular among those who have yet to shed the mentality of missionary-style universalism—a mentality of the premodern, from his viewpoint.

However, is this modern "schema by which to grasp international relations,"[40] which assumes the equal and horizontal coexistence of nation-states, in effect, incompatible with colonialist universality? As we have seen, Maruyama recognizes in Ogyû's political philosophy a sense of distinction between "the self" and "the other," and a possibility to jolt the continuous worldview and optimistic universalism, such as Song Neo-Confucianism (*Shushi-gaku*), which sees the world as "emanating from a single center." Yet, for him, the split between the self and the other is a symmetrical and commensurate one between "Japan" and "anti-Japan," and the other here is no more than a symmetrical other that secures the identity of Japan. It is merely an other that is required in order to guarantee the self-referentiality of the Japanese.

For Maruyama, the West is certainly not an other nation-state that coexists with Japan on the same plane. Thus, Japan's relationship to the West cannot be represented according to "the schema by which to grasp international relations." He does not fail to admit incommensurability to the West as "a non-Japan," so that he can postulate the West not merely as an object of cognition but also as the other with whom to have *personal* relations. The West as an empirical "anti-Japan," and the West as an Idea or as an Ideal in the sense of *an idea in particularity* (though it is definitely a Person, too) of "the non-Japan" itself, are thus given simultaneously and overlap one another. The West insofar as it is an "anti-Japan" carries with it many defects and weaknesses that can be objectified and criticized as gaps between what the West ought to be and what it actually is. Since the West as "the non-Japan" should be a perspective or a transcendental subject, the Japanese too should be able to participate with equal status in criticizing the West from the viewpoint of what the West should be. In this respect, the universality of the West seems open and nonexclusive to those who are outside the West. Surely, this is what underlies Maruyama's commitment to modernity.

But, should we suspect that the ekstatic movement of self-transcendence, of the actual West toward the ideal West, which is propelled by representations of gaps between what it should be and what it actually is, may be the very process of self-constitution of the Subject called the West? As an other of the West, the Japanese, then, would simply contribute to the process of the self-constitution of the West, which is also a process of excluding the non-West for the sake of Western identity that is, in fact, far from definitive. Therefore, Maruyama has to avoid carefully the question of the identity of the West and what is excluded or repressed in this movement of self-transcendence.

Indeed, we cannot forget that the relationship envisaged by Maruyama between "the West" and "Japan" is perfectly resonant with what Robert Young calls the "narcissism of the West,"[41] by which all the others are grasped essentially as "homogeneously different" in symmetrical contrast with the center of the putative West. Even in its praise of "extraordinary cultural achievements by other civilizations," the narcissism of the West seeks only to find in other cultures and civilizations what distinguishes the West from the rest of the world, and continually expects the others to respond to its narcissistic demand for acknowledgment of its distinction. And, as this narcissism is a simple reversal of paranoia in structure, it turns into a paranoiac fear of the others when such a narcissistic demand cannot easily be met (as in the last few decades globally). In this respect, Maruyama's work, perhaps unwittingly, is a response to such a demand (and we must remember that there were times when most non-Western and Japanese intellectuals had no other choices).

What has been evaded at any cost in this transferential exchange of desires between the West and the non-West is any interruption, any questioning of the very distinction between the two domains of the world. According to this schema, hybridity, excess, or the otherness of the other at large, which is unrepresentable and incommensurate in the given regimes of representation and translation, must first be excluded, just as in Ogyû's Learning in which differences and distinctions were predetermined in order for them to abide by the regime of translation, and in which singularity that is incommensurate with the Same has to be eliminated.

Neither colonialist universalism nor "the principle of equality among modern sovereign states" allows for "the Other." The schema of the co-existence among nation-states serves to conceal the complicity of the West and Japan in the transferential formation of respective identities; because of this complicity, the obsession with the West warrants self-referentiality for the Japanese. An uncritical endorsement of such a schema prevents us from detecting the hidden alliance of the narcissisms of the West and of Japan. It conceals the working of the regimes in which a paranoiac impulse to identify with the West, and another with Japan, are simultaneously re-produced and mutually reinforced by one another.

A History of Japanese Thought That Calls "Japanese Thought" into Question

Essential in the history of Japanese thought is the need to call into question how "Japan" is constructed and how the desire for "Japanese thought" that has sustained this discipline has been invoked. Through this questioning, we will think about how the production of knowledge in the history of Japanese thought has been at work in politics. Hopefully, this will serve as an occasion to link this discipline to the old problem concerning the relationship between knowledge and practice. But although such questioning is always expected of any student, who should never stop asking about the conditions that make knowledge possible in her or his field of expertise, it is an attempt, of a historical nature, to assess the role played by the history of Japanese thought in the reproduction of the nation-state and of the extremely problematic subject called the West. Perhaps here we will be able to find a conjunction between an inquiry into the practice of scholarship and an art called history.

3

Return to the West/Return to the East:

Watsuji Tetsurô's Anthropology and

Discussions of Authenticity[1]

What did we see in the prolonged and excessively sentimental expression of a nationwide sorrow staged by the Japanese mass media in the fall of 1988? A case of passion, perhaps. Through billions of copies of daily, weekly, and monthly publications and hundreds of programs broadcast by television networks, the look of the entire nation seemed fixed on the body of Emperor Hirohito, which in fact remained completely invisible throughout. Every hour, the emperor's physical condition was reported by television broadcasting stations as if everyone in Japan were desperately worried about Hirohito's life and demanded to know about it.

I cannot speak of what might be called the "Emperor Boom" in its socio-logical details because I was not in Japan at that time and was therefore not exposed to the avalanche of information about the emperor and the emperor system firsthand, and also because I have had no access to the ways in which that information was generated, processed, and presented. However, I think that it is possible to extract a few traits that characterize the presentation of the emperor in the Japanese mass media and how it was inherently embedded in the formation of postwar Japanese cultural nationalism.

The image of the dying emperor being entirely a work fabricated by the mass media, a definite structure of visibility was at work in the presen-tation of his body. Regardless of whether people watched the television screen or read articles in daily newspapers and weekly journals, the subjective and imagined positions of the people and the emperor were clearly delineated. In this structure of visibility, which was also a structure of invisibility in the double sense of the term, the people were assigned to the position of "the one who saw," of an active agent, whereas the emperor was invariably regarded as "the one who was seen," as a passive object of seeing. There was no doubt that, technologically and politically, the people were solicited, seduced, and eventually forced to see; the people in fact did not have an ability to initiate the act of seeing spontaneously. Nevertheless, insofar as this specific action of seeing was concerned, the people were put in a position in which they were assumed responsible for initiating the action of seeing; they played the role of the subject of seeing in this structure of visibility. In due course, the emperor was supposed to play the role of the object of seeing. Possibly the fact that he was critically ill, and most of the time unconscious, also served to affirm the presumption that he was not capable of initiating the action of seeing and remained deprived of the ability of seeing as a subject; he remained completely passive and helplessly exposed to the look of the people without the slightest possibility of looking back at those who saw him, of reflecting back the gaze. In this regard, unlike the nude prostitute in Édouard Manet's painting *Olympia*,[2] he was unable to protest or even refuse the impudent look of the spectators. Hence, as a critically ill person always is, he was deprived of his spontaneity and had to be at the mercy of those who looked at his suffering body. One cannot imagine a better example of serving the typical conservative notion of *passive* femininity than this case of the dying emperor: he was totally passive, docile, and even pitiable in that he could in no way assume a commanding position or the position of the Subject.

It goes without saying that the structure of visibility as I depict is independent of the actual states of the emperor or what he did, thought, or felt. What is referred to as "the structure of visibility" is a consequence of a certain coordination of technological and discursive arrangements according to which the curiosity and attention of people are solicited, directed, and focused. It consists in a series of suggestions that lure viewers into identifying themselves with prearranged subjective positions.

I repeat that, despite the structure of visibility I have just outlined, the emperor's body remained invisible throughout. To my knowledge, not once was his body, or even his bedroom, shown to the public during the period of what one might call a premortem wake. Yet, precisely because of this invisibility of his body, his bodily presence in its absence reinforced the structure of visibility in which he was assumed to be a rather feminine object of seeing. This structure of visibility appears to have reproduced the structure of what Michel Foucault outlined as that of the modern subject in reference to Bentham's Panopticon.

For more than three months until the possibility of actually seeing the body of the emperor was finally announced as impossible, the people continued to strive to see it in its absence. In other words, the "nation" was redefined as the group of those who would supposedly desire to see the emperor's body in its absence. It was an attempt, the success of which I am not sure about, to define the nation as those who share the same desire, who are concerned with and curious about the same object, and who would act for the same purpose. Sometimes it was suggested that those who would not subject themselves to such a desire were antipatriotic or *hi-kokumin*, and people were forced to yield to that suggestion since many tactics, including intimidation, were made use of in order to repress contestation of any sort that might reveal the essential arbitrariness of the suggestion. The whole affair was presented as though the authentic Japanese had to accept the suggestion without query, as though a good Japanese was one who knew no resistance to it, and as though the Japanese were those who could easily live with and content themselves with the suggestion.[3] The invisible body of the emperor was presented with a certain mechanism of suggestive power, and served as a focal point around which to gather together the disparate looks of the people.

During this period of the premortem wake, it was frequently reported that people expressed the sense of togetherness by virtue of the fact that they were collectively concerned for the life of the emperor. They were solicited to feel sympathy toward the emperor, but what they achieved in feeling sympathy toward the absent body was a sense of camaraderie among those who sought to see it. They were somehow led to believe that their sympathies communicated with one another because they were all concerned over the same object. In this respect, their sympathy toward the emperor was apprehended as a passage to the synthesis of their feelings, which would otherwise be indifferent to one another; their sympathies were "made into one body" (*ittaika*) in which the sharing of feeling was immediate. While the simultaneity and commonness of their sympathies toward the emperor's suffering or passion found their guarantee in the identity of the object of their seeing, they could in turn enjoy the sense of shared emotion not so much toward the absent body as toward their fellow countrymen.

In other words, as long as one commits oneself to this form of sympathy generated by the economy of the figural, which I would like to call the emperor system, one can persuade oneself that one's sympathy toward the emperor is, in effect, an entry to the shared suffering whose communality is sustained by the self-enrapturing mechanism of sympathy. In this sense, the structure of visibility evoked the self-induced feeling of sympathy in which the subjectivity of the people, as opposed to the absence of subjectivity in the emperor, was confined to autoaffection. It was a typical form of sentimentality in that feeling was created without the interruption of otherness or alterity. In other words, this structure of visibility erected around the invisible body of the effeminate emperor gave rise to an opportunity for the people to commiserate among themselves, and, in this sense, allowed for a collective self-pity of the nation to emerge. Feeling was given rise to within the restricted economy of the closed and fully homogenized community as an aesthetic work in which one feels sad because one is supposed to feel sad; one feels sympathetic because one is supposed to feel sympathetic: the sharing of the supposed suffering coincides with conformity. Thus feeling was nothing but an effect of communalist transference from which the otherness of the other was deliberately sealed off.

There were many, of course, who did not feel any sympathy toward the emperor, as they were free from this sort of sentimentality. But is the emperor system, after all, this restricted economy of aestheticization in which reverence toward the emperor who is supposed to "symbolize national unity" cannot but be sentimental? Is it, in the final analysis, a system of sentimentality? Has the emperor system always worked this way, even under the Meiji Constitution in which the emperor was defined as the Subject of subjects? Do we not need to call into question the widely held presumption that the emperor was imagined to be a father figure, commanding and authoritarian?

In order to respond to this question, I should perhaps move away from this happening. As I believe that the structure of visibility that was clearly manifest in the Shôwa emperor's premortem wake in fact illustrates the basic feature of modern subjectivity and confirms what Foucault outlined as the form of subjection, it cannot be dismissed either as particular to a temporary Japanese situation or as lacking the inertia of an institution. Its implications should be examined in related areas such as cinematic presentation, academic knowledge, education, and so forth, in postwar Japan. Leaving these areas of investigation for other occasions, I would like to focus on an intellectual attempt to legitimate the emperor system on an ethico-philosophical ground, an argument that tries to legitimate the emperor as an aesthetic expression of national unity. What I have in mind is a discussion about the emperor presented by Watsuji Tetsurô after Japan's defeat in 1945. But, first of all, I will read Watsuji's prewar discussions on the concept of national totality and ethics, on which much of his postwar articles on the emperor system depended.

Since the publication of *The Study of the Human Being in Pascal* by Miki Kiyoshi in 1926, the question of the human being as *ningen* or the "being-between" has been repeatedly asked by Japanese writers who were engaged in philosophical debates both inside the academia of national colleges and universities and outside it, in intellectual journalism, which was rapidly growing with the increasing number of subscribers to newly founded intellectual journals such as *Shisô, Kaizô,* and *Risô. The Study of the Human Being in Pascal* probably marks the first serious and systematic attempt in Japan to introduce Heideggerian *Dasein* analysis, with which Miki Kiyoshi had familiarized himself by studying with Heidegger in Germany in the early Weimar era. In this monumental work, Miki conducted the existential analysis of the human being or *ningen sonzai* in terms of Heideggerian *Dasein* as "state of mind"[4] and argued that the human being should be understood as "being-between" or "being-thrown-between," an essentially unstable middle entity or *chûkansha* suspended between infinity and void. Here already, one of the concerns that would dominate discussions over the human being in the late 1920s and 1930s is clearly delineated: the human being is comprehended as unsure of itself, as an entity who inquires about itself and relates to itself not through necessities but through possibilities. Miki Kiyoshi continued to ask the question of the human being, first in the context of Marxism in his attempt to synthesize hermeneutics and Marxism, and second, after the collapse of Marxism in the mid-1930s, in his exploration of historical being or *rekishi-teki sonzai*. Perhaps, with the exception of Lukács, no contemporary thinkers of Europe were more extensively and intensely read by Japanese intellectuals than Heidegger during this period. Many, including Tanabe Hajime, Kuki Shûzô, Nakai Masakazu, and Nishitani Keiji, engaged themselves in the problem of the human being through their reading of Heidegger. I believe it appropriate to argue that, in this respect, the variety of readings of Heidegger reflected the intellectual situation of Japan from the late 1920s through the late 1930s; a different reading of Heidegger's works indicated a different political possibility, and conflicts among the interpretations of Heidegger were closely related to the issue of praxis. Partly in contradiction to Miki, for example, Watsuji Tetsurô attempted to modify Heideggerian hermeneutics into a philosophical anthropology as ethics with a comprehension of social praxis that is different from Heidegger's.

In reading Watsuji's texts, I do not want to follow the culturalist scheme of questioning that tends to reduce philosophical problems raised by Japanese or any foreign intellectuals to the matter of cultural difference: many specialists of Japanese thought in Japan and North America, as well as in Europe, are still inclined to let their inquiry be guided by such questions as "Did Japanese scholars who were Oriental understand Western philosophy correctly?" and "How did the Oriental tradition distort their understanding of Western philosophy?" The fact of being brought up in the so-called West might help one to be more familiar with Western philosophy, which is, nonetheless, diverse and heterogeneous. But it is very difficult to find grounds to claim that the fact of one's birth guarantees one's "correct" understanding of it. Furthermore, the arbitrariness of the identity "the West" must be subjected to thorough scrutiny. Of course, the same can be said about "Japan" and "the East." I do not want to read Watsuji Tetsurô within the framework of culturalism in which, as I will illustrate, Watsuji himself was trapped; I would not try to reduce Watsuji's philosophical discourse to an example of the Japanese national character. Instead, I will show the practical and political significance of what the culturalist might call "distortion" and "misunderstanding" peculiar to the national culture in Watsuji's reading of Heidegger, rather than judge Watsuji in terms of a "correct" and "incorrect" binary, although I do admit that simple distortion or misunderstanding is not only possible but also frequent in the comprehension of thought. Sometimes "incorrect" comprehension can be caused by the failure of the reader to take into account regional, class, political, historical, and other heterogeneities. But the diversity of those factors cannot be uniformly and exhaustively attributed to national character and nationality. We must be critical of many sorts of social stereotyping underlying cultural essentialism, which has been increasingly favored in the name of respect for local particularity.

Watsuji's project in philosophical anthropology as ethics was first outlined in a 1931 publication titled *Ethics (rinrigaku)*.[5] In this book, the central question of ethics is defined as that of the human being. It is argued that the question of the human being cannot be addressed merely as the question of what the object designated in this questioning is, since the study of the human being cannot be subsumed under the study of nature. The opposition between the human being and nature operating in Watsuji's insistence on the irreducibility of the human being into nature derives from the distinction, somewhat reminiscent of Neo-Kantianism, between the two mutually heterogeneous domains of scientific investigation, the human sciences and the natural sciences. Watsuji attributed to Marx this distinction, which was fundamental to the initial formation of his idea of human science, *ningen no gaku* as ethics.

Interestingly enough, the itinerary of the argument by Watsuji, who earned credentials as an anti-Marxist liberal, shows how much he owed to *The German Ideology* in the initial formulation of the question of the human being:

> As is well known, Marx rejected eighteenth-century materialism because that materialism neglected the moment of historical and social activities in the human being. "The chief defect of all previous materialism is that things, reality, sensuousness are conceived only in the form of the object, or of intuition [*chokkan*], and are never grasped as sensuous and human activity, that is, as praxis. This is to say that [the old materialism] never grasps such reality subjectively [*shutai-teki ni*]." A Thing [*taishō*] as nature is grasped as an object, that is, as what is posited as something opposed [to the epistemo-logical subject]. In contrast, Marx insists on grasping reality subjectively [*shutai-teki ni*] as praxis.[6]

Here Marx's conception of the human being is presented as introducing a new understanding of sensuous and human reality. Thus, Watsuji claimed that Marx rejected materialism that treated the human being as a natural object, and instead emphasized the subjective being or *shutai-teki sonzai* of the human being as practical activity. While congratulating Marx on the basic conception of human essence as "an ensemble of social relations" on which, as we will see, he would build his *Ethics*, Watsuji gave the first de-termination of the central issue, the human being or *ningen*, as the subjec-tive being or *shutai-teki sonzai* and subsequently characterized the path his inquiry would have to take as a philosophy of praxis. His philosophical an-thropology was thus identified as a philosophy of praxis about the subjec-tive being of Man.

Two points should be noted. First, Watsuji followed Marx, particularly in the First Thesis on Feuerbach, to the extent that the practical and sub-jective activity of the human being is affirmed. However, when it comes to what we know by the critique of humanism—of which there are many readings today, of course—Watsuji shifts away from Marx's argument. This is even more evident when we examine the other, later versions of his *Ethics*, in which fewer and fewer references are made to Marxist literature in general, until many of the traces of his theoretical struggle with Marx are erased in the postwar versions. As will become clear when I examine Wat-suji's discussions of the authentic self in the 1937 and 1942 versions of his *Ethics*, the repression of his theoretical deficit toward Marx, and eventually toward what was perceived to be the West as a whole, will be shown to be an essential component in the constitution of cultural identity in his and others' culturalist discourse. In Watsuji's anthropology, his uneasiness with certain philosophies and social thoughts is immediately molded into the dichotomies the West versus the East, and the West versus Japan. Indeed, one is fully entitled to feel ill at ease with some existing ideas, and without the moment of uneasiness, any critical reevaluation of them would hardly be possible. The trouble is that disagreement with the existing modes of thought is explained away solely in terms of the Orient's or Japan's cultural difference. The concept of culture is appealed to as an excuse not to think through the uneasiness one feels with an existing view. This feature is not exclusive to Watsuji but to culturalism in general. It goes without saying that the same structure with the reversed terms exists in cultural essentialism in North America and Europe, which most often testifies, as does Watsuji, to a certain repression of anxiety that almost inevitably arises from the encounter with any heterogeneous other.

Second, despite Watsuji's emphasis on sensuous and human activity, he did not see much of a problem in allying the sort of praxis thematically dealt with in *The German Ideology* with the basically Kantian notion of praxis. Consequently, although he coined one of the main philosophemes in his *Ethics, kôi-teki jissen renkan* or "practical relationality in [social] action" after Heidegger's conception of "equipment,"[7] almost no attention is paid to social relations that are mediated by equipment. It seems that Watsuji's undue insistence on the irreducibility of his human science or "the study of the human being" to natural science led to the sanctification of Man, totally independent of nature and free of any contamination by materialism. Surely his philosophy cannot be characterized as hostile to carnality, as is unequivocally evidenced by his enthusiastic endorsement of sexual affection and his adamant denunciation of puritanism because of which he has often been portrayed as a liberal and cosmopolitan thinker of modern Japan.[8] But there is a peculiar spiritualism operating in Watsuji's discourse. What one might refer to as the materiality of the social is deliberately excluded in his ethics. And, his conception of the social relation cannot afford to entertain the possibility of overdetermination in that relation at all.

The term "subject" or *shutai* itself was thus posited as the central philosopheme around which topics related to praxis, on the one hand, and the determination of particular social relations, on the other, would be woven together in Watsuji's study of the human being. But here a glance at the history of the term "subject" in modern Japanese language seems necessary.

This particular rendering of the word "subject" in Japanese is inconceivable beyond the context of what was then called *jikaku sonzairon* or the ontology of self-awareness.[9] To my knowledge, no equivalent of "subject" had played any major role in the intellectual world in Japan prior to the importation of European philosophical vocabulary during the Meiji period, although the problems that later received rearticulation in relation to "subject" had certainly been addressed, for instance, in Buddhist discourses of various periods, in pre-Meiji Japan. And, in the process of translating the term "subject," *sujet*, *Subjekt*, and so on, questions internal to the conceptions of subject in modern philosophy—questions that demanded a philosophical, and not a philological or linguistic, response—were inevitably raised.

As this issue has been seriously called into question—for example, in the contexts of psychoanalysis and the critique of ontology in Europe, Japan, and elsewhere for the past several decades—the translation of the term "subject" must have had to do with the peculiarity of a convention in which the subject in the sense of the nominative case (*shukaku*) was assumed to be identical to the subject of a proposition (*shugo*). And in a proposition, the subject is linked to the predicate by the copula, thereby entering the register of being. The situation is further complicated by the fact that the word "subject" is frequently used to signify an individual who speaks or acts. "Subject" is often used for both that which is thought or the subject in the sense of theme (*shudai*) and the one who thinks.

The problem of *jikaku sonzai* or the being-aware-of-self was put forth in relation to the topic of modern subjectivity in Japan when the question about the subject's thinking or perceiving itself as a theme was asked. Already in this questioning itself one can detect some uncertainty as to the status of the verb "to think," for two different ways to posit the subject in relation to this verb are available. One is confined to the formation of knowledge, so that the subject of thinking is exclusively epistemological; this sort of subject was rendered as *shukan*. In contrast, the other is linked to the issue of action and subsequently to praxis in general, and, as thinking was taken to be an act (as in "thinking act"), the verb "to think" was included in the group of verbs "to do," "to make," "to act," and "to speak." The consequence is that the subject of thinking is taken to be the subject of action. In this case, the term was translated *shutai*. What distinguishes the subject as *shutai* from the subject as *shukan* or the epistemological subject is primarily the practical nature of *shutai* because of which the subject as *shutai* cannot be accommodated within the subjective-objective opposition. For this reason, Watsuji could argue that, insofar as the subjective (*shutai-teki*) being of Man is concerned, it should not be grasped as an object opposed to the epistemological subject (*shukan*).

The distinction between *shutai* and *shukan* has been proven very precarious, as is attested to by the frequency of the cases in which these two terms are used interchangeably in Japanese philosophy. Watsuji, who tried to stabilize the distinction by basing it on the opposition of the human sciences and the natural sciences, was, nevertheless, no exception on that score; for he appealed to the Kantian exposition in order to explicate the social nature of the human being, with which he claimed natural science could not deal and for which the term *shutai*, not *shukan*, was necessary.

The social nature of the human being, that is, the fact that the human being is primarily the subject as *shutai*, was deduced from the empirico-transcendental dual structure of the human being. Following Kant's argument about the concepts of transcendental personality and person, Watsuji argued that the social nature of the human being lay in its character:

> The human being finds himself in his object. The ground for such a possibility should be in the fact that the human being is [at the same time] "I" and "you" in himself. When the human being finds an object, he finds in it his "I" that has been externalized into "you." We must agree [with Heidegger] that the primordial scene of "going out," that is, the scene of *ex-sistere*, of transcendence, has been found in the human being.[10]

Thus, Watsuji superimposed the Kantian empirico-transcendental double onto the Heideggerian ontico-ontological double. Since this superimposition was a possibility that Heidegger himself had entertained,[11] let me sketch the path of Watsuji's argument. Starting with the determination of the subject in terms of the "I think" that should be able to accompany all "my" representations, Watsuji stresses the formal character of the transcendental subject[12] as stated by Kant as follows:

> We can assign no other basis for this teaching [about the nature of our thinking being] than the simple, and in itself completely empty, representation "I"; and we cannot even say that this is a concept, but only that it is a bare consciousness which accompanies all concepts. Through this I or he or it (the thing) which thinks, nothing further is represented than a transcendental subject of the thoughts = X. It is known only through the thoughts which are its predicates, and of it, apart from them, we cannot have any concept whatsoever, but can only revolve in a perpetual circle, since any judgment upon it has always already made use of its representation. And the reason why this inconvenience is inseparably bound up with

it is that consciousness in itself is not a representation distinguishing a particular object, but a form of representation in general, that is, of representation in so far as it is to be entitled knowledge; for it is only of knowledge that I can say that I am thereby thinking something.[13]

Following Kant's paralogisms of pure reason, Watsuji demonstrates the fundamental mistake involved in the application of categories to the "vehicle of those categories," to the transcendental subject, in order to show that the transcendental subject or transcendental personality, the determining subject in the application of categories to manifolds of senses, can never be determined to be an object to which categories are applied. Therefore, the transcendental "I" or transcendental personality must be *mu* or nothingness insofar as it is sought for as an object (*taishô to shite wa mu*). It is worth noting that *mu* or nothingness, which would repeatedly be appealed to in the wartime and postwar culturalist discourse as if, from the outset, it had been the mystical concept issued from some profound Oriental religious consciousness, was first given as a philosophical term in the reading of Kant.[14] In contrast to the transcendental personality, which can never be a being, the person is the thinking being to which the category of substance is applied. Therefore, person is partly a being (*yû*) as opposed to personality (*mu*). Yet, person and personality are always combined in the human being as *jikaku sonzai* or the being-aware-of-self.

> The "I," who is conscious of the objectified "I" according to the form of inner sense, that is, according to the "I" in itself, is nothing but the I of the "I think," that is, the subjective ego. Furthermore, the "I think" is empty, without any content, and is the "transcendental personality," but it is never a "person." Therefore, person is neither simply identical to the "I" as an object nor identical to the subjective "I" [*shukan ga*].(*Watsuji Tetsurô Zenshû*, vol. 9, pp. 332–33)[15]

Watsuji attempts to legitimate the use of *shutai* by showing that what is at issue is something that cannot be construed within the scope of *shukan*. Precisely because of the limitation inherent in the conception of the epistemological subject, neither the social nature of the human being nor the being-aware-of-self of *ningen* can be addressed in terms of the classical epistemological subjectivity. And to pose the social nature of the human being as an authentic question indispensable in the study of the human being requires something like a "schematism" about the combination of personality and person, a schematism by means of which to think the internal relationship between *homo noumenon* and *homo phaenomenon*.[16] But, for Watsuji,

Kant's formula was understood to point out both a clue to the possible way to articulate the social nature of the human being within his anthropology philosophically, and the limit of Kantian philosophy, which must be overcome in order to give an adequate account for the "being-with" of the human being (*ningen sonzai no kyôdôtai*). In *Critique of Pure Reason*, the duality of personality and person is given in the "self-consciousness in time." Hence, "in the whole time in which I am conscious of myself, I am conscious of this time as belonging to the unity of myself; and it comes to the same whether I say that this whole time is in me, as an individual unity, or that I am to be found as numerically identical in all this time."[17]

The "I" in which time is, is the "I" of apperception, while the ego in time is the objectified "I." For the "I" of apperception, it is impossible to say that it is in time, whereas insofar as the "I" is objectified, it must be in time since any entity outside time cannot be an object of experience. These two I's are not identical, but they are synthesized in the person through the schematism of time. "Insofar as the objectified ego is concerned, the ego is in time. Since time is in the ego that is not objectified, however, it is in the stage [*bamen*] of time that the ego, which is *mu* or nothingness insofar as it is sought after as an object, objectifies itself" (*Watsuji Tetsurô Zenshû*, vol. 9, p. 334). Watsuji then claims that the dual structure of the human being should be understood in a manner similar to the way Kant demonstrates the duality of empirico-transcendental subjectivity in schematism. But here again he draws attention to the practical nature of *ningen* by pointing out that, although transcendental personality does not relate itself to a subject other than the one to which it is "numerically identical," the human being is essentially with the others and, therefore, necessarily a communal "being-with": as far as the human being is concerned, the subject must be *shutai*, not *shukan*, since *shukan* only relates to itself and lacks the moment of communality with other subjects. In thus addressing the social nature of the human being in relation to schematism, Watsuji believes he has explained the inadequacy of the Kantian framework in which the duality of the transcendental "I" and the empirical "I" is persuasively laid out, but the "being-with" of person is ignored.[18] And he insists that, whereas in the theoretical employment of reason the transcendental subject is indeterminable and unknowable (hence, the subject is *shukan*), the transcendental subject is given immediately and concretely (as *shutai*) in its practical employment. (Thus, by ascribing the uncertainty of the "I" only to the theoretical employment of reason, thereby trivializing it, Watsuji refused to acknowledge the abyssal nature of the "I"; he resisted the cognizance that the "I" is groundless, a cognizance without which the resoluteness of *Dasein* in its authenticity in Heidegger, for instance, would be incomprehensible. At this stage, Watsuji refused to deal with the issue of either "historicality" [*Geschichtlichkeit*] or "cohistorizing." I will return to this problem.) Furthermore, from the outset, the transcendental subject as *shutai* is given as "being-with." The human being understands its social relationality with others, and this understanding is essentially a practical one that is anterior to theoretical understanding. "The human being exists in such a way that it produces communal life, which is mutually understood [by one and the other] prior to consciousness."[19] Rephrasing Marx, then, Watsuji argues that, because of the inner structure of the human being, human consciousness is predetermined by man's social being. Now his study of Man acquired a specific direction by which the being of Man should be investigated: the dual structure of the *ningen* or "being-between."

In his analysis of the concept "human being," Watsuji again proved himself to be an earnest disciple of Heidegger. An etymological method was applied to the Japanese and Chinese terms concerning *ningen* in order to reveal the social nature of *ningen*. The compound *ningen*, which consists of two characters, *nin* (*hito*) and *gen* (*aida*), is subjected to etymological analysis.[20] *Nin* (or *hito*) and *gen* (or *aida*), respectively, mean a person recognized from the third person's perspective or people in general (English "one," French *on*, or German *man*), and space between or relationality. Hence, Watsuji says, the term *ningen* already implies the space between people that simultaneously separates and relates one person and another. In addition, *hito*, the specifically Japanese pronunciation for the first character of the compound *ningen*, contains the viewpoint of another person in that *hito* can never be used to directly designate the self. *Hito* is used for *das Man* ("the 'they'" in the English translation of Heidegger) to show the averageness of "they-self" in some Japanese translations of *Being and Time*. It either signifies the other or others in general who are opposed to "me," or designates "myself" seen from the other's viewpoint. Therefore, *nin* of *ningen* should be understood to imply the mediation of the other in the human being. Yet, it is misleading to regard the human being merely as a composite of individuals mutually mediating one another, because the second character *gen* of *ningen* shows that the mediation of the other in the human being is essentially spatial in character. By virtue of its openness as space, *ningen* cannot be confined to a one-to-one relation between two identities. *Gen* or *aida* is associated with the world (*yo*) of people (*seken*), the world of the social space (*yo no naka*) in which people are thrown (although Watsuji would no doubt evade such an expression because of the theological implications of the term "thrownness"). Together, the compound *nin* + *gen* should signify that the human being is a being that is in the world of people and that is always mediated by the other. The "being-between" of *ningen* was thus analyzed in order to disclose two moments in the social being of Man: the "being-with" determined as the mutual mediation by each other, and the belonging to society as an essential mode of the being-in-the-world.

What justifies Watsuji's move to equate the world (*yo*) with society? I cannot find any reasoning on his part to explain on what grounds society can be conceived of as a whole. Are we witnessing an obstinate tendency in Watsuji to substantialize social relations, as Sakabe Megumi noted?[21] Watsuji said: "However, how is it possible for *ningen*, which means the totality of the human being (in other words, *seken*), to mean the individual human being at the same time? It is thanks to the dialectic of whole and part. The part is possible only within the whole, and it is in the part that the whole manifests itself" (B, in *Watsuji Tetsurô Zenshû*, vol. 9, p. 19). The human being is construed as the dual structure of subjectivity in which the subject *shutai* is at the same time an individual and specific subjective position and the totality in relation to which the fixity of that subjective position is determined. The concept of totality serves two different ends: First, it enables one to conceive of community as an organic and systematic whole in which one's subjective position is given;[22] second, totality serves to guarantee that the fixity of a subjective position is immanent in the person anterior to his or her conscious recognition of it. Accordingly, the human being exists as the particular relationality of one subjective position to another, on the one hand, and as the coherent whole of systematicity among those subjective positions, on the other. Furthermore, the understanding of relationality is mutual. It takes the form of "I am conscious of you," but: "In this case, the act of seeing you is already prescribed by your act of seeing, and the act of loving you by your act of loving. Hence, my consciousness of you *is interwoven with your consciousness of me*. As distinct from the intentionality of consciousness, we call this *aidagara*" (C, in *Watsuji Tetsurô Zenshû*, vol. 10, p. 73; emphasis in the original). *Aidagara* is not mutual in the sense that two intentionalities of consciousness coincide with each other from opposite directions. It is more of a chiasm. Two consciousnesses are mutually prescribed by one another; in the relationality of subjective positions, each consciousness is permeated by the other (C, in *Watsuji Tetsurô Zenshû*, vol. 10, p. 73). For this reason, Watsuji argues that the "being-between" or human being is also the relationality of subjective positions (*aidagara*), and that, even if one may not be conscious of it, the human being cannot exist outside the relationality as such. Yet is it possible to do justice to the chiasmic aspect of sociality within Watsuji's anthropology of subjectivity? Does Watsuji's ethics not have to exclude the very possibility of conceptualizing chiasm in order that the whole of community be conceived of as systematicity?[23]

Just as the consciousness of an empirical subject is always accompanied by the "I think" he says, any consciousness of a particular relationality in which the individual is placed must be preceded by the individual's "being-between." The relationality of subjective positions is an a priori condition for the human being (aidagara sonzai).

> Even in the expressions of relationality [aidagara] such as gesture or behavior, the relationality of subjective positions is already anterior. The relationality can be deployed in its expression, but it is never brought into existence by being expressed. . . . Hence, the expression of a certain relationality is the objectification of an already existing relationality. The presence of many different forms in expression simply means that relationality is articulated [wake] in many different ways. In other words, what has already been comprehended [wakatte] about relationality a priori is objectified in each instance of expression.[24]

Relationality has always been comprehended prior to the objectification of it, because the subjective (shutai-teki) relationality of the human being is mu or nothingness. 'The 'articulation of relationality' [koto wake] is potentially comprehended prior to speech. And in speech, it discloses itself [arawa] as 'being—' [de aru].' The anteriority of relationality is explicated in reference to the mode in which relationality exists. If it discloses itself in social expression, how does it exist prior to disclosure? This issue is closely related to the Japanese verb aru, Watsuji declares.

Another Heideggerian move. Here, Watsuji relates the "articulation of relationality" to the issue of ontology, the subjectivity of the human being as articulated in the relationality of subjective positions to the etymological analysis of a verb aru, which means "to be something" (copula) or "to exist." He first points out the difference between the term sonzai (being), an equivalent of ningen, and German Sein, so as to exemplify the grammatical limitation of European languages that Western ontology has taken for granted. The compound sonzai is never confused with the "copula" in the languages of the Far East, says Watsuji. Instead of the ontotheological determination of "being," he proposes his analysis of a Japanese verb ari or aru as an equivalent to the copula, and shows that this verb can clearly indicate two distinguished uses among the various European terms corresponding to English "being." When it is used as a copula, the verb aru takes a particle de to form de aru, and it takes another particle, ga, to form ga aru when it is used in the sense of *existentia*.[25] Following Heidegger's argument on *ousia*, Watsuji relates *ga aru* to the character *yû* meaning "there is" or "to exist," and establishes a passage from *ga aru* to *motsu* ("to own" or "to have") since the Chinese character *yû* equates existence with possession. Thus, he asserts, the question of the meaning of being in the sense of *existentia* can be communicated to that of having. Since property can be ascribed only to the human being, one who has it is always the human being. In this regard, every being is being owned or had by the human being. Any statement that affirms the existence of a thing necessarily connotes the fact that the thing is in the possession of the human being. It follows that ultimately, for Watsuji, every ontological question should be an anthropological and, subsequently, an anthropocentric question. The project of the study of the human being as "being-between" asserts itself as an anthropocentric anthropology.

That anthropocentrism now reproduces the dual structure of subjectivity can be seen when one reflexively applies his equation of "to be" and "to have" to the being of the human being: if the statement "there is a thing" can be equated with the human being's having it, that the human being has itself or owns itself should be inferred from the statement "there is a human being." This is to say that the existence of a particular human being is already in the possession of the systematicity governing the relations among subjective positions within the totality: *shutai* owns itself. For this reason, the subject as *shutai* discloses its proper self in praxis, whereas in knowledge the subject does not reveal itself to intuition. The authentic self derives from the fact that the subject is always proper to the designated position in, as well as the property of, systematicity as totality. This is the primary setting within which Watsuji's ethics was further articulated.

For Watsuji, conscience that deters the individuality of the human being from taking its arbitrary path is equated with the voice of the totality. The totality in "me" declares, "Thou shalt not." And the conflict with the totality immanent in the individual presents itself as a supposedly dialectic interaction between the individual and the totality (I am extremely suspicious of Watsuji's appropriation of the term "dialectic"). Here, the individual is defined as follows: "The act of retention that unifies a variety of other acts has been taken to be essentially most individual. But, only because one presumes individual consciousness can it be taken to be individual. The act of retention itself does not belong to the individual. The same can be said about the unity of the act or the agent of the act" (C, in *Watsuji Tetsurô Zenshû*, vol. 10, p. 83). Of course, many acts that are too frequently predicated on the subject as the individual need not be related to the individual at all. As is often the case with individualism, the concept of the individual is kept artificially ambiguous, and the extremely dubious convention of substituting the subject for the individual as its equivalent is let pass unnoticed in most cases. For Watsuji, too, the concept of the individual is far from self-evident.

> He [Max Scheler] said that absolute solitude is the inevitable negative essential relation among the finite persons. A person can be individual not because he is the center of the act but because he negates communality. The essence of individuality is the negation of communality.(Ibid., p. 84)
>
> What is communal in essence can manifest itself in the mode of the absence of communality. This is individuality. Therefore, individuality cannot exist independently. Its essence is negation and emptiness [sunyata]. (Ibid., p. 83)

Since communality (kyôdô-sei) presumes the relationality of subjective positions, individuality is given rise to only when a person fails to identify himself or herself with the designated subjective position. Hence, it is impossible to construe individuality in positive terms: it could only be described as a series of negations. Watsuji does not seem to assume, however, that individuality is the inevitable consequence of human finitude. It can only be apprehended to be a deviation from what the person immanently is. Thus, individuality is comprehended primarily as a transgression of the existing relationality according to which one's duties are defined in accordance with one's subjective position. It follows that, whereas individuality negates the relationality of subjective positions, individuality affirms and endorses the relationality through the negation of it just as the transgression, insofar as it is the transgression from the already existing norm, affirms and sanctifies it. Consequently, in Watsuji's Ethics, individuality has to be viewed as a rebellion or as the guise of a rebellion that is always launched in anticipation of a prearranged resolution: it is a moment of deviation, but it always assumes the return to normalcy. Hence, Watsuji attempts to reduce the whole issue of individuality to what Lacan calls the "demand for love" on the part of the individual (one might call the individual sekishi or baby in this instance) toward the totality (which one might consider associating with the emperor),[26] but this "demand" is expected to be responded to when the individual returns—through confession perhaps—to his or her authentic self. Thus, this particular conceptualization of individuality makes any contest or rebellion against the totality a sinful act that could be redeemed by confession or return.[27] Watsuji's ethics, then, provides a very clear view of the ethical imperative. It is a call of totality to urge a person to return to his or her authentic self.

Therefore, what constitutes the ethical is the negation of individuality, the negation of negation, which brings a person back to what totality inside that person dictates. And it is a return to the subjective position of the authentic self that can be anticipated and understood by others since the mutual understanding among the people of a given communality is warranted by the very relationality of subjective positions (aidagara).

> One who rebels against one's origin by deviating from a certain communality wishes to return to one's origin by negating the rebellion. And this return takes place through the realization of some communality. The movement of this return is a human action that signifies the sublation [shiyô] of individual personality, the realization of social communion [jinrin-teki gôitsu], and the return to the original source of the self. Therefore, this is approved of [yoshi to serareru] not only by those people who participate in that communality but also by the profound essence of the self. That is "good" [yoshi]. Accordingly, it is not on the basis of "good" [yoshi] feeling but rather because an action indicates the return to the origin that the value of good is constituted. It follows that one can argue that it necessarily rejects low value for high value. The highest value is absolute totality, aspiration [in English in the original] toward which is called "good." This is why one's subjugation to the authority of the whole—abandonment of individual independence, and love, devotion, or sacrifice—has always been regarded as "good." This is illustrated by the fact that, in simple everyday language, the state in which social communion [jinrin-teki gôitsu] is achieved is called naka yoshi [on good terms]. (C, in Watsuji Tetsurô Zenshû, vol. 10, pp. 141–42)

Watsuji proposes a kind of ethics whose central guiding principle is to be "on good terms" with others: it is a kind of ethics that permits one to neglect other social and ethical concerns in order to remain on good terms with others.

But Watsuji's ethics also clearly and systematically delineated what Louis Althusser would describe thirty years later as the practical nature of ideology in which we "live, move and have our being." [28] Here, to be sure, we are not impressed by Watsuji's farsightedness: we are astonished at the high accuracy with which Watsuji's Ethics conforms to Althusser's description of ideology, in which, in fact, ethics is included. Watsuji's anthropology is decorated with so-called Oriental cultural costumes. But, it can effectively be analyzed by the critique of ideology that originated in Western Europe. And the call of totality to urge a person to return to his or her authentic self in Watsuji's anthropology can be explained as a detailed exposition of the function of ideology, which "hails or interpellates concrete individuals as concrete subjects, by the category of the subject";[29] and, as we will see, his philosophy of praxis is an authentic humanism that determines Man as a subject owned by the totality, that is, the state.

For Watsuji, therefore, the ethical is a return, a restoration of what a person originally is. But it is not only a return to the original moment in time; the return to the authentic self cannot be construed exclusively in terms of temporality.

> Space is the juxtaposability of subjects, the externality of one subject to another. Insofar as it is grasped directly and abstractly, it does not contain determining differentiations. So it is simply continuous, and the self and the other are not differentiated in it. Such subjective externality that is at the same time differential and nondifferential corresponds to what we have been discussing in terms of *the spatiality of the human being*. . . . As it is understood to mean the subject [*shutai*], the structure of [Hegelian] Spirit has both temporality and spatiality. Heidegger has already pointed out its temporal nature [of the Spirit]. According to him, the negation of negation that is the essence of the Spirit cannot be understood without reference to temporality. It is according to temporality that we understand the significance of the term "return" in the statement "Idea returns to itself through negation." For our part, however, we must go further and ask whether or not the return is possible only temporally. What, after all, makes the return (*Rückkehr, zurückgehen*) possible is partition, separation. And partition and separation are originally (*kongen-teki ni wa*) grounded on the spatiality of the subject [*shutai*]. (C, in *Watsuji Tetsurô Zenshû*, vol. 10, pp. 243–44; emphasis in the original)

As his work *Fûdo* or *Climate and Culture* amply indicates,[30] the totality to which a person belongs is circumscribed in terms not only of historical, political, and sociological factors but also of climatic, geographic, and ethnographic specificities. It would be an injustice merely to extract the geocultural sense of space from Watsuji's discussion on the spatiality of human being. But, given the distribution of his statements in his other works, it would be equally misleading to deny that the totality here means a particular geographical place, and the return invariably implies a move in the geographic space. Immediately, such a determination of the return evokes the geopolitical and cultural distinction between the West and the East, particularly between pastoral Europe and monsoon Asia, to use the basic categories coined in Watsuji's work *Climate and Culture*. Therefore, the return to the specific totality could imply the departure from another specific totality if the identities of these totalities are defined exclusively in geographic terms: an ethical choice could be made to represent an alternative between geopolitical and cultural areas in Watsuji's discourse. In this regard, one might naturally observe that geocultural categories are highly charged with ethical value. In a sense, geocultural categories begin to serve as ethical categories to the extent that the ethnic-national identity is taken to be the ground of science. At one point during the war, Watsuji went as far as to advocate that sciences, including physics, must be delimited by ethnic nationality (*minzoku*).[31] The international collaboration of scholarship is possible when each scientist works as a representative of his or her nation. Only through nationalism, Watsuji argues, can internationalism become possible. Therefore, those who do not belong to the nation and who do not work on the basis of the identity of *minzoku* in fact make internationalism impossible. (Yet it is important to keep in mind that many of his contemporary thinkers explicitly used the same term *minzoku* in the sense of the nonethnic or multiethnic nation, and, in this respect, Watsuji was not necessarily following the trends of the Japanese state's official argument. This is one of the reasons why Watsuji could become a dominant intellectual figure in postwar Japan when all those advocates of the multiethnic Japanese nation were disqualified after the loss of the empire.)

Imitating the restorationist move in the West toward Eurocentricity, which was to a great extent motivated by an anxiety concerning the putative loss of the West's superiority over the non-West in the 1930s[32] and which found its cumulative expression in the obsessive emphasis on the idea of the distinctiveness of the West and on the separationist distinction of "we the West" from the rest of the world, Watsuji seemed to produce an equally ethnocentric move toward the East. The impulse to imitate Heidegger and European philosophy now resulted in a desire to react to the West, a desire for symmetry between the West and the East, and eventually for the ethical absolutization of the East in the face of the restorationist declarations by Valéry, Heidegger, Husserl, Pound, Eliot, and others.[33] No doubt, this is a reactive return to the authentic self, but when the subject (*shutai*) is construed in spatial terms, the demand of symmetry in the name of equality among civilizations and nations seems to trigger this return to the East in the face of the return to the West in the West. After all, is all return to the original self reactive? Is it not exactly the other side of mimetic identification?[34] Then, for Watsuji, what is the totality to which one is urged to return?

In his study of the human being, totality is not immediately equated to an existing community. A sociomoral community (*jinrin-teki kyôdôtai*) may be family, corporation, neighborhood community, or the state. But they are all finite totalities in contrast to the absolute totality, the ultimate principle of emptiness or *sunyata*, to which the ethical is attributed in the last instance (*Watsuji Tetsurô Zenshû*, vol. 10, p. 126). A person may well live simultaneously in different finite totalities. Therefore, one's subjective position is determined in its multiplicity. In this regard, in spite of his hostility to individualism, which he regards as a modernist fallacy, Watsuji endorses the wide variety of choices on the basis of the division of labor.[35] Nevertheless, the absolute totality is not transcendent with regard to its accessibility to a person since absolute negativity can be found in the person's belonging to a specific and existing finite totality. After all, the highest and most encompassing finite totality should be found in the nation-state, where its communality consists not of associations but of individual citizens, so that the individual citizen participates directly in the whole (ibid., p. 156). Therefore, in the nation-state, the relationship between the individual and the totality, the relationship determining the ethical in the subject, must be most clearly revealed.

> Regardless of whether the totality at issue be family, friends, corporation, or the state, it is pointless to talk about individual impulse, individual will, or individual action outside the context of separation and independence from such a totality. . . . The independence of the individual can be sublated in the negation of the negation, and, without exception, this is achieved by belonging to some particular sociomoral totality. (C, in ibid., p. 127)

After all, for him, individuality is nothing but mere selfishness. The negation of the sociomoral totality, therefore, cannot imply the transformation of that totality, or its reform: it is preordained that the negation of the totality is ascribable to individual impulse so that it can be recuperated by the totality through moral acts such as conversion (*tenkô*) and confession. In Watsuji's conception of "negation," there is no moment that alters the very relationship of the individual and the whole: it is negation in the static opposition affirmation—negation. His use of the term "dialectic" sounds odd, partly for this reason.

> The individual dissolves into that sociomoral totality. Again, it does not matter whether it be family, friends, corporation, or the state. After all, it is

> pointless to talk about transindividual will, total will, or dutiful act unless in one's assimilative identification with the totality. It is precisely in this realization of a finite totality that the absolute negativity returns to itself. (Ibid.)

Among the existing finite totalities, the nation that has realized itself in the institution of the state is most important and sacred because of its sovereignty expressed in the legal institution. It is into this finite totality that the individualistic individual is urged to dissolve through his or her assimilative identification with it. Furthermore, as Takahashi Tetsuya has argued extensively,[36] Watsuji defines the nation (*minzoku*) as a cultural community "delimited by the communality of blood and soil" (D, in ibid., p. 585). And the identity of this community can be formed by its closure and exclusionism: in principle, a cultural community can be "an open society," but the formation of its identity requires closure (ibid.).

The same argument about national particularism, which is most systematically developed in *Climate and Culture*, is also deployed here. However, Watsuji does not seem aware at all that, in order to juxtapose one national character with another, he has to take up a transcendent viewpoint, a bird's-eye view, flying high above the ground where one encounters another. In spite of his dependence on Kant and his abhorrence of unmediated universalism, Watsuji does not recognize that the characterization of the other's particularity is simply impossible unless his own ethnocentric universalism is accepted. Here we are not concerned with the observation of other national cultures on the basis of the exoticism of international tourism. Watsuji does not seem comprehensive about cultural and social incommensurability. It is no accident that his respect of other national characters would result in certain racial stereotyping.

As an authentic culturalist, Watsuji continues to argue that the cultural community forms the substance of the state, and that the state must be kept in touch with absolute negativity through the living totality of the nation.[37]

But let's not jump at an easy condemnation of Watsuji. Before coming to any concluding remarks about the totalizing tendency of Watsuji's humanism, the issue is to envision the probable consequences of what is signified by the return to the authentic self and how the "dissolving into totality" is actually to take place.

It is amazing that, in Watsuji's conception of the relationality of subjective positions, no conflict is to result from the simultaneous overlapping of totalities. Not the slightest possibility of indeterminacy is expected when a person is said to belong to anything from the community of a married couple at the minimum level up to the nation-state at the maximum. If the return to the authentic self is definitive as to the ethical value judgment, what would ensue in the situation where one must identify with contradictory subjective positions simultaneously? Or are those finite totalities synthesized in such an organic way that a smaller totality may be assimilated into a larger one, just as an organ is assimilated into a larger system in a living organism? (D, in *Watsuji Tetsurô Zenshû*, vol. 11, p. 593). Is the possibility of overdetermination in the relationality of subjective positions entertained at all in Watsuji's ethics? Obviously not. In this sense, Watsuji's Man does not have "the unconscious." Thus, his anthropology uncritically inherits another feature of humanism—that is, of modern constructive subjectivism.

Authenticity is prescribed in terms of the totality's immediate immanence in the person, so that the person's authentic self is given as conforming to the systematicity governing the relationality of subjective positions from the outset. A preestablished harmony is always already implied in the concept of authenticity. As a corollary, one might as well infer that, unlike Heidegger's authenticity, Watsuji's retains no ex-static or pro-jective—or decentering—character. Perhaps it is because Watsuji conceives of the dual structure of the subject mainly in spatial terms: the subject goes outside of itself, but spatially toward the other person already retained in the relationality (*aidagara*) and not temporally toward the future. As a result, the subject can return to its authentic self through the mutual understanding secured by the very notion of the relationality between the self and the other. Predictably, Watsuji's critique of Heidegger goes as follows: "[Heidegger's] *Dasein* is, in this sense, "beyond itself" [*über sich hinaus*]. Yet, *Dasein* is not concerned with other beings than itself, and is concerned with the possibility of being proper to itself. . . . *Dasein* is always the end in itself" (C, in *Watsuji Tetsurô Zenshû*, vol. 10, pp. 226–27). *Dasein* returns to itself through its authentic possibilities, but the being that discloses the totality through the project toward its own death is merely an individual being. According to Watsuji, it is never a human being. Hence, "Heidegger dealt with the death of an individual as the phenomenon of human death, ignoring [the social manifestations of human death such as] deathbed, wake, funeral" (ibid., p. 233), and so on. In passing, let me note that he ignores unnatural death, whose image is not fixed within the network of social customs; he ignores violent death.

What Heidegger called authenticity is inauthenticity. Only when such inauthenticity is negated in the merger of the self and the other [*jitafuji*], that is, when the "self" is forgotten, can authenticity be realized. Retrospectively, one may call the totality of the human being thus realized the "authentic self." But, in this case, the authentic self is more like Kant's transindividual subject than Heidegger's individual self that becomes totality through death. (Ibid., p. 237)

Now Watsuji is thinking in the rather regressive language of culturalism in which the formula the individualistic West = being versus the collectivist East = emptiness or nothingness is accepted as a truism. From this standpoint, Watsuji seems to reject Heidegger's argument about "temporality and historicality" and ventures to announce that Heidegger did not address the issue of "being-with" at all. Is he completely blind to the question of historicality, and to the implications of the famous passages (Part II, chapter 5, section 74, "The Basic Constitution of Historicality," of *Being and Time*) about the being-with in the destiny of community and *Dasein*'s resoluteness to its own death, passages about themes that would be repeatedly discussed by Japanese writers in the late 1930s and early 1940s?

Perhaps what Watsuji said about Heidegger's authenticity equally applies to Watsuji's authenticity from Heidegger's viewpoint—that is, what is authentic for Watsuji is inauthentic for Heidegger, and that the reverse is also true; for the relationality of subjective positions (*aidagara*) suggests an affinity with Heidegger's "they" rather than the authentic potentiality-for-Being. Watsuji seems to seek the ground for his ethics in the averageness of "they," which Heidegger describes as follows:

> The Self of everyday Dasein is the *they-self*, which we distinguish from the *authentic Self*—that is, from the Self which has been taken hold of in its own way [*eigens ergriffenen*]. As they-self, the particular Dasein has been *dispersed* into the "they," and must first find itself. This dispersal characterizes the "subject" of that kind of Being which we know as concernful absorption in the world we encounter as closest to us. . . . *Proximally*, factical Dasein is in the with-world, which is discovered in an average way. Proximally, it is not "I," in the sense of my own Self, that "am," but rather the Others, whose way is that of the "they." In terms of the "they," and as "they," I am "given" proximally to "myself" [*mir "selbst"*]. Proximally, Dasein is "they," and for the most part it remains so. (*Being and Time*, p. 167; translators' brackets)

It may appear that Heidegger's statement that "authentic Being-towards-death—that is to say, the finitude of temporality—is the hidden basis of *Dasein*'s historicality" simply does not apply to Watsuji's ethics. If this is the case, resoluteness toward death would not be the essential moment in the return to the authentic self in *shutai* since the social as Watsuji conceives of it seems devoid of uncertainty. This point is made most explicit by the example of his analysis of trust as a moment of subjectivity.

Watsuji ascribes trust to the relationality of subjective positions, so trust is primarily an expression of the already existing relationality, that is, of the totality as *shutai*. As a matter of fact, trust is not defined as a moment in generating a new social relation, but it is assumed that it can be known only in its absence. Just as individuality is the negation of totality in his ethics, so trust is a derivative effect of the totality that is always already there. What is deliberately eliminated from Watsuji's conceptualization of trust is its aleatory aspect. In due course, he argues against Nicolai Hartmann that trust occurs only where social positions are guaranteed by the relationality of subjective positions and that it should be taken not as the basis of society but as its consequence. Therefore, trust is directed to the systematicity guaranteeing the mutual understanding of subjective positions rather than to a particular person. According to Watsuji, therefore, one is not supposed to trust another person, but one is to trust sociomoral totalities like the corporation and the state. In principle, trust cannot be extended to those whose subjective positions are uncertain within the network of given social relations. Watsuji's ethics declares: "You ought not trust strangers." Such a conception of trust does not allow for the conception of sociality, which cannot be integrated into the restricted economy of totality. Furthermore, as Watsuji conceives of the chiasm of "you" and "I" only in terms of symmetrical exchange, he cannot allow for a surplus in the social. If sociality means the impossibility of symmetrical mutuality—or transference—between the self and the other, the possibility of sociality as such must be in contradiction to Watsuji's trust.

It is often said that, in contrast to the Heideggerian *Dasein* analysis, Watsuji's ethics is much more attentive to, and even perceptive of, the sociality of the human being. My reading is diametrically opposed to that. What is absent in Watsuji's anthropology is the very concern for sociality. Even as a common word, sociality connotes much more than the relationality of subjective positions. Normally, we do not ascribe sociality to a person who can only operate within prearranged social relations such as parent-child and teacher-student. Sociality is understood to mean the ability to leave behind the sort of trust warranted by the already existing relations, to "go out in the world" and to establish new relations with strangers. Figuratively speaking, this ability can be compared to the capacity to learn and pluralize a language rather than to the capacity to repeat and maintain a language conceived of as a closed system. By the same token, it should be evident that one's relation to the other must of necessity contain the possibility of betrayal and contingency without which trust would be empty. Only within the element of uncertainty does trust make sense. I trust a person precisely because I recognize him or her as one who is potentially capable of betraying me. Here, trust is one's resoluteness to confront the possibility of betrayal; it is a decision to expose oneself to the possibility of being betrayed. Even when their relation appears secured by the institution of a certain *aidagara* or relationality of subjective positions, uncertainty can never be eliminated. This is to say that chiasm with others can never be reduced to a transparent mutuality of intersubjectivity. The inner construction of Watsuji's argument of ethics, which should be summarized as a sort of systems theory, did not allow but for him to misconstrue the very experience of chiasm. Therefore, his claim that trust is always preconditioned by the relationality of subjective positions must mean disavowal—disavowal in the psychoanalytical sense, too—of the moment of uncertainty, which, because uncertainty is always interwoven in every social relation, necessitates one or another form of "alea" in order to be engaged in any relation with others. Moreover, it is not because of a rebellious attitude toward the totality, or of an "individualistic" impulse, or individuality as an expression of "selfishness" that uncertainty arises. Uncertainty is inherent in every *aidagara*; uncertainty is inevitable in every social encounter, as Emmanuel Levinas often emphasizes by his phrase "transcendence of the Other." Therefore, in order to preserve room for sociality in our discourse, totality should never be conceptualized as systematicity as in systems theory; the simultaneity of the social must never be collapsed upon the synchrony of relationalities that is obtained through transcendental analysis or phenomenological reduction.[38]

It follows that the repression of uncertainty in the relationality of subjective positions amounts to a refusal of the otherness of the other, of respect for the other, and, after all, of sociality itself. For example, in her relation to me, my wife's subjective position is "comprehended and articulated [*wakatte*]" as such, but she is not merely my wife. The situation does not change much even if other relationalities are taken into account. In her relation to a shop owner, she occupies the subjective position of customer; in her relation to the teacher of her child, she is a parent; in her relation to her junior staff in the office where she works, she is regarded as boss. Her subjective position is further articulated as the number of "practical relationalities in social action [*jissen-teki kôi renkan*]" that she is involved in increases. But, however many predicates one may wish to attribute to her, she cannot exhaustively be defined as the subject of those predicates. She always exceeds the subject: she always retains some surplus over her subjective determination. Thus, she can never be exhaustively identified with a subject. And, precisely because she cannot be exhaustively identified with any subject, there can be sociality between her and me. Needless to say, the same applies in my relation to myself. Not only am I an other to myself (Watsuji was fully aware of this sort of otherness, which can easily be contained by the scheme of *shutai* or subjectivity), but I am also other to the dual structure of subjectivity; that is, my relation to myself always bears a surplus that is irreducible to the dual structure of the whole and the individual. Thus, I am never reduced to an identity, an individual who identifies with the whole. I am not a unity fashioned after the unicity of the whole. In short, I am not an *individuum*.[39]

And if the putative systematicity of totality as the human being is always threatened by sociality, the return to the authentic self would require a much more violent decisiveness toward an ecstatic leap into communality, something like the Heideggerian resoluteness, without which the very sense of communal belonging that our original selves are always already understood and embraced in the *shutai* would be lost. In order to believe that one is able to return to the authentic self or to keep one's nostalgic sense of belonging insulated from sociality,[40] one would have to take a blind leap into what might be called the destiny of the community. At this stage, Watsuji Tetsurô had to face the problem of one's own death, of the kind of death that is not the death of the average "they" fixed within the network of social relationalities and customs; he could no longer avoid the problems of unnatural, violent death.

Until the publication of his *Ethics (I) (C)* in 1937, Watsuji's anthropology bore a fundamental shortcoming as a typical theodicy for the modern Japanese state. In spite of its conservative character, particularly in comparison to Heidegger, Watsuji's philosophy lacked one essential insight into the mechanism of the modern state formation and its reproduction, that is, the relationship between national community and death.

It is well known that the modern nation-state invents such apparatuses as national history, literature, and national education, and thereby projects the image of a homogenized and universalized national community. Among those features peculiar to the modern nation-state is the idea of universal conscription. This idea dictates that the adult male population—in some cases, the female population as well—over a certain age be subjected to military service, and it thus determines national community in a specific fashion: all the legitimate members of this community are defined as potential soldiers.

As Carl Schmitt and others have asserted, the national community acquires the most explicit self-determination in the extremity of war. National community is then unequivocally determined as to the constitution of its membership: one's belonging to the nation is immediately facilitated by one's willingness to join in the act of killing a group of people designated as the enemy. Of course, the possibility of killing is always accompanied by the possibility of being killed. Therefore, the possibility of belonging to a national community by killing may also be accompanied by the possibility of belonging to that community by being killed. It is noteworthy that the verb "to belong" has gained some transitive as well as transitory quality in this context, and, in this regard, neither belonging to the national community nor identification with it designates a static state of affairs: rather, both designate a historical process in which one is urged to act. Historicality cannot be excluded from the issue of belonging to the national community since belonging, in fact, is always a matter of becoming and acting: belonging is a sort of historizing. Thus, the idea of universal conscription teaches the masses that they can belong to their nation through the possibility of their own death. Until recently, the nation-state could not shed its determination as the community of death.

The history of modern Japan is nothing but a history in which a national community was formed as the community of "unnatural" death. Under the Tokugawa regime, only the administrative class of the samurai, some 5 percent of the population, possessed the right to kill and be killed for the sake of the polity. Through many reforms in the late nineteenth century, that right and/or duty was extended to about the half of the adult population. Finally, during the 1930s and early 1940s, it was given to the entire population. Literally, total war became possible.

It is all too obvious that the antihistorical stance of Watsuji's anthropology proved to be a fatal shortcoming insofar as it claimed to be the theodicy for the prewar Japanese state: historicality had to be regained in order for his anthropology to continue to serve as the state ethics.[41]

In the attempt to identify oneself with the national community through one's own death, one would have to be "brought back to [one's] ownmost potentiality-for-Being-[one's]-Self" in order to die one's own death as a cohistorizing in Being-with-Others.[42] Here, since one dies alone, one is relentlessly individualized. "The unwavering precision with which Dasein is thus essentially individualized down to its ownmost potentiality-for-Being, discloses the anticipation of death as the possibility which is *nonrelational*" (emphasis in original)—nonrelational, that is, outside *aidagara*. One would then have to face "the lostness of the 'they'"—that is, one would then be expelled from the world of the "they" warranted by *aidagara* or the relationality of subjective positions; for, when one is "resolute, [one] takes over authentically in its existence the fact that [one] *is* the null basis of one's own nullity" (*Being and Time*, p. 354). But for this recognition about the aloneness of one's own death and the groundlessness of one's existence that are disclosed by anticipatory resoluteness toward death, the theodicy for the state would never be able to acquire the coercive force with which to command the nation to "die for its country."

In order to serve to legitimate the membership of the national community sanctioned by the state, Watsuji's anthropology should have recuperated all its shortcomings.

This is exactly what I find in the second volume of *Ethics*, published in 1942. First, historicality and the destiny of the nation:

> We have said that there cannot be a human totality higher than the state, but have never implied that there is not the ultimate absolute totality thanks to which the totality of the state continues to be a totality. Each state and the relations among the states express the way this absolute totality exists, and cannot be apprehended without reference to this origin. From this, however, we cannot conclude that the totality encompassing many states has been formed in the human being. These states are moments in the human being, but the human being is a fluid scene in which they cannot be unified into one. Such a human being may be called "World History" after Hegel, provided that it is not merely the "history" of the world but also the historical "world." (D, in *Watsuji Tetsurô Zenshû*, vol. 10, p. 432)

Second, the people's self-sacrifice to the state:

> The state is the absolute force for the individual, and demands unconditional devotion from the individual. The individual can return to his or her own ultimate totality through devotion to the state. Therefore, it is said that duty to the state means loyalty [*chûgi*], according to which one devotes everything one owns in order to serve the sovereignty of the state. (Ibid., p. 434)

Many have attempted to distinguish Watsuji's anthropology from Heidegger's philosophical project by stressing the former's concern with "being-with" and a certain resemblance of his concept *aidagara* to intersubjectivity. Yet, as far as the appropriation of an individual's death by the state is concerned, both Heidegger and Watsuji seem to have reached an almost identical conclusion.

Jean-Luc Nancy showed that the remnant in Heidegger of subjectivism and individualism—Nancy is primarily concerned with the indivisibility

of the individual—led him to the blind submission of the individual to totality through the logic of communalist identification.[43] Watsuji Tetsurô,
who was a disciple of Heidegger and who believed himself to be most rigorously opposed to the individualism of his mentor (Watsuji is primarily
disagreeable with regard to the singularity of the individual), followed the
same path also through the logic of communalist identification. It seems to
me that, unless one resists this logic of communalist identification, one
could easily be drawn into a violent jingoistic sentiment. One need not
abide by the logic of communalist identification: one need not "belong" to
a national community this way.

What I have pursued in my reading of Watsuji's *Ethics* is a peculiar reversal of his logic, a reversal that somewhat resembles what Adorno called
the "cult of death": he argues that, because of the totality immanent in
each of the people, they volunteer to devote and sacrifice themselves to
the totality. But, if the existence of the systematicity of the totality and its
immanence in the people is seriously questioned, the only answer would
be that, because the individual member of the people sacrifices and "dissolves his or her individuality" into the whole for "World History," the totality can manifest its existence. At the limit, such a logic could easily produce an argument that the sense of totality is given because people die for
it, and that the resoluteness toward one's own death sustains the existence
of such a totality. In this sense, since I argued that Watsuji's *Ethics* can be
characterized by the will to *return*, it is typically an ethics of immanence.
Jean-Luc Nancy defines immanence as follows: "What the community has
'lost'—the immanence and the intimacy of a communion—is lost only in
the sense that such a 'loss' is constitutive of 'community' itself."[44]

There is no doubt that, during the fifteen-year war (1931–45), "dissolving into the whole" immediately suggested the physical erasure of the self
or *kyoshi*, which could mean one's own death. The slogan *ichioku gyokusai* or
"the total suicidal death of one hundred million," another version of "the
final solution," was propagated all over Japanese territories toward the end
of the Second World War, and, in view of the manner in which Watsuji
conceptualized authenticity in his ethics, it was no coincidence that the
final moment of the total suicidal death was imagined as the aesthetic experience of ultimate communion.[45] Death was appropriated into an experience in which one dissolved and got integrated into the body of the nation: death was transformed into the imagined experience of togetherness
and camaraderie; the resoluteness toward one's own death was translated
into the resoluteness toward identification with the totality. Death was
consequently aestheticized so that it could mediate and assimilate one's

personal identity into national identity. Finally, the nation was turned into the community of destiny (*unmei kyôdôtai*) toward death. To use Watsuji's vocabulary, absolute negativity equals absolute totality and was internalized into the finite totality of a nation-state. In this sense, the absolute totality lost its transcendence and infinity and became "expressible." Watsuji's ethics of *nakayoshi* (being on good terms) transformed itself into the ethics of *ichioku gyokusai* (the total suicidal death of one hundred million).

At many levels of discourse, the transformation of a polity calls into question some of the assumptions on which that polity hitherto justified itself, and forces it to come up with a new set of protocols according to which it will produce its new legitimation. It is the time when some questions concerning the foundation of the polity that would otherwise not be addressed at all are allowed to be posed. But it is also the time when many seek to prevent damaging questions from arising, or to dilute them into more docile ones, so that certain assumptions may remain repressed.

It goes without saying that the several years immediately following Japan's defeat in 1945 marked such a period of transformation. And many questions that had been suppressed until then were openly raised and discussed. For instance, the existence of the emperor system itself could now be debated, and Watsuji Tetsurô's articles on the *ten'nô-sei* or the emperor system could hardly be appreciated without taking into account the ongoing debates surrounding the status of the emperor in the supposedly new polity in postwar Japan and in its new Constitution around that time. Yet, speaking in the present, some forty years after their publication, I am sure that one could easily recognize, albeit in embryonic form, some of the themes that would continually dominate the discussion about the emperor system in postwar Japan. Although I have no intention of attributing the initial articulation of these themes to Watsuji's ingenuity, retracing his argument will hopefully disclose what was and still is at stake in the debates on the emperor system.

In this series of articles written during the time when the future of the emperor system and of Watsuji himself were uncertain (both were vulnerable to the charges of war responsibility), it is not difficult to discern the central topoi in which Watsuji invested much of his intellectual effort. In "Hoken shisô to shintô no kyôgi" (Feudal thought and the doctrine of Shinto), the first in chronological order after the war (October 1945), he attempts to distinguish the emperor's reign from the characteristic of samurai loyalty, which he regards as essentially a private relationship between the lord (*kun*) and the vassal (*kashin*) within the institution of *Ie* or a kinship organization, and which, according to him, was mistakenly appropriated into the Meiji imperial reign. Because of this feudalistic legacy, some historians incorrectly conceived of the nation's relationship to the emperor, and demanded that the subject (*shinmin*) devote himself directly to the emperor. Dissociating the "reign of the emperor" from feudal samurai ethics allowed Watsuji to suggest, if not explicitly, the fundamental problem inherent in the prewar emperor system, and to redefine the significance of the emperor in modern Japanese society. Although he did not mention it, we cannot help noticing the complete change of his attitude about the terms *chûgi* (loyalty) and *chûkun* (loyalty to the lord), which he not only endorsed but also promoted vehemently in the 1942 edition of his *Ethics*.

While loyalty (*chûkun*) served to regulate the relationship claimed by Watsuji as a personal one between the lord and his maximum of several hundred vassals, the emperor does not relate himself to the nation on an exclusively personal basis. Assuming the theoretical construct he had developed in his study of ethics (*Rinri-gaku*), he described the emperor as the unifying agent of a complex whole that consists of many different social organizations. The individual serves the totality through the various social organizations to which he or she is committed. "As a member of the family, as a friend, as a citizen, as a member of the church, as a researcher of the research institute, one serves the totality by fulfilling duties assigned according to one's social rank." The emperor is made to symbolize something like the Durkheimian organic solidarity of the society. Therefore, respect for the emperor does not entail one definite way of acting; rather, it should comprise the sum of different ways of acting in different social organizations. The trouble with loyalty lies in its indiscriminate application of an imperative that is peculiar to a specific social relation to all the other social relations. From this derives the misleading notion of the family state, which is utterly inappropriate to the reign of the emperor, Watsuji claimed.

In "Kokuminzentai-sei no hyôgensha" (The one who expresses the national totality), this topic receives further conceptual articulation. While endorsing the definition of the emperor in the new Constitution—the symbol of national unity—Watsuji denies the emperor the status of commander in chief or *sôran-sha* precisely because the emperor and the nation are not related to one another in their respective roles of issuer and receiver of any order. In the authentic reign of the emperor, he argues, the emperor does not command at all. One implication of this determination, a determination of the emperor's status in terms of the indetermination of the emperor's command, is obvious: the emperor does not relate himself to the nation in a relationship that can assume the question of responsibility; he cannot be held responsible for his command over the nation, for he neither executes nor expresses the will of the nation as a whole in his command addressed to the nation; he does not perform an act of enunciating on behalf of the nation what the nation as a whole wills or wishes. Therefore, according to Watsuji, the emperor is not a spokesperson for the nation or even a representative of it. On the condition that it is accepted that the emperor has always served the nation this way, regardless of various political structures in which he happened to be involved, including of course the structure of the Meiji state, one can in fact argue that the emperor can never be responsible for any particular political consequence brought about by a particular political structure such as the defeat in the war or atrocities caused by the national forces. It is not the emperor himself but only misguided and misguiding officials that can be held responsible for the execution of the nation's will. Here Watsuji is not trying to prove that the emperor was innocent of the war and Japanese governmental policies; as far as his argument goes, it does not seem that he is particularly concerned with the fate of the emperor as an individual. What he strives to demonstrate instead is the fact that the definition of the emperor as it is promulgated in the new Constitution already implies the impossibility of ascribing political and legal responsibility to the figure of the emperor. The persuasiveness of his argument hinges on the premises that the status given in the new Constitution of the emperor as "the symbol of national unity" in fact describes more accurately what the emperor has actually been and what he ought to be.

What does this symbol do when it neither represents the will of the nation as a whole nor executes it on behalf of the nation? On what ground can one claim that the emperor is the symbol of or symbolizes the unity of the nation when he can never be put in a relationship to the nation in which he is responsible to and, perhaps, for the nation? It is in this context that Watsuji carefully drew a distinction between the general will—*la volonté générale*—of the nation as a totality and the specific determination of that will.

> If the sum of the nation's opinions [*kokumin no sôi*] can be equated to the general will [*zentai ishi*] of the group called the nation, the general will exists wherever the group exists. It need not be formed. . . . The representatives are elected by vote, and the representatives thus elected decide on something in the parliament. The general will is not formed in this process. What

happens is that the general will is determined with respect to something. In other words, a specifically directed general will is formed with respect to a determined content.[46]

Thus, the existence of the general will, which is equal to the totality of the nation, must be distinguished from what the nation as a whole wills to do. On the one hand, Watsuji maintains the concept of the subject (*shutai*), which, as we have seen, he first articulated in his discussion of Kant, and posits the nation as a subject, thereby preserving the connotation of the Kantian subject as the agent of will and of praxis. On the other hand, he deliberately deprives that subject of any ability to posit itself in concretizing its will, that is, he deprives the subject of all freedom. Therefore, although he defines the nation as a living totality, the general will as the totality of the nation does not realize anything but its existence: the general will does not express its being by doing something, but merely expresses its being. It is a will (*ishi*) that wills to do nothing.

> The problem concerning the means by which to express such a living totality or the general will of the nation is different from the problem about the determination of the general will or about how to enunciate the general will thus determined in concrete terms. The core of the problem is how to bring into visibility "the living totality," which is neither objectifiable nor visible. In our country, it has been expressed in the emperor.[47]

In the attributes to the living totality, "neither objectifiable nor visible," the conceptual determination of the totality of the nation as *shutai* is still alive. As in Kant, the subject as Watsuji understood it cannot be posited as an object because the subject is the agent who posits the object. Neither can it be visible because it is an agent to see but not to be seen. However, a strange twist in his argument occurs here. If the living totality of the nation is expressed (*hyōgen suru*) in the figure of the emperor, the emperor himself cannot be identified as a subject. In this expression, which is nonetheless a sort of act, and, of course, a willed act, it is the nation as a whole and as *mu* or nothingness that objectifies and sees the symbolic representation of its totality: it is not the position of the emperor but that of the nation that is *mu*.

Therefore, it is the nation that is active in this act, and the emperor must remain passive; his role is described as a figure of passivity or even passion. Accordingly, Watsuji argued at one point prior to the promulgation of the new Constitution: "If, in the decision to come, it is clarified that 'Only the emperor expresses the general will of our nation,' to say that sovereignty consists in the general will of the nation will be no different from saying that the sovereign is the emperor who expresses the general will."[48] (The decision here means a decision by the Allied Powers as to whether or not the emperor system would be allowed to continue.) Because the nation recognizes its totality in the figure of the emperor and because there are no other ways to express such a totality as a totality, the emperor is immediately the expression of the people as a whole. Furthermore, Watsuji put an emphasis on the fact that the decision about whether to continue the manner of expressing the totality of the people in the emperor or to adopt a presidency was left to "the freely announced will of the Japanese people," who, under occupation at the time, held no sovereignty legally or politically. Later the parliament, consisting of members elected by vote, reached the decision to continue the emperor system. Therefore, on behalf of the General MacArthur occupation administration, and offering support to the United States political authority in East Asia, Watsuji concluded that the nation *had chosen* to express its general will in the emperor. The flaw of his argument is only too obvious. But what is important lies not in the tautological structure of his argument but in the implicit positing of assumptions without which even his circular argument would not be intelligible. The point at issue here is the existence of the totality of the nation itself: "No matter whether or not the individual is aware of his freedom, it is predetermined that the nation is a whole and accordingly has a general will."[49] Although the totality of the nation cannot be objectified or made visible— that is, brought into cognition without expression—it is predetermined that it exists. It has to be noted that Watsuji was not merely saying that many people existed in the country but that those people living there had already formed a unified whole as a nation with a synthesizing will. This unity cannot be attributed to the unity of a particular polity, for there were periods in Japanese history when many different polities coexisted. He asserts that, independent of political organizations, which changed throughout historical time, there has always been the totality of the nation with a general will. Hence:

> The people belonging to the group voluntarily started the system in which the living totality of that group is expressed in the emperor. It was not forced [on the people] by a few conquerors. . . . When the emperor was judicially instituted as the expression of the general will [during the Nara period (the eighth century)], it was not done irrespective of the will of the nation.[50]

Watsuji claimed that, just as the Japanese people freely and voluntarily chose to continue the institution expressing its totality in the figure of the emperor after the Second World War, the same entity freely and voluntarily started the same institution at the initial stage of the imperial tradition. That the people could freely and voluntarily choose the emperor system was testified to by the fact that the state was first organized on the basis of unification by religious authority without the use of military coercion. As those who are familiar with the general field of Japanese studies in the United States would probably note, this is a prevailing hypothesis that has been repeatedly stated by some historians of Japan.

They have claimed that a state was unified without the use of military violence because they are unable to avoid assuming that the Japanese nation had already been there to legitimate it. They have simply repeated what Watsuji and a few others argued in order to legitimate the new emperor system immediately after the war. What sort of lethargy allowed them to argue that the state was first organized without the use of military coercion, I do not know. Yet, let me stress that their argument for the non-violent formation of the Japanese state invariably but implicitly assumed the existence of the Japanese nation in antiquity.

More important, it is very hard to comprehend the presupposition underlying Watsuji's assertion. How can one possibly accept the thesis that the state is acceptable simply because it is organized without the use of military means? Is he saying that nonmilitary means such as religious authority are not coercive, and that it is therefore acceptable without further qualification?

After the initial stage, the power base of the state gradually changed from a religious authority to a military force. And, as the ancient Japanese state collapsed, political organizations based on military superiority became dominant. But there had always been the general will, which even the most powerful feudal lords could not ignore. Thus, the imperial court survived many historical transformations while it was impoverished politically and financially. Thus, in Watsuji's argument, the continued existence of the imperial court was equated with the continued existence of the Japanese nation.

It should not be difficult to dispute Watsuji's account of the imperial tradition, which does not differ much from the imperial historiography (*kôkoku shikan*) sanctioned by the prewar Japanese state and whose legitimacy was already very fragile when it could no longer receive legal support from the state after the war. This sort of historiography is viable only when the system of state censorship is at work. However, when we examine what is at stake in Watsuji's account, we cannot simply say that his argument has lost its validity. In a variety of forms, the censorship of historiography has continued in the hands of the Ministry of Education officials in postwar Japan.

By choosing two separate periods in Japanese history, one at the beginning and another in the present, Watsuji extrapolated the continual existence of the unity of the people between the two points. No doubt the continuity of the imperial genealogy, which had once been the preoccupation of the imperial historiography, was reasserted, but in a different guise. If the emperor sided with the nation and not with the state, the whole legitimation procedure should likewise have been pursued within the nation. By this I do not necessarily mean that the emperor was perceived to belong to the state before the war. What Watsuji attempted to achieve was a reformulation of the status of the emperor so that the emperor could be given an important role in the legitimation procedure of a so-called democratic Japan.

Moreover, and perhaps more important, by implicitly relying on the continuity of the imperial genealogy, Watsuji deproblematized and depoliticized the existence of the nation itself, erased the past of the multiethnic imperial state of Japan prior to the loss of the empire in 1945, and posited the nation as a given entity, as if the totality of the nation had not been constituted and reconstituted politically. Logically, it is not sufficient to say that because the nation existed in the eighth century and in the nineteenth century, it must have existed in the tenth or fifteenth centuries. Its existence at one point in history does not guarantee its existence a century later. Insofar as it is a social organization, it has to be reproduced to ensure its continued existence. As a matter of fact, it is equally possible to argue from the same set of premises that the Japanese nation existed in the eighth century and that a different Japanese nation emerged in the nineteenth century since the nation does not designate a population occupying a certain geographic territory but an internally organized unity of the people. One may also pose another question: Is the idea of the nation as Watsuji posited it a modern invention? Is it anachronistic to talk about the nation in the fifth century in Japan in spite of the fact that the term "nation" may indeed be traced back etymologically to Greco-Roman antiquity?

Since it was evident that there was hardly any political cohesion among the people who lived in ancient Japan, the unity of the nation had to be sought somewhere other than in political organizations. Neither could it be found in social organizations as historical materials indicated that the country was divided into many local communities. The only sphere Watsuji could possibly appeal to was that of culture.

If the concept of "the nation" [*kokumin*] presupposes the state, one might as well use the word people [*jinmin*] or folk [*minshū*] instead. In any event, [the emperor] is the symbol of the Japanese people [*pīpuru*; English in the original]. But [the nation] definitely continued to exist even when the Japanese state was divided and destroyed, so it must be understood as belonging to an order different from that of the state. Therefore, its unity is not a political but a cultural one. The Japanese people have formed a cultural community in language, historiography, custom, and all other cultural activities. What the emperor symbolizes is the unity of the nation or folk as a cultural community. The tradition of revering the emperor [*son'nō shisō*] that has existed throughout Japanese history indicates the very awareness of the unity.[51]

Watsuji has to make a series of assertions about the putative unity of the nation in ancient Japan in order to demonstrate a culture shared by all the people. Although many of the historical materials to which he referred in order to illustrate the cultural unity of the nation were in fact produced by a very small number of people, who were mostly of the ruling class, he says, the sentiment expressed in them was actually shared by all the people. They were part and parcel of the national expression (*kokuminteki hyōgen*). It is not necessary for the masses to be engaged in the production of such a national expression; it could very well be produced by a single genius. If the people recognize the expression of their own sentiment and will, and if their desire for self-expression is satisfied in it, it must be called national expression. During the Middle Ages, many tales only depicted conflicts within the ruling class and paid little attention to the everyday lives of the people. "Nevertheless, these works were narrated in front of the temple and shrine gates all over the country. It is an undeniable fact that people in villages listened to them and were deeply moved by them."[52] Thus, it now appears clear that, by culture, Watsuji mainly meant aesthetic works, and literature in particular. Accordingly, what was referred to by the cultural community was the people whose unity consisted in the shared aesthetic sentiment. But again one can notice a circular argument here. Is it not because Watsuji assumed a certain homogeneity in aesthetic sentiment expressed in literary works of a given period that he could argue for the commonness of aesthetic sentiment? Could he discover the existence of a cultural community whose unity was given by the shared aesthetic sentiment precisely because the unity of the nation was presupposed in the selection and appreciation of literary works?

However trivial this analysis may be, it shows why the figure of the emperor is so important in Watsuji's understanding of the unity of the nation.

Contrary to the way he organized his reasoning, we must reread it the other way around, for the relationship between the emperor and the totality of the nation is in reverse order in his argument. Literally, the emperor expresses the totality of the nation. This is to say that the totality of the nation is not anterior to the emperor and that it (here the pronoun "it" designates not the nation but its totality) does not express the emperor; the figure of the emperor in a sense creates its totality.[53] Needless to say, the totality thus created is an imaginary construct.

Can we think of a better example of the totality as an imaginary than this case of the emperor? What is expressed in the figure of the emperor is nothing but the imaginary nature of the totality of the nation. It goes without saying that not only the nation but also much of the social institution in general is of an imaginary nature. To say that the nation is essentially an imaginary construct does not amount to saying much. Yet, what is important in Watsuji's argument is the manner in which he ascribes to the figure of the emperor the function of erasing and concealing the imaginary nature of its totality. Contradictory though it may sound, its imaginary nature is best concealed when the totality is expressed solely in aesthetic terms. Because it is not defined in practical terms, because there are no procedural rules by which to evaluate the appropriateness of the expression of the general will, it is given as if it were always and already there. For this reason, it seems that Watsuji's account of the emperor presumes a functionalism.

Therefore, the national community had to be defined in terms not of the state, whose existence was regulated by a set of stipulations, but of the ethnic nation (minzoku; here minzoku unambiguously designates an ethnic nation), which supposedly had existed independent of the state: it was necessary to substantialize national culture, thereby guaranteeing the eternity and communality of it. Here, cultural essentialism, that is, discourse based on the substantialization of national culture, reveals its political effect. It is not without connection to the emperor system that the type of cultural essentialism generally referred to as nihonjin-ron or the discourse on Japanese uniqueness flourished after the Second World War both in Japan and other parts of the world, particularly in the United States. And Watsuji's argument about the emperor system is a specific instance in which cultural nationalism is mobilized for its legitimation.

As Watsuji admitted, his use of the term "nation" (kokumin) frequently changed,[54] but we must agree that he had been fairly consistent in his efforts to define the term in close connection with the substantialized culture. During the war, by appealing to the particularism of "community with character," he criticized the universalistic and expansionist logic of *Hakkô Ichiu* ("Eight Corners of the World under One Roof"), which was to assimilate other peoples into one unity.[55]

In *Ethics (II)*, originally published in 1942, Watsuji argued as follows:

Thereupon, he [Alexander] created a situation in which many nations [*minzoku*] were integrated into one state, directly out of the situation in which the single nation was divided into many states. The Roman Empire inherited this situation. Under such circumstances, it was a matter of course that the totality of the state did not coincide with that of the nation. Alexander created his empire by military force. Caesar did the same. The power of the state created in this way was severed from the sacred. Into this fissure crept the god of the Jewish nation [*minzoku*]. This god grew into a god that transcended nationality by pushing aside the gods of other nations living within the world empire of the time, and it eventually dominated the entire empire. Then, the sacred that was to express the totality of the Jewish nation absorbed the sacred for other nations with the empire, and caused the irredeemable separation between the totality of the state and its sanctity.

Against such a historical background emerged the problem of the difference between monarchic right and democratic right. When the state is severed from its sanctity, it rules not by "leadership" [*tôsotsu*] but by "dominion" [*shibai*]. For example, a conquered nation was simply "dominated" by the power of the state. In this kind of state, and if it is a monarchy, the sovereign is not an authority but merely "one man with power." As such a dominion is institutionalized, not only the conquered nations but also the conquering nation would be ruled by "dominion." Then the monarch would cease to express the totality of the state, and he would be a private person who monopolizes the power of the state.[56]

Watsuji attributes the source of violent domination to the severance of the state from the national (*minzoku*) community. The separation of the state and the nation gives rise to a split between the state and the cultural community that would result in "dominion" instead of "leadership." In order for the state to maintain itself not by "dominion" but by "leadership," the state must be continuous with the national community, whose communality is based on the enduring identity of culture.

Watsuji resorts to a certain racist scapegoating in the preceding quote. The insane atmosphere during the war might have lured him into writing those passages that held a single nation (*minzoku*) responsible for the drastic change in world history. I do not wish to draw a simple conclusion from this alone because the passages are obviously overdetermined and have to be read in various contexts (I will examine this problem in the next chapter). Nonetheless, I cannot dismiss the presence in his anthropology of what would allow him to slide easily into racism. This is, I think, manifest in that Watsuji does not hesitate to classify all sorts of humans according to racial stereotypes through an analysis of the climatic and historical being of Man. Furthermore, it is disclosed by his insensitivity to what I have called sociality, to that movement that decenters subjective positions fixed by *aidagara* or the relationality of subjective positions, on the one hand, and by his *nihonjin-ron*, which always posits the cultural community as a closure. For this reason, although his study of Japanese culture bears witness to vicissitudes that nation and culture undergo and does not hesitate to admit the hybrid nature of Japanese culture (his famous thesis of *nihon bunka no jūsōsei* or the multilayered nature of Japanese culture),[57] Watsuji's argument reveals many inconsistencies when it is read in the light of the question "Are the notions of the 'nation' [*kokumin*], the ethnos [*minzoku*], and culture (in the sense of a substantialized closure) historically constructed?" The notions of "Japanese culture," "Japanese language," and "the Japanese"—as an ethnos—in terms of which he defines the transhistorical identity of the national-ethnic community, seem to me to be rather recent historical constructs; to my knowledge, they were conceived of first two to three centuries ago, as archaic forms that had been lost, and as the nation-state was formed they came to be regarded as existing in the present.[58]

Accordingly, the sanctity of the state that "leads" but does not "dominate" the national community must be designated by the emperor, who supposedly expresses the totality of the nation. Moreover, since the emperor expresses the existence of the substantialized cultural community on which the national community is grounded, we would be led, as long as we adhere to Watsuji's logic, to the thesis that to accept the emperor as the expression of the national totality is to believe *dogmatically and arbitrarily* in its continual existence since antiquity. Thus, the continuity of the national community must be posited beyond all possible contestation based on empirical evidence, and would be perceived as some "spirit" devoid of any institutional stipulations.

First, the expression of national totality is supposed to have been given in the form of a festival in which politics and festivity were one (*saisei itchi*). Watsuji insists that the identity of politics and festivity can be attributed only to the emperor and that, as both archaeological and historical materials testify, this tradition preceded the formation of the state in the jurisprudential sense. Therefore, the totality of the nation has always been there or immanent in any cultural activity, just as the emperor has continued to exist since antiquity. Immanentism, which we witnessed in Watsuji's discussion of *aidagara*—the relationality of subjective positions—is reproduced intact here. Second, precisely because this unity of the people or People-as-One should be understood at the level at which the people form a sense of shared aesthetic experience, it is constituted neither as the commonness of legal or even social institutions nor as the participation in the same set of ethical imperatives. The totality of the nation is expressed in sympathy, in the sense that the nation finds itself in the communality of "communion." Therefore, the emperor expresses the very possibility that the people can feel sympathetic to one another and communicate with one another in "communion." Through the figure of the emperor, therefore, the nation feels together, and this sense of national communality or of national "communion" is given rise to in an aesthetic experience.

In his study of ethics, as we have seen, Watsuji outlines a theoretical framework within which the individual relates itself to the totality. Although Watsuji is most adamantly hostile to individualism on the grounds that individualism regards the individual as an atomic and autonomous entity completely deprived of its communality, in the final analysis he assimilates many of the theses from individualist philosophies. Because the individual is the negation of the totality and the totality the negation of the individual, the individual is absolute only insofar as the totality is absolute. Yet, his conception of the individual is not much different from that of atomistic individualism in which the individual is simply an *individuum*, an indivisible unity containing no fissure within it. In other words, his individual is more like an entity definable in terms of the subject (*shugo*) in the sense of the propositional subject: for Watsuji, the individual is the subject whose position is predetermined within the fixed and static totality of the functionalist kind. Hence, he had no other way to conceptualize the individual and totality but as totality being immanent in the individual and the individual immanent in totality. In his *Ethics*, according to which the individual is a fixity, the individual does not differ, delay, or flee but is confined to the subjective position predetermined by the totality through the being-between of the human being. Furthermore, because the totality is immanent in the individual, the ultimate ethical imperative can only be found in the discovery of the true and authentic original "self" in which the equally original totality is already immanent.

Assuming this predetermined harmony expressed by his concept of *aidagara*, one could easily understand why Watsuji defines the being-between of the human being as the transferential and mutual penetration of consciousnesses and as the symmetrical reciprocity of you and me. Of course, such a reciprocity cannot be attained in an ordinary situation, but the predetermined harmony of totality and the individual suggests the possibility of symmetrical reciprocity, pure sympathy, and eventually "communion" as the presence of national totality.

The emperor expresses nothing but the predetermined harmony of this symmetrical reciprocity, pure sympathy, and "communion" in aesthetic experience. This way of understanding sociality or ethics does not need to posit the emperor as commander for the totality, as an authoritative figure who orders. Here the emperor is an absolutely arbitrary— hence absolutely unreliable—guarantee of reciprocity, sympathy, and "communion." But precisely because his status is arbitrary (he expresses only the totality without any content), people can project their communalist desire onto his figure. It seems to me that, unless one resists this logic of communalist identification, one could easily be drawn into a sentiment such as the following: "Some might say that there has never been a nation in the true sense of the term or the true general opinion of the nation in our country. Whatever they may wish to say, they would not be able to deny the fact that it was the general will of the nation to declare war against America, and that it was the nation as a totality that fought America."[59] Watsuji no doubt surrendered himself to this violent manifestation of communalist desire. Yet, once again, Watsuji is not being accurate. If, by the nation as a totality, he means the people of postwar Japan, the nation that had fought during the Fifteen-Year Asian-Pacific War included many who were now outside that nation. The war was fought in the name of the emperor under the slogan "Eight Corners of the World under One Roof" and the figure of the emperor was appealed to in order to mobilize those in the annexed parts of the Japanese Empire too. Those who would not be included in the nation of postwar Japan were also sacrificed under the name of the emperor. Watsuji's (self-serving) forgetfulness, whose political astuteness can never be underestimated in the postwar context of the loss of the empire, amply demonstrates the very arbitrariness of the notion of national totality itself and of the relationship between the emperor, the expression of the people's unity, and the totality of the nation. As a matter of fact, this forgetfulness of Watsuji doubly erased the historical conditions under which Watsuji's cultural nationalism acquired a certain hegemony in the Japanese intellectual world, after the loss of the empire in 1945. First, committed to the task of assimilating the plurality of ethnic groups into one nation-state, the Japanese government could never adopt the stance of particularistic nationalism in which an ethnic unity is immediately equated to the unity of a nation prior to defeat. Japan was an imperialist nation, and—although I am theoretically suspicious that any sustainable distinction between the monoethnic and multiethnic social formations could ever be drawn—it was a multiethnic nation-state before August 1945, so that the Japanese state could never afford to justify its policies on grounds of so-called particularism. Retroactively, Watsuji's culturalist legitimation of the emperor system helped the Japanese elites as well as intellectuals disavow the past of Japanese imperialism and its multiethnic policies. Second, under the guise of culturalist nationalism, it erased the fact that Watsuji's particularism served not to reject or denounce but to accommodate Japan within the United States hegemony in postwar East Asia. Far from being a critique of American universalism, it was a supplement to it: his cultural nationalism was one of the best testimonies to a complicity between postwar Japanese particularism and United States universalism.

The relationship between the emperor and the totality of the national community is, in fact, doubly arbitrary. Perhaps what the emperor expresses best is this arbitrariness of the second power and the opportunistic irresponsibility inherent in it. Nonetheless, the emperor system is not an exception. As Ernesto Laclau asserted, there is always arbitrariness between the totality as a social imaginary and social and political structures. The emperor system is another example that attests to this arbitrariness.

It is worth noting that Watsuji paid no attention to Article 9 of the new Constitution, which prohibits Japan from appealing to military means to solve international conflicts, although he enthusiastically endorsed the status of the emperor in the new Constitution given by the United States. He is not interested in the theoretical implications of Article 9, which strongly suggest the possibilities of the state outside the logic of communal death and of channeling the subject's freedom away from cohistoricizing through the resoluteness toward death. And, he continued to seek the only evidence that guarantees the immanence of totality in the individual in the nostalgic aestheticization of the totality.

Today, it may appear that the assimilative power of the prewar emperor system has dissipated. Possibly the discourse of Japanese uniqueness (*nihonjin-ron*), of which Watsuji can be counted as one of the founding fathers— not unique at all in its insistence on national uniqueness among modern nationalistic discourses—has concealed the possibility of talking about the emperor system as a modern state assimilationism and thereby protected this institution from critical scrutiny. But if one regards the emperor system not as a *unique* institution particular to the last twenty-six centuries of Japanese history, but as one form of modern assimilationisms, one cannot so easily feel confident that it has completely severed itself from the violent manifestations of communalist identification in patriotic fury.

Has modern patriotism ever been free from this logic of communion?

4

Subject and/or *Shutai* and the

Inscription of Cultural Difference[1]

If Bentham's theory of life can do little for the individual, what can it do for society? It will enable a society which has attained a certain state of spiritual development, and the maintenance which in that state is otherwise provided for, to prescribe the rules by which it may protect its material interests. It will do nothing (except sometimes as an instrument in the hands of a higher doctrine) for the spiritual interests of society; nor does it suffice of itself even for the material interests. That which alone causes any material interests to exist, which alone enables any body of human beings to exist as a society, is national character: *that* it is, which causes one nation to succeed in what it attempts, another to fail; one nation to understand and aspire to elevated things, another to grovel in mean ones; which makes the greatness of one nation lasting, and dooms another to early and rapid decay. . . . A philosophy of laws and institutions, not founded on a philosophy of national character, is an absurdity.   John Stuart Mill

From the outset, I must insist that the problem of theory and Asian Studies is primarily a political one. It is political in the sense that this problem must be posed in such a way that it can explicitly indicate, rather than conceal or neutralize, the antagonistic nature of the social conditions due to which it is able to be enunciated. That the enunciation of the problem is always foregrounded by antagonism is indeed a truism that need not be repeated here. However, I must venture to mention it since, I think, the apolitical accommodation of "theoretical approaches" has never been as popular as nowadays. Confronting the blatant and undeniable reality of ethnocentrism and Eurocentrism in the social and epistemic formations that for the past few decades have been rendered explicit as a result of "theoretical efforts," and in which we have nonetheless had to continue to live, we are apt, perhaps more than ever, to be lured into the hegemonic logic of unmediated reconciliation and synthesis that serves to neutralize and render invisible the antagonisms and innumerable instances of injustice that we have been witnessing around us. Under such circumstances, what is referred to as theory can be utilized as an authority in whose name to repress those questions and the sense of anxiety that can remind us of historical aporias we are locked into, and, also, theory can help insulate academic discussion about Asia away from the nagging issues concerning the very relationship of the student of Asian Studies to the object of his or her study.

Theory is often turned into something that does not trouble us or make us feel ill at ease. Instead of disclosing the sites of anxiety in our supposedly epistemic relationship to Asia, theory would then serve to neutralize or silence the questions that might incite us to further inquiry about the enunciative positionality of experts in Asian Studies.

In order not to lose sight of the politicalness of theory, therefore, it is necessary to keep asking questions about the constitution of Asian Studies as an assembly of particular academic fields, and about one's involvement in them: it is necessary to continue to call into question what Pierre Bourdieu calls "the place designated in advance as that of the objective and objectifying observer who, like a stage manager playing at will with the possibilities offered by the objectifying instruments in order to bring the object closer or move it further away, to enlarge or reduce it, imposes on the object his own norms of construction, as if in a dream of power."[2] To problematize the enunciative positionality of the observer is to remind ourselves that the object does not exist out there of and by itself, and that, even if it is merely to be described, of necessity it demands a certain participation on the part of the observer. The object of such an epistemic relationship, or what Tokieda Motoki referred to as "the observational stance" (kansatsu-teki tachiba), can take place only on the basis of "the subjective and participational stance" (shutai-teki tachiba).[3] The observation of the object is always accompanied by the observer's "practice," and unless the student has a practical relation to his object, he or she cannot have an epistemic relationship to it either.

My proposal, therefore, is that the sense of theory should be steered toward evocation by questioning rather than settlement by solution, to what Homi K. Bhabha calls the repetition of iterative stoppage rather than the fixity of identity in synchronicity.[4] Underlying this proposal is the fact that theory always operates in a twofold manner: it takes advantage of the essential ambiguity inherent in any description of cultural differences, and it announces itself in a forked tongue as though it were inhabited by something like Sartrean "bad faith."

In this intersection of epistemology and practice, what Bourdieu argues in reference to the "logic [sense] of practice" seems to intercept with the by now classic conceptions of subjectivity in modern Japanese philosophic and linguistic discussions of the interwar period, and to disclose the political blindness inherent in them.

Similar to Bourdieu's distinction between the worked work (*opus operatum*) and the working mode (*modus operandi*), I would like to introduce a tentative differential between the two determinations of subjectivity, the epistemic subject (*shukan*) and *shutai* (the practical subject or agent of practice), in the context of the analysis of culture and cultural differences, although whether *shutai* can be subsumed under the generality of subjectivity is highly problematic and far from having been settled.

Shutai was introduced into Japanese intellectual vocabulary as a neologism, as one of the translations for "subject," *sujet*, or *Subjekt*, other translations being *shugo* (propositional subject), *shukan* (epistemic subject), *shudai* (thematic subject), *shinmin* (the subject of the emperor), among others. I would like to stress that the translation into English of *shutai* in particular frequently does not coincide with "subject." The cycle of translation from English into Japanese and, again, back into English—subject→ *shukan* or *shutai*→ subject—generates an inevitable surplus that cannot be explained away by the difference between the two conceptions of "subjectivity" in English and Japanese. In other words, being other than a *Japanese* conception of subjectivity, *shutai* is that which cannot be contained in the economy of equivalence in a transnational translational exchange. In this respect, *shutai* is not subject to the unity of either Japanese or English: it is a hybrid from the outset. It is because of this hybridity that *shutai* must be denied or disavowed in order for the subject to constitute itself. *Shutai* itself is of hybridity that is inevitable in the *process* in which the subject is constituted, but it is erased and disavowed in the subject thus constituted. In this respect, the hybridity of *shutai* is its unrepresentability. Partly because of this, I have been trying to render *shutai* as "the body of enunciation," a translation in which the word "subject" is avoided, in order to draw attention to a certain metaphysics concerning the concept of subject. Although these two determinations of subjectivity—the epistemic subject and *shutai*—can by no means be taken to be two definitive conceptualities, the differential distinction of the practical agent from the epistemic subject, as a difference inherent in the subject, as a difference whose economy could potentially be delineated in many different senses or directions—toward empirico-transcendental and ontico-ontological differences, for example—will, I think, serve to explicate the politicalness of *theory* in the performativity of Asian Studies.

In addition, the difference between the epistemic subject and *shutai* is far from being singularly determined even within prewar Japanese philosophical discussion. On the contrary, already during the 1920s and 1930s, the issue of how to distinguish these two senses of subjectivity was a political problem concerning practice and knowledge.[5] Taking into account the instability of this distinction, I will explore the possible connections between the problem of subjectivity, as it is raised in prewar Japanese philosophical discourse, and our problem of theory and Asian Studies, and try to think through the problem in the reading of the Japanese philosophical discussion on subjectivity.

This differential *of and in* the subject enables me to address the duality of temporality in the articulation of cultural difference, a duality according to which it can be demonstrated that the description of cultural difference is always the acknowledgment and endorsement of a particular enunciative positionality in the student's relationship to the object of study. To describe cultural difference is to establish a specific enunciative position from which the student is to observe it. But we cannot emphasize too much that one cannot encounter cultural difference without encountering other people; one never experiences it in a social vacuum; to encounter other people is to be engaged in some social relation with them. Thus, the description of cultural difference is always correlative with an act of inscribing and instituting specific social relations that necessarily involve the student himself or herself. And it is through the duality of temporality that the description of it is a poietic act of cultural manufacture. To that extent, it is legitimate to claim that the description of cultural difference produces and institutes cultural difference.

It is in practice, which is essentially social, that cultural difference is encountered, so that the description of it is always a delayed and posterior reaction to it, because, in order to be grasped as an object of description, it must be apprehended and transformed into a *phenomenon*. To describe the characteristics of some aspects of the social world that the student observes is invariably a process (of signification), or what Jean-François Lyotard called "performativity," in which the student's position (as a subject of enunciation that is essentially imaginary) is represented or thetically posited in relation to the object thus constituted in that observational and scientific description. As Jonathan Crary argued with regard to the historical changes of the regimes of vision, an epistemic subject or *shukan* who observes cultural difference is also an *observer* who observes the rules of the regime, and therefore is a subject who is subjected to the rules.[6] But the positing of the observing subject (or the fixation of that subject in the context of the present argument) and the constitution of the object do not take place on the same plane, so to speak.

In this respect, it is important to note that the distinction I tentatively draw between cultural difference as it is encountered and thereby given to "us" in its immediacy (or more precisely in its originary repetition) and cultural difference as it is described does not correspond to the distinction between primordial perception and its secondary representation in the description of it because such a difference, insofar as incommensurability pertains to it, is not given as *percept* in its primordial givenness, a percept in the phenomenological sense: one cannot *perceive* cultural difference unless as an already determinate object of description. It is encountered rather as "feeling" or *jô* according to a certain Confucian terminology, "that which moves," something like the Lacanian *réel*. which cannot be arrested in the *li*, in the synchronicity of signification.[7] In other words, one comes across cultural difference as an unobjectifiable "feeling" of anxiety or of the uncanny that cannot be contained within the economy of spatialized time governed by the pleasure principle. For this reason, it must be *articulated* in enunciation and be repressed so as to be perceived as *determined* cultural difference, as an identifiable difference between entities. Being endowed with the status not of the original but of the originary, cultural difference is necessarily given as a repetition in the general text, and therefore cannot evade the politics of and in articulation.

In this process of signification in which cultural difference is transformed into a phenomenon concerning the object of study, what happens is the arrest of the practical and nonsynchronic encounter of cultural difference and the *letting it stand* in front of one who gazes at it, contemplates it, and recognizes it, namely, in front of the epistemic subject (*shukan*). Simultaneously, it is the insertion of a certain distance and detachment from the phenomenalized datum thanks to which the epistemic subject is able to fashion itself as the self-effacing guarantor of universal objectivity. The epistemic subject is detached from practical relations and becomes an abstract subject who is a formal condition necessary for the observation of a phenomenon. Here, the problem necessarily arises as to whether *shutai*, or the agent of practice, can be registered within the purview of subjectivity since, of course, the practical subject or *shutai* cannot be equated with the epistemic subject, that is, an ontological requirement for the possibility of phenomenality. Moreover, the description or recognition of cultural difference itself occurs as a practice, as an enunciation that is not let stand in front of one who gazes at it or phenomenalizes it. Hence, the process of signification should not be confused with that of externalization and alienation, which can be retraced or returned to the primordial perception. No cultural difference is given in and of itself. Without the process of signification, cultural differences themselves would never be there as ontologized differences between beings. The enunciation of cultural difference always mobilizes various fragments from the existent discourse that are heterogeneous to one another, and connects them in new and accidental ways; even if it is represented in the name of an acknowledgment of difference and separation, it is necessarily an inauguration of the being-in-common, of a *communism* in the sense specified by Jean-Luc Nancy.[8] This is to say that practice in which we encounter cultural difference and enunciate it can also be what Ernesto Laclau and Chantal Mouffe called "articulation."[9]

As against "mediation" in which the organization and the fragments to be organized are necessary moments of a totality that transcends them, Laclau and Mouffe specify the type of "organization" in which fragments are unified in such a way that the organization "is contingent and, therefore, external to fragments themselves."[10] It is "an *articulatory practice* which constitutes and organizes social relations."[11] Fragments on which an articulatory practice works cannot be reduced to moments of a closed and fully constituted totality. "The incomplete character of every totality necessarily leads us to abandon, as a terrain of analysis, the premise of *society* as a sutured and self-defined totality."[12] Accordingly, it is impossible either to extract necessary laws according to which a social relation is fully fixed or to determine whether a social relation is entirely internal or external to a given social or cultural totality. By the same token, it is impossible to conceive of cultural difference as that between one fully constituted cultural unity or society and another. The experience of cultural difference, therefore, is possible exactly because of "the incomplete character of every totality." This is to say that it can be brought into awareness only in the midst of articulatory practice that makes it impossible to conceive of it as a difference between the inside and the outside.

But, it is also important to stress, "in criticizing the conception of society as an ensemble united by necessary laws, we cannot simply bring out the non-necessary character of the *relations* among elements, for we would then retain the necessary character of the *identity* of the elements themselves."[13] Hence, an articulatory practice takes place in "*this field of identities which never manage to be fully fixed*," in "*the field of overdetermination*."[14] And "since the affirmation of the discursive character of every subject position was linked to the rejection of the notion of subjects as an originative and founding totality, the analytic moment that had to prevail was that of dispersion, detotalization or decentering of certain positions with regard to others."[15] Therefore, as to the subjective position for the agent of an articulatory practice who can never be understood as a subject transparently present to itself, articulation has to be a decentering and caesural practice.

Nevertheless, more often than not, in Asian Studies the agent of the description of cultural difference fashions himself or herself as a predetermined identity, a Westerner as against the Asians, for instance, who is supposed to occupy a subjective position exclusively exterior to and separate from the sphere where his or her observation is conducted. In this case, the identity of the Westerner is evoked precisely as the holder of "Imperial Eyes" at what Mary Louise Pratt calls the "contact zone,"[16] a place where the student encounters and observes cultural differences. Obviously, this separatist self-fashioning is often matched by a corresponding fashioning by the Asians about their essentialized Asian identities.

In this way, too, we confront the duality of temporality in the articulation of cultural difference. This contradiction between two temporalities is precisely what is noted by Homi K. Bhabha when he talks about "temporality," which gives the articulation of cultural difference "symbolic access to the social movement of the political imaginary."[17] And what Bhabha calls "time lag" after Frantz Fanon—an iterative, interrogative space produced in the interruptive overlap between symbol and sign, between synchronicity and caesura or seizure (not diachronicity)"[18]—allows me to continue to call attention to the two temporalities. But I would rather call it "an iterative, interrogative *duration*" rather than "an iterative, interrogative *space*." As "an internal multiplicity of succession, of fusion, of organization, of heterogeneity, of qualitative discrimination, or of difference in kind,"[19] Bergsonian duration or *durée* can better express the experience of radical incommensurability between the stability of cultural identity as it is fixed in the representation of cultural difference and the temporality of enunciation in which cultural difference is articulated. The stability of cultural identity is incommensurate with the temporality of enunciation, just as space is incommensurate with the pure duration that is incompatible with juxtaposition, comparison, mutual externality, or any idea of extensity.[20] This is to say that, although it is feasible at all times to differentiate between the epistemic subject (*shukan*) and the practical agent (*shutai*), of necessity they emerge as overlapping one another while never coinciding with one another. Whereas the epistemic subject emerges in the spatiality of synchronicity, *shutai* always flees such spatiality and can never be present to itself either.[21] *Shutai* is always marked by ecstatic temporality. In other words, *shutai* can never be talked about as the self in its specularity. Therefore, I would like to suggest that, although they have often been called by the same name "subject," they belong to two heterogeneous registers, and that the epistemic subject (*shukan*) is instituted in space, while *shutai* is rather in time as duration.[22]

In this regard, Bhabha's intervention is essential because he unequivocally proposes the possibilities of transforming the identities inscribed in the "space" of cultural representation as possibilities inherent in the performativity of enunciation in the articulation of cultural difference. Unless the issues of the formation and possible transformation of subjectivity are mentioned as an integral part of the understanding of cultural difference, we will not be able to bring forth the sort of theory, of political intervention, that works to effectuate the dislocation of fixed identities and to promote a different articulation of cultural difference. When these identities are perceived to be eternal and transhistorical, while the assumed hierarchy among the identities such as the one between the colonial master and the native servant *is imagined* to have undergone a mutation and become inverted as a consequence of general economic and political development, even the most conscientious and self-critical of those former "masters" might find it very hard to resist the temptation of resorting or "returning" to naked ethnocentrism. The current cultural climate of "the return to the West" is no doubt a testimony to it; for, their identity as "the Westerners," "European," or "white" being essentialized, they would in due course feel cornered and begin to demand the recognition of their ethnic authenticity with every appeal to their "neglected" tradition and the "love of Western civilization." This reactive reaction to the imagined change in their position in the changing world is neither accidental nor pathological. In a sense, it is an inevitable corollary of the essentialism of ethnic, racial, national, and cultural identity. Therefore, what is at stake in theoretical decipherment of the epistemic subject and the practical agent in the articulation of cultural difference is how we are to search for the critical intervention that goes beyond the retaliatory disclosure of ethnocentric regimens in the production of knowledge, although such a retaliatory debunking might be necessary at one stage or another; in short, what is at stake here is how we envision the articulation of different social relations that is enunciated together with the different articulation of cultural difference.

In the articulation of cultural difference neither a purely epistemic nor a purely practical relationship to the object is possible; or, one can be neither an outsider positioned completely outside the social world and whose commitment in that world is exhaustively epistemic, nor an insider who simply and blindly lives one's practical relations with it. It follows that, because of the "time lag" and the duality of temporality, the opposition of inside and outside cannot be sustained, or can be reproduced only by means of a series of repressive disavowals. Thus, my inquiry into the continual tension between synchronicity and caesura, and the unstable differential between *shukan* and *shutai*, will disclose the sites of political intervention as well as what I will call "the enunciative displacement," which inscribes and reinscribes various identities in the space of cultural representation.

What bearings, then, can my discussion of the duality of temporality possibly have on theory and Asian Studies?

The untenability of the inside/outside opposition should mean that, regardless of whatever the national, ethnic, class, and gender background of the students of Asian Studies, they are already implicated in the practical relations that involve them in the social worlds of Asia by exposing them to those singular beings there. In this respect, the students of Asian Studies are Asians insofar as they observe, try to comprehend, and enunciate various determinations concerning Asian texts, texts in the broadest sense. Even American students of Asian Studies cannot fashion themselves as pure outsiders to the social worlds of Asia. But, at the same time, it is important to stress that so-called Asians themselves can never regard themselves as purely practical subjects, as genuine natives who inhabit their own social worlds immediately and originally; for the articulation of cultural difference takes place at the very sites where the synchronic opposition of the native and the nonnative, the Asians and the non-Asians, or the non-Westerners and the Westerners, is radically problematized. Only through practical negotiation—indeed, of a political nature—about the continual tension between the epistemic subject and the practical agent can the articulation of cultural difference be enunciated; only by wagering putative identities fixed in the synchronicity of the sign can those identities be reinstituted, if this is possible at all.

Of course, the students' exposure to the social world they study does not suggest that they are accepted or assimilated into that society that the inhabitants of the object social world identify themselves with. The practical relation does not at all exclude the possibility of conflict. On the contrary, practice is essentially antagonistic. For this reason, in order to construct their national communal identity, many people in Asian countries have had to exclude so-called Westerners and colonials by granting them outsider status, as well as by cynically accepting the exclusively Western identity of those Westerners and colonials. (Should we call this Occidentalism?) By inverting the Eurocentric taxonomy imposed on them, they could construct the mythic subject of their own nation. Similarly, the students of Asian Studies are obsessed, more often than not, with asserting the irreparably non-Western characteristics of Asian social and cultural formations, or even physiological constitutions, in order to convince themselves of their own Western identity, whose attributes have been called into question in their practical relations to those social worlds. Have we not too frequently witnessed a strange complicity between Asian cultural essentialisms that willingly internalize the stereotypes imposed on them by racism and what Robert Young refers to as the narcissism of the West?[23]

What pronounces itself in these transferential and countertransferential exchanges between Asian cultural essentialisms and the narcissism of the West is the urge for a displacement of anxiety caused by the liminality of the agent who enunciates the articulation of cultural difference. In order to articulate the very cultural difference they participate in, the students of Asian Studies, like immigrants from Asian societies in Western Europe and North America, are obliged to occupy the liminal positions of "in-between" and, as a result, they find themselves in the midst of an antagonism inherent in their practical relations to the object of their study. Imagine a situation in which an anthropologist from an old or currently colonizing country is working on a region in which the absolute majority of the population recognizes the devastating effects of its colonialist violence as unmistakable and undeniable in everyday actuality. In such a case, the anthropologist would find the impulse to introduce the purely epistemic relation to the object society, culture, or people and to substitute "the observer's relation to practice for the practical relation to practice"[24] almost irresistible. As Kang Sangjung demonstrated, the most typical "Orientalist" perspective, which imitates the narcissistic exclusion of the non-West by the West, has been reproduced in Japanese state-sponsored high school history textbooks in order to disavow the historically inevitable anxiety resulting from Japan's past engagements in Asian countries.[25] It may well take the form of an urge to displace the anxiety brought forth in a specific practical relationship with the general binary opposition between the two pairing identities, the West and Asia, or Japan and Korea, thereby continually reproducing and reifying these identities. It is *not* that in this liminal topos of "in-between" the students of Asian Studies come across the crisis of their identity; rather, it is that they are forced to face their *identity as crisis* in this critical "contact zone" of liminality. It is because they are in crisis that they obsessively identify themselves with their "own" West or Japan. The identity thus installed through the disavowal of anxiety cannot but be an identity based on "homosociality," an identity that, in the final analysis, can be installed only in negative, exclusionistic terms.[26] And, the mutual transference between Asian cultural essentialisms, which were called for by the historical necessity to build modern nations against the onslaught of colonialisms and imperialisms at one stage or another, and "the narcissism of the West," is, in fact, underwritten by the mutual need for complicity between these two "homosocial" demands.

By now it should be only too obvious that there are traps in questions like "Can and should theory recognize its own limits in advance and take precautions so as to confine itself to a particular geopolitical, local, and historical moment outside which it ceases to be relevant?"[27] What appears to be a gesture of modesty in this question serves to eradicate rather than underline the antagonistic nature of the *practice* of Asian Studies. To fail to notice this danger would amount to losing sight of the historicity, local specificity, and politicalness of practice in Asian Studies. The assessment both of the limits of the validity and of the conditions, epistemic as well as historic, of the possibility of a theory cannot be obtained without theoretical mediation. I agree that a theory, or a regimen of certain theoretical discursive strategies, must be delimited and should not be upheld as an uncritical "universalism" that assumes itself to be ubiquitously applicable; but neither am I oblivious to the complicity between "particularism" and the very universalism it proposes to reject.

Therefore, the first question that must be asked about theory and Asian Studies questions the relationship between theory and a group of objects that are given rise to by the primarily geopolitical designation "Asian Studies" itself. Because of the historically negative and oppositional determinations within which Asia has been defined as an exemplary non-West, as an other of Europe or the West, the question concerning theory and Asian Studies inevitably invites a chain of queries about the exclusionist and separatist nature of this dichotomy the West/Asia, and the enunciative positionality in which the act of this questioning is invariably implicated. All too often is it presumed that theory is always an appropriation of, if not necessarily an imposition on, Asia by the West, as if by law it would follow the trajectory of "the strategy of containment" of which Homi K. Bhabha speaks.[28] Such a view of theory serves not only to affirm the rather familiar quasireligious opposition of universalism and particularism, whose political uses are analyzed by Catherine Hall, for instance, in the case of nineteenth-century Jamaica,[29] but also to prohibit different employments of theory that would gradually dismantle the very opposition of the West and the non-West, together with its political implications. The rejection of theory would be my recommendation if such a view of theory were the sole choice. Notwithstanding the Orientalist division of labor whereby theory is registered or ordained as the exclusive property of Western man, both the universalism and the particularism of theory are within the register of the synchronicity of the sign. Unless *shutai* or the agent of practice is completely absorbed into *shukan* or the epistemic subject, neither the universalism nor the particularism of *theoretical practice* can be a significant issue.

As a prolegomenous step toward asking questions about the plurivalent connectedness of theory and Asian Studies, I want to circumvent the prevalent confusionism about the definition of theory. The theory that I am to discuss does not designate a set of propositions predicated in the element of universality in the sense of universal generality (distinct from *infinite universality*), as opposed to the object to which theory is applied and which is predicated in the element of particularity.

What is at stake in theoretical practice is the interaction of various forces in the constitution of the spatiality of synchronicity prior to which neither universalism nor particularism is comprehensible. Of necessity, theoretical practice is concerned with the task of discerning those forces. But it should be emphasized that one can never be able to bring into awareness all the forces operative in the constitution of the spatiality of synchronicity; the claim for the exhaustive view, a view in which all the forces are discerned and identified, would inevitably require the postulation of an impartial and omniscient ego, who is imagined to reside outside the site in which cultural difference is encountered. This is why *shutai* is said to be in history because of its essential openness or incompleteness, whereas the evasion of practical relation makes *shukan* essentially ahistorical. Therefore, theoretical practice must interrupt the representation of cultural difference and thereby attempts to disclose the politics at work there by asserting what Deleuze calls an essential forgetting of the very *shutai* of such theoretical practice, as well as the equally essential partiality of the epistemic subject in front of whom cultural difference is supposedly displayed.[30] What theory as I understand it takes upon itself is more an intervention rather than the mastery of its application to putative objects.

And since "Asian Studies" is understood to consist of geopolitical designations of smaller units such as "Chinese Studies," "Japanese Studies," and so on, my second question, as a corollary of the first, is about the constitution of the field according to the unity of the nation-state, which is more often than not imaginarily projected as a homogeneous interior.

Fûdo (*Climate and Culture*) by Watsuji Tetsurô has been upheld as one of the key works in the field of Japanese cultural history. Since its initial serial publication in the academic journal *Shisô* between 1928 and 1934, it has enjoyed an astonishingly wide popularity among Japanese readers. In many respects, *Climate and Culture* has been read and interpreted as a canonical work that has played a decisive role in the development of Japanese cultural history both as an academic discipline and as a genre of popular writing often referred to as *nihonjin-ron*, or the discourse on Japanese uniqueness.

In *Climate and Culture*, Watsuji attempted to establish cultural typology by means of two basic categories: climate and the national character. Yet, despite its global scope, this hermeneutic and existential study of the human being as the resident of a particular climate is written from the perspective of a traveler who had observed cultural differences during brief sojourns in China, Southeast Asia, India, the Middle East, and Europe and on returning from Germany to Japan. In this book, one would most likely discover the author's surprise in the face of foreign cultures, his curious gaze, his anger, and his perception of contemporary international politics. Yet, at the same time, the reader can hardly ignore the fact that the author also wished to construct a national narrative in which the identity of the Japanese nation could be constituted by means of the observation of cultural differences between Japan and other regions in the world. Consequently, one could conclude after reading the book that all other climates, cultures, and peoples are viewed as moments cumulatively synthesized toward a final objective: the cultural identity of the Japanese nation. In an interesting way, *Climate and Culture* seems to be guided by a narcissism not entirely different from that of the West. As a matter of fact, Watsuji does not hesitate to adopt European scholarship in dealing with culture, climate, and their analysis insofar as it helps construct the native into "a narcissistic, self-consolidating other" for the Japanese readership.[31] His reliance on Europe goes beyond the realm of scholarship. He seems to adopt European politics toward the non-West, too. For instance, he analyzes the Indian's resigned relationship with nature from the perspective of a colonial administrator: "The fullness of feeling of the Indian comes from out of this attitude of resignation. The attitude of resignation is at the same time one of submission."[32] After demonstrating that the fullness of feeling of the Indian is a general and transhistorical characteristic of the Indian culture, he asserts:

> And even in the case of night festivals, behind the gay bustle of the crowds or of the processions of myriad lanterns, there hovers plaintiveness which cannot be disguised. This fullness of feeling, instead of promoting our admiration, as in the case of the India of the past, for example, simply pains our heart in respect of the lack of will and the submission to oppression that we see here. Although we may well see no actual evidence of oppression, we feel that the Indian himself is in a way a symbol of suffering from oppression. . . . Because of his receptivity and resignation, or, to put it in another way, because of his lack of an aggressive and masterful nature, the Indian, in fact, prompts in us and draws out from us all our own aggressive and masterful characterization. . . . although his cotton may well glut the world's markets, the Indian is as receptive and resigned as ever,—witness his policy of non-resistance and passive obedience.[33]

Today, some might not find it easy to be convinced that those passages were written by a Japanese visitor to India in 1928, since the viewpoint he adopted seems so typically that of the British colonial authority and of nineteenth-century European Orientalists. There is little doubt that Watsuji acquired much of his knowledge about those Asian regions from European ethnographic and geographical scholarship. He appears content with an exclusively colonizer view of India. (Watsuji, in fact, did not hide his indebtedness to European Orientalist scholarship in writing *Climate and Culture*. However, it seems important that the chapter on European scholarship on climatology is excluded in the English translation. I will return to this point.)

Nevertheless, as if noting Japanese Pan-Asianists' works on colonized Asia, which called for the liberation of Asian peoples from European imperialist ambition, Watsuji was not entirely oblivious to the fact that there were some non-Indians who would not put up with the colonial injustice to which the people of India were being subjected: "the visitor to India is made to wish impulsively that the Indian would take up his struggle for independence."[34] Thus, Watsuji at least acknowledges that his practical relation to the object of his observation could generate anxiety in him and that, in his practical relationship to the object, he had to occupy a specific position that would demand some political decision. It is undeniable that this anxiety was closely related to the contemporary political situation of colonized India. However, the sense of historical specificity is lost a few sentences later when Watsuji says, "The physical strength of the Indian laborer is said to be far less than even that of the Chinese, and no more than a quarter or a third of that of his Western counterpart; but neither this, nor his distinctive nature, can be transformed overnight." Citing Indian classics since Veda and Buddhist rhetoric of the pre-Christian era as evidence of the immutable Indian national character, Watsuji's analysis of Indian climate and culture serves to dehistoricize his practical relation to the object of his observation. In addition, by ascribing the Indian's submission under colonial rule to the Indian's national character, he projects all the anxiety he must have felt in his practical relation to the object, into the object itself. On behalf of the British colonial administration, he even argues that it was not British colonialism but the transhistorical essence of India's national character itself that placed the Indian under oppression. Watsuji here tries to produce the most typical objectivism in which the social conditions of observation are all ascribed to the object.

Partly because of his dislocated and ambiguous status (nonwhite and a visitor in India), Watsuji had to confront a certain undecidability in his practical relationship to the Indians living under British rule, an undecidability to whose elimination, as we will see, his entire scholarship on ethics would soon be devoted; he was put in the site of what Laclau calls the "dislocation" of structure, which endowed him with a certain freedom. However, precisely at the moment when he gained an access to "temporality" that disrupts the spatiality of synchronicity, that is, when it was possible for him to identify with the Indians, Watsuji in fact *decided* to identify himself with the West.[35]

Watsuji's subsequent encounter with Europe was rather traumatic. Initially, in 1927, Watsuji Tetsurô was sent to Europe by the Ministry of Education to study in Germany for three years. But, after one year in Germany, he decided to return home as the result of a "nervous breakdown."[36] As one of the possible causes, one might speculate that, perhaps, for the first time in his life, he came across the reality of racial discrimination from the side of those who were discriminated against.

Watsuji's relation to the West, or to the British, had always been problematic. His essays "Amerika no kokuminsei" (American national character)[37] and "Nihon no shintô" (The way of Japanese loyalty) reiterate his strong condemnation of Anglo-American imperialism. Even in *Climate and Culture*, one finds his explicit denunciation of Eurocentrism: "We can never accept World History like Hegel's, in which the Europeans are upheld as *the chosen people*."[38] (In the late 1930s, Watsuji changed his philosophical position with regard to Hegelian World History, and started to modify his *Ethics* to accommodate the idea of the mission of the Japanese nation-state in World History, as was in chapter 3.)

"Amerika no kokuminsei" begins with a remark to the effect that the modern world was formed as a result of European military superiority over the non-European world. Watsuji notes that, in the history of the American continent, European military superiority defeated kingdoms in Mexico and Peru and annihilated the majority of the local population.[39] In the Spanish conquest of the American continent, "any means would have been accepted as not being cruel if it had been for the purpose of destroying the deeds of devils and spreading the gospels. This was the principle behind their massacre of the aboriginal."[40]

The Anglo-Saxon colonization that followed the Spanish conquest of America was conducted with a different Christian attitude. Protestant settlers upheld the idea of faith as a matter of personal choice, and did not dare to kill for the sake of Christianity. But, in order to colonize newly acquired land, they had to annihilate the aboriginal's resistance. In this respect, they had no choice but to massacre the aboriginal. However, the Anglo-Saxons needed a different principle in the name of which the massacre of the aboriginal could be accomplished. According to Watsuji, it was the idea of natural right that justified the settlers' killing of those American Indians who violated peace treaties and agreements they had signed but which were written exclusively in the settlers' terms. They could continue to kill the aboriginal because,

> the distinction between justice and injustice not existing in the state of nature that prevailed prior to the establishment of a contractual relationship, it was always the aboriginal who *violated justice*. Therefore, they could expel and slaughter the aboriginal *in the name of justice* and colonize farther into the new continent. Compared with the Spanish, who slaughtered the aboriginals in the name of Christianity but who began to mingle with them as they were converted, the Anglo-Saxons were much more *cruel, merciless,* and *vicious*. However, they were determined enough to be proud of this attitude. It is said that only the Anglo-Saxons could build a large and powerful state in the American continent because of their determination, a determination of the Hobbesian character.[41]

If one were to accept the date of its first publication (1937) given by the editors of Watsuji's *Zenshû* (Complete works) volume 17 (which seems to be a mistake, according to more recent accounts), one would find it hard not to detect some allegorical strategy at work in this argument since the publication date was set prior to the outbreak of warfare against the United States and Britain. Unwittingly, perhaps, this article could have disclosed the generality of the structure of the power relationship that exists in a colonialist situation, and the blindness typical of those colonizers who legitimate their "universal" justice in a tautological manner. Given the contemporary situation in East Asia and the history of Japanese imperialist diplomacy, particularly in China, therefore, the word "Anglo-Saxons" could easily be a substitute for the word "Japanese." Yet, we cannot say that this article *discloses* the generality of the structure of the colonial power relationship. That is because it failed to be *enunciated*. It would be plausible that this article was conceived of with a view to its "boomerang" effects. Yet the possible mimetic relationship between the Anglo-Saxons and the Japanese is never noted. The colonial power relationship is ascribed exclusively to the "national character" of the Anglo-Saxons. For reasons I will come back to, the recognition of the similarity between the Anglo-Saxons and the Japanese is repressed throughout this article. Watsuji deliberately tried to dodge the boomerang effects of the critique he initially aimed at the Anglo-Saxon.

This sort of conscious forgetfulness often serves to construct the sense of national fraternity. By excluding those who might break an unwritten vow and mention the very existence of such a repression, people would even be able to establish a channel of identification with all those who potentially share the same need for the disavowal of such anxiety. Thus, with respect to the formation of a national narrative, Homi K. Bhabha says, "It is through this syntax of forgetting—or being obliged to forget—that the problematic identification of a national people becomes visible."[42] But one must not overlook the other political effects that might help empower the groups in adversity. "Being obliged to forget becomes the basis for remembering the nation, peopling it anew, imagining the possibility of other contending and liberating forms of cultural identification." Yet, I find it very hard to imagine that Watsuji's tactic of wittingly forgetting would ever lead to the liberating forms of cultural identification.

In "Gendai nihon to chônin konjô" (Present-day Japan and the merchant mentality), Watsuji cast a critical glimpse at the relationship between Japan and Asian countries since the Russo-Japanese war of 1904–5 and imperialism. "In the Russo-Japanese war Japan deflected the spearhead of imperialism that was to turn every corner of the East into a colony. But, with the victory in this war, Japan's impulsive rejection [of imperialism] that meant 'the liberation of the East' was over. Japan herself joined the imperialist race."[43] The development of Japanese capitalism may appear to serve to liberate [the peoples of the East] from colonial domination by Europe and America, but it is not aimed at "the liberation of the East" in the true sense. The Japanese have never recognized their own achievement "as the liberation of the East from imperialism. See how indifferent the Japanese were to the Racial Equality Provisions proposed at the peace conference [at Versailles] after the world war."[44]

Even the writing of this kind of fairly short article was an example of articulatory practice in which an acknowledgment of a mimetic relationship, on the one hand, and of antagonism, on the other, could have been worked out. The acknowledgment of the mimetic relationship with the Anglo-Saxons, whose relation with the "aboriginal" was undoubtedly antagonistic, would present another acknowledgment of the antagonistic relation the Japanese must have had with the Chinese and other minorities within the empire. Yet Watsuji never reached this awareness, and, as we will see, the mimetic relationship with the Anglo-Saxons and the West in general would be guided by a different economy in which the *shutai* is completely repressed, an economy that is regulated and sustained by a format called "the national character." Precisely because Watsuji adamantly disavowed this mimetic relationship, he was all the more vulnerable to its adverse effects, and obliged to further imitate the least appealing aspects of the Anglo-Saxons and the West.

Not surprisingly, in "Nihon no shintô" (The way of Japanese loyalty), which was published during the final stage of the Fifteen-Year War, in the same year as "American national character," Watsuji exercises even more powerfully the repression of such "boomerang" effects, which would disrupt the constitution of the Anglo-Saxons as the "narcissistic self-consolidating other" and the very distinction between "them" and "us." What we can see in these articles is a displacement of a certain colonial guilt about the imperialism of his own country that finds its outlet in the description of the brutality of Anglo-American imperialism. Just as the talk of "white slave traffic" serves to displace anxiety over racialist violence practiced on peoples of color, so his condemnation of British and American imperialisms seems to relieve Watsuji of his anxiety. (With regard to his anxiety over the Sino-Japanese situation, as we will see, he found a way to evade the issue altogether by presenting himself and the Japanese in general as *victims* of supposed Chinese shrewdness!) Instead, the disavowal and displacement of collective colonial guilt worked to consolidate the fraternity of the "Japanese Empire" against "the Anglo-American demons." As far as "The Way of Japanese Loyalty" and "American National Character" are concerned, it should be argued that Watsuji simply followed the government's policy of demonizing the enemy. In this respect, his condemnation of "white" imperialisms is one more testimony to Japan's involvement in "what Kipling called the 'Great Game'" of "the imperialist superiority complex"— "playing off, in other words, 'their' natives, rebellions against one another and, above and beyond this, all priding themselves, in competition with one another, on their particular humaneness, by projecting the image of racism on to the colonial practices of their rivals."[45]

Thus, in Watsuji's works on cultural typology, we are forced to face the strange coexistence of an uncritical identification with the West and an equally uncritical rejection of the West. In most of his published articles in the 1930s, therefore, Watsuji maintained an anti-imperialist posture. However, the "imperialist discourse" is not merely a matter of opinion; it also consists in a certain positionality of the observer or a set of regularities thanks to which the institution of an imperialist subjective position is sustained. Few claim themselves racist in their "opinions," but racism is present in so many aspects of our lives. Similarly, few argue positively for imperialism or colonialism, but many nevertheless behave as imperialists or colonizers; for imperialism is constituted not at the level of statement in the narrow sense of the word but at the level of discourse. I am not seeking to determine here whether or not Watsuji as a person was immanently colonialist or racist; it is not my business to issue the final judgment on the person of Watsuji Tetsurô as a coherent and systematic author. The point is to ask how, in spite of his anti-imperialist stance, Watsuji often ended up identifying himself with a specific position of observer equals subject that was sustained by imperialist discourse; that is, it is to bring to light the dynamism because of which one often cannot get out of imperialist regimes of behavior despite being consciously opposed to imperialism.

Perhaps, the part of the 1929 edition of *Climate and Culture* that was later dropped and rewritten (chapter 3, section 1) might help us to better understand this ambivalence in Watsuji. In this part, he tries to define the Chinese national character. He points out the Chinese inability to form a homogeneous national community because they have never been able to get rid of their "anarchistic tendency." This anarchistic tendency manifests itself in the fact that foreign colonial powers controlled many parts of China in the 1920s. However, he rejects the historical explanation of the

Chinese political situation in favor of an explanation in terms of trans-historical cultural traits.

> The Chinese apathetic attitude may be explained by their anarchistic social situation. However, the social situation of anarchy does not necessarily produce an apathetic attitude similar to theirs. For one and a half centuries since the Onin era, a similar state of anarchy had prevailed in Japan. Yet did the Japanese become apathetic then? . . . In Japan, this one and a half centuries of an anarchistic state could produce an exceptionally vigorous and emotionally intense period in Japanese history.[46]

Finally, Watsuji reduces the particularly anarchistic character of the Chinese to those factors that remain relatively constant throughout historical time. But he also argues that, because of their anarchistic character, the Chinese are resilient as independent individuals and can survive well without the protection of the state. They may not be able to appreciate the subtlety of emotion, but:

> The Chinese are a pragmatic people [= nation] who would not appreciate the aestheticization of life, whereas the Japanese are a nonpragmatic people who tend to aestheticize life too much. . . . If the Japanese should lose their unity and compete with the Chinese on an individual basis, the Japanese would be no match for the Chinese. And the Chinese victory would signify the regression of humanity.[47]

Watsuji's personal observation of people in a few colonized cities in East Asia with large Chinese populations is completely overshadowed by his anxiety about the Sino-Japanese relationship of those times, which was undoubtedly antagonistic. I am almost certain that Watsuji as a Japanese tourist was forced to confront turbulent and discomforting facts about his practical relationship to the object of his observation. Whether he liked it or not, he had to occupy a specifically imperialist position in relation to the people in China. Anti-Japanese movements proliferated, and the Japanese government had already been expanding its imperialist control over China politically and militarily. Not even once, however, did he attempt to respond to the nagging anxiety generated in his relationship to the Chinese by calling into question the very opposition between China and Japan, between the two national identities, in terms of which cultural differences had been inscribed and essentialized. In this respect, Watsuji took a hostile stance against other intellectuals, including Japanese writers and filmmakers such as Kaneko Mitsuharu and Yokomitsu Riichi, who discussed topics relating in one way or another to Sino-Japanese relations in reference to the situation in Shanghai. Later, in 1943 when the new edition of *Climate and Culture* was published, with a revised chapter on China, he explained his political stance as follows: "I wrote the original version of this chapter in 1929 when leftist thought was popular, so I included a refutation of leftist theory in my investigation of the climate and culture."[48]

Watsuji stayed in Shanghai in February 1927.[49] His visit to Shanghai took place during the period when an anti-imperialist labor movement, which started on May 30, 1925, was gaining momentum. The capital of the Japanese spinning industry, which had rapidly become dominant in the Chinese market in the 1920s, was confronted with a severe protest by the Chinese nationalist movement, prompted by the murder of a striking worker by Naigai Men Kaisha, a Japanese concern based in Shanghai.[50] I believe I can detect a doubly antagonistic relationship between the colonizer/the colonized and the capitalist/the worker behind what Watsuji tried to describe exclusively in terms of the differences between the Japanese and Chinese national characters. Indeed, he was merely a tourist in the Shanghai of the late 1920s, a city to which Maeda Ai attributed "the craftiness typical of the colonial situation,"[51] but Watsuji could not have avoided the sense of threat in certain practical relations to the majority of the residents who were discriminated against in the system of extraterritoriality as long as he identified with the subjective position called "the Japanese." In those relations, he must have confronted the anxiety of being labeled one of the colonizers and capitalists, an anxiety arising out of a direct confrontation with the consequences of Chinese articulatory practice, thanks to which, as Mao Dun's *Rainbow* depicted, the fragmented masses had gradually *articulated themselves* against imperialist forces.[52] In reference to *Shanghai* by Yokomitsu Riichi, Maeda Ai argues:

> By the time *Shanghai* was written, that notorious notice board of "Dogs and Chinese" was already a legend of the past. Yet, only those in Western clothes or Japanese kimono were allowed to enter the park. There still was a rule by which those citizens and tourists in Chinese costumes were excluded. The subtlety associated with the position occupied by the Japanese, who were an important yet novice member of the international community of extraterritoriality, is captured in the scene where Koya, who never entertained any doubt about such a system, was obliged to acknowledge his sense of inferiority toward Westerners as well as his sense of superiority toward the Chinese.[53]

To use the terminology of Watsuji's *Ethics*, there must have been a "practical relationality in social action" (*kōteki jissen renkan*) between Watsuji as a

Japanese tourist in Shanghai and Chinese residents there. Watsuji as a "person" should have occupied the subjective positions of the colonizer and the capitalist in his *aidagara* (relationality of subjective positions) to the majority of Chinese residents who then should have occupied the subjective positions of the colonized, the worker, and so forth.

Unlike the "anarchistic" Chinese and like "foreigners" who "were accustomed to living under the protection of the state,"[54] Watsuji decided to take up the position of an observer and continue to describe the apathetic characteristic of the Chinese as if no practical relation had existed with people in Shanghai. What happened in February 1927 in Shanghai was not difficult to discern, even in Watsuji's account. It was the collapse of the system of separation. Watsuji reported: "The foreigners, who had been accustomed to state protection, felt an acute fear and a sense of insecurity when they were confronted with the possibility that *they might have to get out of state protection*."[55] It was therefore doubly necessary for Watsuji to erase his practical relations to people living in Shanghai altogether, and to observe them only as objects of his observation from a protected viewpoint regulated by the positionality of an epistemic subject (*shukan*). First, in order to fashion himself exclusively as the epistemic subject who observes, he had to rely on the semicolonial system that maintained the separation of the colonizer from the colonized, a system of apartheid in which Watsuji's inclusion on the colonizing side was guaranteed by the Japanese state.[56] Second, "getting out of state protection" would oblige him to cease to identify with the subjective position dictated by the Japanese state, and live among "the Chinese": it might well have rendered it impossible to separate "the Chinese" from "the Japanese" and resulted in an "anarchistic" mixture of Japanese and Chinese people and in the collapse of the binary opposition between the two nationalities. Watsuji warns: "We, who customarily ascribe every bit of our life to the state, could not predict such a state of affairs."[57] As long as Watsuji continued to ascribe every bit of sociality to the state as the subjective totality, as he would do in his *Ethics*, he had to refuse to seek an articulation of different social relations that could be enunciated together with a different articulation of cultural difference. What he did was to stigmatize and destroy any social relation that was not confined by the dictates of nationality, of an identity sanctioned by the state.

In this instance too, Watsuji was drawn into a dialogic struggle with other possible enunciative positions in spite of the disavowal of his anxiety. He was opposed not only to "leftist thought" but also to those who attempted to confront rather than repress the anxiety generated by the practical relationship to people in Shanghai. Yokomitsu's novel *Shanghai* depicted the scenes of international mingling involving the behaviors of international capital and the mass movements, which, like a flood, swept away the system of separation. Yokomitsu attempted to outline an imagined political possibility by depicting the main characters of the novel as liberating themselves from the subjugation and subjection to an imperialist state and thereby constructing different relations with people in Shanghai.[58] Perhaps the most interesting attempt along these lines made in the Japanese mass media around that time can be found in a documentary film by Kamei Fumio, also called *Shanghai*, in which the position of the observing—Japanese—subject was so disrupted and inverted that the subject was solicited to "cross to the other side," although the film itself was released nearly a decade after Watsuji's visit to the city.[59] What one sees in the novel *Shanghai* and the film *Shanghai* is an attempt to seek an articulation of different social relations with the object of viewing, the kind of attempt that Watsuji could not afford not to block, so to say, by any means.[60] In what he called "leftist thought" around that time, therefore, we can still recognize an attitude of intellectuals in which they managed to face the anxiety being generated in the Japanese state's relationship to peoples on the continent without disavowing it, and were determined to remain in the fundamental aporia of their historical existence without taking refuge in their cultural identity, despite the fact that so-called leftist thought then was far from being free of many defects of imperialism. Thus it is essential to note that Watsuji's *Climate and Culture* was enunciated against emerging cultural and political practices whereby intellectuals dared to confront the reality of their own historical aporias, and were ready to "cross to the other side," if necessary, through carefully designed cultural and intellectual tactics, and "to see themselves as they were, to cease fleeing reality and begin to change it."[61]

At issue in the separation of "foreigners" and the "Chinese" is not merely the relationship between the visitors from foreign lands and the residents, but also the power relationship between the colonizers and the colonized. And, needless to say, it is what was meant by Watsuji's identification with the "foreigners" in this power relationship. But, on the grounds that he was immediately and essentially an Oriental and a Japanese, Watsuji refused to acknowledge that he would have to accept the unfavorable aspects of the mimetic relationship between Japan and the West if he wished to endorse its favorable aspects. The mimetic desire for the West thus disavowed was somewhat communicated by his fear of "anarchistic" confusion and hybridity. Eventually, the desire comes back as "a return of the repressed": "The Chinese are more Jewish than the Jews, while the Japanese are more Greek than the Greeks."[62]

Is there anything that indicates the locus of Watsuji's disavowed anxiety better than the rather odd parallelism between the Jews and the Chinese and the Greeks and the Japanese? Watsuji's anti-Semitism was first published before Nazism became popular among a very small group of intellectuals in Japan, and continued to be expressed sporadically until the end of the Fifteen-Year War. The oddity of Watsuji's anti-Semitism consists, above all, in the fact that it was announced in a country where the absolute majority of its population can hardly tell a synagogue from a church. It seems to consist of the following three emphases: First, the Jews were regarded as an "anarchistic" ethnos (minzoku) who symbolized disparity between the national community and the ethnic community, and the absence of the Jews would thus mean the ideal state of the national community in which national identity was immediately equated with ethnic identity.[63] It is this logic that Watsuji exploited most effectively in order to legitimate the postwar "symbolic" emperor system, which was introduced by the American Occupation Administration after the war, against the universalistic doctrine of the prewar emperor system. Second, the framework of symmetry between the West and the East was installed, and without this the contrast between the Greeks and the Jews in Europe and the Middle East would not correspond to the contrast between the Japanese and the Chinese. Third, Jewish commercial capital was thought to be dispersed beyond "the protection of the state" while, pretending to assimilate into whatever national community they happen to inhabit, the Jews in fact remained absolutely loyal to their ethnic deity, and militantly but secretly disloyal to the deities of the other states. Such a view of transnational Jewish capital inevitably evokes fear of those who migrate irrespective of national borders and identities.[64] Yet, for Watsuji, the image of the Jews remained so vague that he would have no need to modify his argument about the Jews if he had to substitute the Palestinians for the Jews in the 1980s, since by the Jews he designated those who had failed to create their own nation-state, and consequently had to live in diaspora without the protection of their own state, just like the Chinese in the late 1920s. "The Jews" were determined to be those who would "anarchistically" invade and overcome all those barriers partitioning people into many stables and lots, and erode existent, stable national identities. In other words, all the anxiety that might well arise in practical relations in the encounter of cultural differences crystallized into the traumatic figure of the Jews.

Slavoj Zizek's endeavor to analyze anti-Semitism in Eastern Europe in his *The Sublime Object of Ideology* attracts our attention in regard to Watsuji's sinophobia. According to Zizek, "It is not enough to say that we must liberate ourselves of so-called 'anti-Semitic prejudices' and learn to see Jews as they really are—in this way we will certainly remain victims of these so-called prejudices."[65] The traumatic figure of the Jews serves to play the role of the refuge people could possibly take in order to displace the sense of the deadlock of their desire, and gives some coherence to their anxiety, which they had felt rather amorphously until then.

> The basic trick of anti-Semitism is to displace social antagonism into antagonism between the sound social texture, social body, and the Jew as the force corroding it, the force of corruption. Thus it is not society itself which is "impossible," based on antagonism—the source of corruption is located in a particular entity, the Jew. This displacement is made possible by the association of Jews with financial dealings: the source of exploitation and of class antagonism is located not in the basic relation between the working and ruling classes but in the relation between the "productive" forces (workers, organizers of production . . .) and the merchants who exploit the "productive" classes, replacing organic co-operation with class struggle."[66]

Notwithstanding the fact that I find it hard to go along with Zizek's rather dogmatic adaption of Lacanian psychoanalysis in some parts of this book, his insight into anti-Semitism, whose relevance in the East European countries I would not dare to judge, seems to help in understanding Watsuji Tetsurô's anti-Semitism/sinophobia; one could detect the process of displacing the colonial and class antagonism with the opposition between the Westerners and Japanese who lived "under the protection of the state" and the "anarchistic" Chinese in Watsuji's description of cultural differences in terms of the "Chinese anarchistic" character.

Yet, the disavowal of such an antagonism on Watsuji's part was essentially a reactive act and was prompted by the articulatory practice that had rendered it visible. The practical relation between a Japanese tourist and the majority of residents in Shanghai had not been *determined* as a relationship between the colonizer and the colonized, or the capitalist and the workers, until it was articulated as such by Chinese activists and Japanese leftists. Therefore, those practical relations had been invisible and *mu*, to use Watsuji's terminology, or nonbeing in the sense of not-being-ontologized, in daily life before some articulatory practice made it visible and determined it in such a manner as to allow for the formation of a new political collective and for eventual alteration, through such an articulatory practice, of the existing social relations.

Thus, Watsuji's disavowal was a response to an articulatory practice not only by the Chinese but also by some Japanese who dared to admit rather than disavow the anxiety generated by the relations of colonialism with the Chinese in which they were trapped, and who worked to form different relations with them. As far as the acknowledgment of the colonialist relation was concerned, the division was drawn along a line different from that between nationalities in that articulatory practice.

Watsuji's conception of the subject (*shutai*) dictates that immanent in each "person" is a totality as the communality of persons in which social discriminations are sublated and in which the equality of each is realized. Needless to say, "the ultimate totality as the ethical organization of all the ethical organizations"[67] that has been concretized is given as the nation-state, so that, in principle, one cannot and should not have a relationality of subjective positions or *aidagara* with those who, being "anarchistic" and not living "under the protection of the state," do not belong to such a totality. There cannot be a social space of *ningen* or "being-between" (meaning human being) between Watsuji and some "anarchistic" residents in Shanghai without the mediation of an "international" diplomatic relationship between the two nation-states. It follows that any person with a different nationality or no nationality must be excluded from the social space of "human being," although a person with a different nationality can be related to him through diplomatic channels controlled by international treaty, whereas a person without nationality who does not live "under the protection of the state" can never enter the space of *ningen*. Watsuji cannot be a subject in the sense of what he called *shutai* in relation to the Chinese, so that he had to posit himself primarily as an "ahistorical" observer-*shukan*. Precisely because his *Ethics* not only neglects but also refuses what Nancy calls "being-in-common," or the sociality of the relation that is nonrelational, nonmutual, and even antagonistic, with people without Japanese nationality, the only posture he could possibly take was that of the observer-*shukan*. To follow the argument of his *Ethics*, one would be ethically obliged to relate oneself to foreigners by accepting them as the object of observation when there is no international relation between one's state and the foreigners' state.

In order to postulate the nation-state as "the ultimate totality," Watsuji had to eliminate the possibility of the sort of social relations that could be formed independently of "international" relations. That possibility was represented by the figure of the Chinese, and it was necessary for him to first objectify that possibility in terms of the Chinese *national* character and to quarantine it, so to say, by calling it "anarchistic." On the one hand, his description of the Chinese undoubtedly reflects an uneasiness he must have experienced on his first overseas journey. On the other hand, it indicates various relays between the constitution of the national community in culturalist discourse and the dynamics of displacing anxiety. For this reason, I find it very difficult to separate the anti-Semitism and the sinophobia, as clearly expressed in *Climate and Culture* and *Ethics*, from his discussions on national culture. The figures of the Jews and the Chinese were understood by Watsuji as factors that would make the ultimate (corporatist) totality of the nation-state impossible. Zizek analyzes the workings of the traumatic figure of the Jews as follows: "The 'criticism of ideology' must therefore invert the linking of causality as perceived by the totalitarian gaze: far from being the positive cause of social antagonism, the 'Jew' is just the embodiment of a certain blockage—of the impossibility which prevents the society from achieving its full identity as a closed, homogeneous totality."[68]

Just like the Lacanian "Other" who cannot be, the society can exist only as the impossibility of totality. Watsuji had to follow the logic of corporatism, which begins with the assumption of a homogeneous totality, in his cultural studies as well as in his *Ethics*. Zizek continues: "Society is not prevented from achieving its full identity because of Jews: it is prevented by its own antagonistic nature, by its own immanent blockage, and it 'projects' this internal negativity into the figure of the 'Jew.'"[69] Accordingly, the traumatic figure of the 'Jew' is a point at which the antagonistic nature of society "assumes positive existence,"[70] and from the viewpoint of "homosocial" fantasy, which aspires to achieve the homogeneous totality of transparent mutual recognition, and fraternal fusion, which perhaps finds its best expression in Watsuji's concept of *aidagara*, transparent reciprocity between the other and the self, "the 'Jew' appears as an intruder who introduces from outside disorder, decomposition and corruption of the social edifice—it appears as an outward positive cause whose elimination would enable us to restore order, stability and identity."[71] But, "the 'truth' of anti-Semitism is, of course, that the very identity of our position is structured through a negative relationship to this traumatic figure of the Jew."[72] Watsuji's sinophobia paradoxically discloses the "truth" of the cultural identity of the Japanese in his cultural typology and *Ethics*.

In this respect, the formats of cultural typology and national character served to maintain a sort of discursive economy whereby to legitimate the disavowal of the political antagonism that necessarily arose in the Japanese practical relations to the object in Watsuji's description of cultural difference, while at the same time sustaining the mimetic desire to be like "the

Greeks." It has to be noted that these discursive formats did not cease to be effective in the postwar period.

What is perhaps more significant in Watsuji's discussion of cultural differences is that the descriptions of Chinese, Indian, and European national and regional characters are always accompanied by a series of assertions about the Japanese national character. Each of these determinations is predicated within the schema of cofiguration whereby the *self* of the Japanese is always posited as the *other* of the Chinese, Indian, or the European. In other words, the determinations of those *others* serve reflectively to postulate the *self* of the Japanese in specularity. *Climate and Culture* contains a great number of logical inconsistencies and utterly arbitrary evaluations about those object peoples, but they can be overlooked because of the dominant structure of address according to which Watsuji's narration is organized; he was only attentive to the oppositional and spatially determined differences between Japanese and other national identities because, ultimately, he was only concerned with the assertion of his ethnic and national identity. Consequently, each of his observations of other peoples and his moral judgment about them were prescribed by one criterion: the exclusive uniqueness of his ethnic and national identity. (The same sort of culturalism seems operative in a number of recent English-language publications on Japan that, under the guise of critically examining Japanese society and its culture, seem to be guided by an obsession to assert the exclusive uniqueness not of Japan but of some amorphous unity called "the West." One can find a culturalist argument of this sort, for example, in *The Enigma of Japanese Power* by Karel van Wolferen, who, ironically enough, believes himself to be critical of the *nihonjin-ron*-style culturalism.)[73]

Fûdo is delivered from a specific enunciative position or a complex of enunciative positions: it is addressed to "us" Japanese, and Watsuji would never entertain the possibility of addressing himself to those peoples whom he describes extensively. In spite of the fact that *Climate and Culture* was later translated into English and acquired a fairly large audience outside of Japan, the structure of its address excludes the audience beyond Japanese readers. It is addressed to "us" from the positions of "we" whose determination is multiple: "we" as the generalized speaking subject who knows; "we" who have undergone the same experience as Watsuji; "we" who would, because of common cultural heritage, share a subtle sensitivity and the same kind of curiosity; "we" who always occupy the viewpoint of the Japanese nation as an organic totality (*yûkiteki zentaisei*), and so on. Yet, from the beginning of this book to the end, the possible complaints or counter-arguments by those "object" peoples are foreclosed. Despite the variety and multiplicity of "we," the economy that regulates the metonymic and metaphorical shifts of "we" in address does not accommodate the "object" peoples. The entire narration proceeds as though those "natives" could in fact never speak back or refute "our" commentary on them, and one might perceive that Watsuji is enjoying a certain comfort and sense of security that arise from excluding the voices of those who are other than "us." Yet, precisely because it is addressed to "us," the regulative structure of the address obliges the author to seek some response, and even an affirmation, from the readership while allowing him to ignore those outside the assumed community of readership. At the same time, this "homosocial" foreclosure in address posits and marks what I refer to as the "interior called Japan." In this respect, *Climate and Culture* reproduces in its symmetrical reversal the structure of address known as "Orientalism." Just as Orientalism constitutes the subject called "the West," *Climate and Culture* projects the subjectivity of the Japanese nation. Thus, Watsuji's practical relations to those peoples in his description of cultural differences at the sites where he supposedly encountered them are completely absorbed into his epistemic relationship to them, and the practical agent (*shutai*) is substituted for by the epistemic subject (*shukan*) even though he never ceased to emphasize the significance of the distinction between the *shukan* and the *shutai*.

In his philosophical anthropology, which was gradually developed between 1931 and 1949 in a series of publications under the title *Ethics*, he also proposes the conception of *shutai* according to which the practical agent or *shutai* is distinguished from the epistemic subject called *shukan*.[74] In *Climate and Culture* too, the distinction between the agent of practice and the epistemic subject is a guiding principle according to which climate as "a historical and social concept" is discerned from what is understood by that name in natural sciences. Yet, whereas Watsuji stresses the observer's practical relation with climate and posits the observer not as an epistemic subject but as a *shutai*, he completely ignores the fact that the observation of social and cultural traits necessarily involves practical relations to the objects of observation, who are also agents of practice. However much he may wish to avoid being in common with the agents he studies, he is already and always implicated with and exposed to them in the social. As is most explicitly demonstrated in his *Ethics*, what he consistently evades is the undecidability of the social, inherent in the "being-in-common" with others, which cannot be equated to the relational determination of an identity within the spatiality of synchronicity. What is achieved in his use of the term *shutai* is, in fact, a displacement of the practical relation by the epistemic one. In this sense, I think that, in the final analysis, Watsuji's *shutai* is reducible to *shukan* and that *shutai* is a mere corollary of subjectivity. Thus, his cultural typology constructs not the *shutai* but the subject. This subject is ruled by the relationality of subjective positions, or *aidagara*, as well as the structure of address concerning enunciative positionality, and is exactly what Jonathan Crary called "the observer," a subject who occupies the expected and preserved position, thereby observing the rules.[75] It is precisely in this respect that the Japanese are *shukan*, just as Westerners are *shukan* in relation to the people of "the non-West." I believe that one of the functions without which the subjective identity called the West would not gather itself can be found here: the West is a historically specific mode of subjectivity that can be best characterized as *shukan*. Accordingly, the interiority called Japan thus constituted in *Climate and Culture* is fundamentally *Western*. It goes without saying that the concept of "the West" must be elucidated in terms of historically mutable practical and epistemic relations since its referent varies and slides accidentally according to a local and temporary situation. Furthermore, it is misleading to label this construction of the national subjectivity as particularly Japanese, partly because such an urge would inevitably amount to an insistence on the West's distinction and exceptionalism. In many regards, what Watsuji attempted to achieve was the construction of a society of sympathy, an explicit prescription of which can be found in the following, written by an author who would become Examiner of India Correspondence of the East India Company shortly after it was published:

> [As a strong and active principle of cohesion among the members of the same community or state,] we mean a principle of sympathy, not of hostility; of union, not of separation. We mean a feeling of common interest among those who live under the same government, and are contained within the same natural or historical boundaries. We mean, that one part of the community do not consider themselves as foreigners with regard to another part; that they set a value on their connexion; feel that they are one people, that their lot is cast together, that evil to any of their fellow-countrymen is evil to themselves; and do not desire selfishly to free themselves from their share of any common inconvenience by severing the connexion. How strong this feeling was in those ancient common-wealths which attained any durable greatness, every one knows. How happily Rome, in spite of all her tyranny, succeeded in establishing the feeling of a common country among the provinces of her vast and divided empire, will appear when any one who has given due attention to the subject shall take the trouble to point it out. In modern times the countries which have had that feeling in

the strongest degree have been the most powerful countries; England, France, and, in proportion to their territory and resources, Holland and Switzerland; while England in her connexion with Ireland, is one of the most signal examples of the consequences of its absence.[76]

It might well be argued that, following the old recipe of modernization, Watsuji simply explored the cultural strategies for constructing a national community of sympathy.[77] Let me stress that such a community of sympathy was imaginarily constructed by positing the outsiders as objects of observation, of administration to whom, by definition, sympathy should not be extended. In the quote above, the proposed embracement of the Irish was supplemented by the insistence on a separatist distance between "us" and the nonwhite in the British colonies. Similarly, Watsuji could draw the contour of the national community of sympathy by first marking the "homosocial" limit of sympathy.

Watsuji's cultural typology was a version of what I have referred to as *subjective technology* an ensemble of cultural and political techniques to make (*poiein*) the national subject, who could imagine himself or herself to be able to share the suffering of the compatriots. But the sense of this emphatic suffering could only be facilitated by creating the object of observation outside the "homosocial" limit of the communal sympathy.

Thus, Watsuji, "like a stage manager playing at will with the possibilities offered by the objectifying instruments . . . , imposes on the object his own norms of construction, as if in a dream of power."[78] Furthermore, he constantly solicits his readers to enjoy this "dream of power," and tries to establish the identity and camaraderie of "us" on the basis of this secretly shared homosocial enjoyment.

Mary Louise Pratt analyzes travel writings of the eighteenth and nineteenth centuries as a cultural politics of "transculturation" in which the white settler class in Latin America managed to claim its American authenticity against European colonizers while sustaining its status as the ruling class within the local racial hierarchy.[79] In many respects, Watsuji unwittingly repeated the strategies of transculturation. His critique of Western domination represented by the behaviors of the Anglo-Saxon ended up serving to consolidate the ethnic superiority of the Japanese as "the Greeks of the East" in relation to Asian peoples. His discussion of Japanese culture is insistent on the differences between the Japanese and other Asian peoples, just as nineteenth-century (and even present-day) European travelogues are insistent on the separation between the West and the non-West. And his anthropology seems haunted by an obsession with ethnic homogeneity, as well as with the paranoiac fear of refugees, the hybrids, "the an-archistic," and those in diaspora who intrude on the separatist boundaries of apartheid imposed on the local population by colonial regimes.

It is now evident that what Watsuji's culturalism attempted to destroy was the political and social possibilities of what Jean-Luc Nancy calls "communication," the possibilities that, despite inscribed cultural, ethnic, and national differences, people as singular beings can articulate the modes of exposition in which to "communicate" with one another; his culturalism was to repress the possibility of the networks of people that, for instance, made it feasible for Mao Dun to stay in Japan and write *Rainbow*. I do not believe that the Japanese intellectual world has yet recovered from damage thus done to it by culturalism even a half century after the end of the Fifteen-Year War.

What we have been witnessing in *Climate and Culture* is one of the most alluring forms of "homosociality" in which the identification of us with ourselves is facilitated by excluding "them," and by turning "them" into an object of our speculative gaze. Yet the identity of "us" also has to be articu-lated, enunciated, and cofigured in reference to the instituted differences between "them" and "us." And, it is the representation of "us" to ourselves that is achieved in this sort of cultural typology. It is through the descrip-tion of cultural difference that Japanese cultural identity could be rendered representable. Watsuji obediently reproduces the obsessive insistence on the separatist distinction of the West from the non-West. In the final anal-ysis, the subject that posits itself in the inscription of cultural difference is nothing but the interior called *Japan* as the epistemic subject. Japan as a nation that represents itself ("we") to itself ("us") by means of *cofiguration* of another national character and "our" national character.

Theory, as I understand it, is not merely the universal or indiscriminate application of some formulas or categories but, above all, a bringing into awareness of the practical in the formation of knowledge, and of the split between the epistemic subject (*shukan*) and the practical agent (*shutai*). In the context of the articulation of cultural difference, therefore, theory should point to a project to reverse what Watsuji Tetsurô attempted to achieve, a project with the aim of demonstrating the *atheoretical* nature of the enunciative positionality from which he wished to address himself to his "us."

What is the status of my reading of Watsuji in relation to Asian Studies? Does it function in the mode of exemplarity, which, of course, would not be operative unless we presuppose the commensurability of the particular and the general? My reading of *Climate and Culture* is informed with the recognition of a certain general universality of the way in which the practical relation to the object of study is reduced to the epistemic one in the objectivist description of cultural difference. In defying the singularity of Watsuji's enunciation in the writing of *Climate and Culture*, which took place in a historically and geopolitically specific situation or situations, am I to extract from this particular instance some example that can equally be applied to the present state of Asian Studies in North America or Japan? If so, would it be to submit myself to the lure of the universalist pretention of theory?

Let me draw attention to what is implied in the reduction of the practical relation to the epistemic one, the reduction of "feeling" to the synchronicity of signification. What takes place in that reduction is that particularity takes the place of singularity: the singular eventhood of cultural difference is fixed according to the epistemic regime that has already been in place. In this fixing and fixation of cultural difference, the already existing regime remains unaffected and insulated from the dialogic dynamics of the event; that is, the universalism of generality, as distinct from the universalism of infinity, comes from the imperialist inscription of cultural difference, which always and necessarily erases the change and transformation brought about in the encounter between singular beings. Therefore, the universalism of generality has to be adopted as our reading strategy in order to outline the universality of the workings of imperialism/colonialism in general, which reduces singularity to particularity. Accordingly, such a reduction must always be underwritten by an insistence that, regardless of what happens in the encounter with cultural difference, the description of it should be able to be achieved as business as usual. This essay has attempted not to demonstrate the general applicability of a certain interpretative scheme, but rather to point out the working of denegation, which necessarily requires the repression of the singular eventhood of cultural difference, as well as the forgetting of historicity, of what cannot be arrested in the phenomenality of the representable within the economy of chronological temporality. It is in order to disavow the destabilizing "feeling" in the encounter of cultural difference—an encounter always among singular beings, that is, an encounter such as what Nancy calls "communication" (which necessarily undermines all those "communication theories")—that universalism and particularism, oppositional stances that demand one another in their complicity, are brought forth in due course. It must be shown that the universalism of theory is already operative in the very description of the particularities of the object culture or people: uni-

Subject and Inscription of Cultural Difference
≈ 149 ≈

versalism is not something one can consciously add or withdraw in the articulation of cultural difference.

It is partly for this reason that I must introduce the difference between the *shukan* and the *shutai*, an essentially asymmetrical difference between what can be accommodated within the discursive economy of general universality and particularity and what flees as soon as an attempt is made to arrest it in the "spatiality of synchronicity." By *shutai*, therefore, I like to suggest the impossibility of the full saturation of any identity and, particularly, the identity of the agent of action, as well as an undecidability that underwrites the possibility of social and ethical action. Yet the *shutai* is not the agent of action possessing free choice as it is understood in liberal humanism because freedom is neither owned by it nor in it. Freedom *of* and *as* the *shutai* comes from its materiality in that the *shutai* is the body of enunciation. Consequently, I think, *shutai* can be defined only as a differential of the *shukan*. What happens in Watsuji's cultural typology is the erasure of this differential characteristic of the *shutai*, and his attempt to close off the identity of the Japanese subject who represents the other nations, thereby representing itself to itself.

In this respect, it is necessary to ask students of Asian Studies whether they are repeating what Watsuji Tetsurô attempted to do some sixty years ago. Such an anachronistic question, which links one instance of reduction to another instance in spite of the undeniable heterogeneity in historical and geopolitical settings, must be raised in order to disclose the essentially universal generality of the working of this denegation that is called for whenever a desperate attempt is made to evade problems inherent in the practical relation to the object of study, and to erase the singularity of cultural difference as an event.

Perhaps what happened in the English translation of *Climate and Culture* is symptomatic of the discipline of Asian Studies: dropped in its entirety is the last chapter, in which Watsuji evaluated his own scholarship of cultural typology in relation to previous scholarship and located it within the genealogy of Western climatology since Hippocrates, through Jean Bodin (*De la république*), Montesquieu (*L'Esprit des lois*), Herder (*Auch eine Philosophie der Geschichte zur Bildung der Menschheit, Ideen zur Geschichte der Menschheit*), Kant, Fichte (*Reden an die deutsche Nation*), Hegel to Marx and Rudolf Kjellén (*Der Staat als Lebensform*). Clearly, in spite of his insistence on the Japanese national character embodied in Japanese *fûdo* (climate and culture), Watsuji never hesitated to admit that the genre of climatology itself was of a *Western* origin. This is to say that, in its insistence on its non-Western origin and Japanese uniqueness, Japanese national character is particularly *Western*.

What is disavowed in the English translation is nothing but the modernity of this form of knowledge shared by both "Western" and Japanese writers of the modern world, of knowledge that includes such fields as physiognomy and pathognomy. In this translation it is rather difficult not to notice a gesture, on the part of the translator, of disavowal of the universality of cultural essentialism prevalent in both the West and the non-West, a gesture of disavowal similar to Watsuji's attempt to dodge the "boomerang effects" of his critique of Anglo-American imperialisms in "American National Character" and "The Way of Japanese Loyalty." The author of *Climate and Culture* and its translator had to disavow the mutual transference of cultural essentialism and, consequently, inscribed the distinction between the West and the non-West as if it were an essential and immutable distinction. I believe, therefore, that, unless the identity of the West and that of its opposite, the non-West, as analytical categories operative in Asian Studies are called into question, cultural essentialism of Watsuji's type will continue to be reproduced on both sides of the great divide.

Similarities that can easily be noticed between the cultural essentialism of Watsuji's cultural typology and more recent ones are not merely accidental, of course. As I will discuss in the next chapter, both stress the oppositional distinction between "the West" and "the non-West," take the unities of national culture, nation, and national language as three aspects of the single substantialized essence of the object people, and insist on the historical immutablity of that essence. The recent publication *Japan* 2000, for example, cannot be overlooked as insignificant political propaganda, for, without inhibition and with a certain frankness, it manifests not only the features of a certain anti-Semitism (which, just like Watsuji's sinophobia, does not necessarily focus on the figure of the Jews) but also all the traits of the repression of anxiety in the reduction of practice from which Asian Studies has never been entirely free.[80] And it is deceiving to dismiss such a publication merely as a piece of irresponsible journalistic gossip since even so-called scholarly work can easily degenerate into this sort of racialist stereotyping, as is amply exemplified by Watsuji's scholarship— although Watsuji's ethnocentric expressions appear rather civilized compared with some in *Japan* 2000.

In Watsuji's *Ethics*, the fear of foreigners or those whose social status is not predetermined, and the psychology of hypersensitivity toward others (*uchibenkei*—a lion at home and a mouse abroad mentality), find some theoretical elucidation. In that respect, the dictates of his *Ethics* do not have the appearance of "militancy," which he attributed to the "desert type." Yet, in spite of its "passive and tolerant character" (which he attributes to the "monsoon type"), we cannot but admit that his *Ethics* justifies cruelty toward those in diaspora and without their own state protection—refugees, immigrants, foreign laborers, and so on in our present-day world—a cruelty that is the reverse side of the fear of those who would approach "us" and create social relations with "us" in disregard for national borders and identities. Since Watsuji's national narcissism neglected the possibilities of making social relations beyond the national community and refused to keep that community exposed to the outside, it eventually ended up endorsing colonial and racist power relationships between the inside and the outside of the national community, despite his declared hostility to imperialism and racism. Thus, some of his works seem to teach us a great deal about a mechanism that allows an alliance to be created between imperialism and a fascistic social formation through the self-enclosed corporatist desire for "homosociality."

5

Modernity and Its Critique:

The Problem of Universalism and Particularism[1]

Even though I will predictably reach the conclusion that the postmodern, an other of the modern, cannot be identified in terms of our "modern" discourse, it should not be utterly pointless to question what constitutes the separation of the modern and the postmodern—that is, what underlies the possibility of our talking about the modern at all. Similarly, it is essential to deal with another other of the modern, the premodern, with reference to which modernity has also been defined in a great many instances. This series—premodern-modern-postmodern—may suggest an order of chronology. However, it must be remembered that this order has never been dissociated from the geopolitical configuration of the world. As is well known by now, this basically nineteenth-century historical scheme provides a perspective through which to comprehend the location of nations, cultures, traditions, and races in a systematic manner. Although the last term emerged fairly recently, the historico-geopolitical pairing of the premodern and the modern has been one of the major organizing apparatuses of academic discourse. The emergence of the third enigmatic term, the postmodern, possibly testifies not so much to a transition from one period to another as to the shift or transformation of our discourse as a result of which the supposed indisputability of the historico-geopolitical pairing (premodern and modern) has become increasingly problematic. Of course, it is not the first time the validity of this pairing has been challenged. Yet, surprisingly enough, it has managed to survive many challenges, and it would be extremely optimistic to believe it has finally been proven to be ineffectual.

Either as a set of socioeconomic conditions or as an adherence of a society to selected values, the term "modernity" can never be understood without reference to this pairing of the premodern and the modern. Historically, modernity has primarily been opposed to its historical precedent; geopolitically, it has been contrasted to the nonmodern, or, more specifically, to the non-West. Thus the pairing has served as a discursive scheme according to which a historical predicate is translated into a geopolitical one and vice versa. A subject is posited through the attribution of these predicates, and thanks to the function of this discursive apparatus, two kinds of areas are diacritically discerned: the modern West and the premodern non-West. As a matter of course, this does not mean either that the West was never at premodern stages or that the non-West can never be modernized; it simply excludes the possibility of a simultaneous coexistence of the premodern West and the modern non-West.

Already a cursory examination of this sort about modernity amply suggests a certain polarity or warp among the possible ways to conceive of the world historically and geopolitically. As many have pointed out, there is no inherent reason why the West/non-West opposition should determine the geographic perspective of modernity, except for the fact that it definitely serves to establish the putative unity of the West, a nebulous but commanding positivity whose existence we have tended to take for granted for such a long time. It goes without saying that the West has expanded and shifted arbitrarily for the last two centuries. It is a name for a subject that gathers itself in discourse but is also an object constituted discursively; it is, evidently, a name always associating itself with those regions, communities, and peoples that appear politically or economically superior to other regions, communities, and peoples. Basically, it is just like the name "Japan," which reputedly designates a geographic area, a tradition, a national identity, a culture, an ethnos, a market, and so on, yet, unlike all the other names associated with geographic particularities, it also implies the refusal of its self-delimitation; it claims that it is capable of sustaining, if not actually transcending, an impulse to transcend all the particularizations. Which is to say that the West is never content with what it is recognized as by others; it is always urged to approach others in order to ceaselessly transform its self-image; it continually seeks itself in the midst of interaction with the Other; it would never be satisfied with being recognized, but would wish to recognize others; it would rather be a supplier of recognition than a receiver thereof. In short, the West must represent the moment of the universal under which particulars are subsumed. Indeed, the West is particular in itself, but it also constitutes the universal point of reference in relation to which others recognize themselves as particularities. In this regard, the West thinks itself to be ubiquitous.

This account of the putative unity called the West is nothing new, yet this is exactly the way in which Jürgen Habermas, for instance, still argues about Occidental rationalism. He "implicitly connect[s] a claim to *universality* with our *Occidental understanding of the world*."[2] In order to specify the significance of this claim, he relies on the historical-geopolitical pairing of the premodern and the modern, thereby highlighting a comparison with the mythical understanding of the world. Within the cultural traditions acceptable to us—that is, within the cultural traditions anthropologists have reconstructed for us—myths of archaic societies

> present the sharpest contrast to the understanding of the world dominant in modern societies. Mythical worldviews are far from making possible rational orientations of action in our sense. With respect to the conditions for a rational conduct of life in this sense, they present an antithesis to the modern understanding of the world. Thus the heretofore unthematized presuppositions of modern thought should become visible in the mirror of mythical thinking.[3]

Habermas takes for granted a parallel correspondence among the binary oppositions premodern/modern, non-West/West, mythical/rational. Moreover, for him the very unity of the West is a given; it is an almost tactile reality. What is most surprising is that while admitting the need for the non-West as a mirror by which the West becomes visible, Habermas obviously does not ask if the mirror may be extremely obscure. Whether or not the image facilitated by ethnographers and anthropologists is the true representation of what is actually there is not at issue. What is worth noting is that he deals with non-Western cultures and traditions as though they were clearly shaped and as though they could be treated exhaustively as objects. Even when he tackles the problem concerning the incommensurability of other cultures, the whole issue of unintelligibility is reduced to the intelligibility of the problem of incommensurability. For Habermas, it signifies no more than that of cultural relativism, a pseudoproblem in itself.

Habermas argues with epistemological confidence in order to reinstall epistemological confidence in us and make us trust in universalism again.[4] Given the most persuasive and possibly most rigorous determination available today of the term "ethnocentricity," one might say he is simply ethno-centric. But if the intrusion of the term "postmodern" bears witness to the inquietude surrounding our identity, if this putative unity of the West, the us, from which and with whom Habermas wishes to speak is being dissolved, what does the fact that his epistemological confidence is not shaken imply? If the possibility of a certain enunciative position, the us, the Occidental *us*, with which his theory of communicative action is so closely interwoven, is in fact threatened, would one be justified to say his epistemological confidence indicates something else? Are *we* then allowed to say it points to an inquietude about *us* that has been repressed?

From this perspective, it is understandable that the discursive object called Japan has presented a heterogeneous instance that could not be easily in-tegrated into the global configuration organized according to the pairing of the modern and premodern. It has been repeatedly deplored or extolled that Japan alone of the non-Western cultures was able to adopt rapidly what it needed from Western nations in order to transform itself into a modern industrial society. Hence, a sizable amount of intellectual labor has been invested in order to render this peculiar object innocuous in the discursive formation. In the United States, the consequences of this labor have usually been collected under the name "modernization theory." In addition to overtly strategic requirements of the state, there was a certain implicit but no less urgent demand to which the production of social-scientific and humanistic argument was submitted. Following Max Weber, who also saw clearly the mission of discursively ascertaining the putative unity of the West and who executed that mission most skillfully, some modernization theorists pursued the mission of ascertaining the unity of America as the central and perhaps commanding part of the West.

What modernization theory has accomplished by introducing the op-position of universalism and particularism into the study of other cultures is, first, to reproduce the same kind of discursive formation within which the unity of the West is constituted—but, this time, with the center ex-plicitly in the United States; second, it has generated a new kind of histori-cal narrative that preserves the dictates of nineteenth-century historicism but rejects its overt reliance on the notion of national history. Here, I has-ten to add that this does not mean that the new historical narrative was less nationalistic or in an antagonistic relation with nationalism. This version of universalism is, like some other universalisms, decidedly nationalistic. Yet, in this new narrative, nationalism had to be articulated differently. On the one hand, modernization theorists certainly inherited the European legacy of a historical time that coincides with the transition, gradual or rapid, from particularity to universality, from abstract universality to concrete universality, and ultimately coincides with the process of increasing rationalization, of reason realizing itself. On the other hand, they saw universalistic elements as being dispersed; instead of stressing the dynamics of conflict between the self and the other, the attempt was made to show that any society is potentially capable of rationalizing itself. But it is also explicit that, in rationalizing itself, that society becomes similar to the United States. Or, to put it slightly differently, progress always means Americanization. In this respect, modernization theorists expressed the vision, most successfully implanted in the mass consciousness of postwar Japan, that modernization was implicitly equated with Americanization. Whereas, prior to this, modernization had been more or less equated with Europeanization, modernization theory at large worked in the service of shifting the center from Western Europe to the United States.

Obviously, it is utterly beside the point to ask which vision of modernization is more authentic. What this reading hints at is that, although the modernization process may be envisioned as a move toward the concretization of values at some abstract level, it is always imagined as a concrete transfer from one point to another on a world map.

Thus, universality and the concept of modernity were even more closely woven together with American nationalism than before. But because of this double structure, universalism often appears free of the well-recognized defects of nationalism. Of course, the claim to universality frequently serves to promote the demands of nationalism. Because of the double structure, an incessant oscillation is generated between universalism and particularism; possibly a certain provincialism and a certain aspiration toward universalism are two sides of the same coin; particularism and universalism do not form an antimony but mutually reinforce each other. As a matter of fact, particularism has never been a truly disturbing enemy of universalism or vice versa. Precisely because both are closed off to the singular, who can never be transformed into the subject or what infinitely transcends the universal, neither universalism nor particularism is able to come across the other; otherness is always reduced to the Other, and thus repressed, excluded, and eliminated in them both. And, after all, what we normally call universalism is a particularism thinking itself as universalism; it is doubtful whether universalism could ever exist otherwise.

Certain conditions have to be met, however, for this universalism to be possible. The center of the West being assumed to represent the most densely universalistic social formation, it ought to be ahead of less univer-

salistic and more particularistic societies in the historical time of rationalization; it must be the most *advanced* particularity, since universality is
equated to the ability to change and rationalize its social institutions. Embedded in this format is an equation according to which one can infer,
from the relative degree of economic rationality, the society's investment
in universalism. In other words, unless a society performs well in such a
sphere as the economy, it would not be able to claim it adheres to universalism. Hence, when the society is perceived to be ahead of other societies, this universalism effectively and powerfully legitimizes that society's
dominion over others. But if its economic and political superiority to the
others in rationalization is not perceived to be certain, it rapidly loses its
effectuality and persuasiveness. By the weight of its commitment to universalism, the society's self-esteem would eventually be put in jeopardy.
Universalism would then appear to be the burden under whose pressure
the image of the society as a totality would be crushed.

The term "postmodern" obliquely attests to this sort of internal contradiction that modern universalism has come to realize. *The Fracture of Meaning*
by David Pollack is one of the best instances in which to observe what
would happen when a naive universalism is confronted with such recognition. It reacts to the perceived change of environment by reinforcing
the already existing rules of discourse according to which universalism has
been naturalized. What is significant here, however, is that, whereas those
rules were previously implicit, assumed, and accepted silently, they have
now to be stated and loudly announced. It is in this point that the importance of Pollack's work lies; furthermore, his investigation of the Japanese
aesthetic constitutes a deliberate attempt to conserve the kind of framework embedded in the accumulated knowledge on the non-West, particularly in the Far East. What makes his work even more interesting is his gesture of respecting and taking seriously the kind of theoretical critique,
sometimes called poststructuralism in academic journalism, that has been
most effective in disclosing a specific, Eurocentric, and humanistic power
relation in the production of knowledge. Pollack's dauntless determination
to eliminate and neutralize the critical impulse of "poststructuralism" is betrayed at almost every point where the authority of such names as Jacques
Derrida and Roland Barthes is appealed to. Yet one must be sensitive to
ways in which his argument collapses, since these reveal much more about
the persistence of that obsolete but arrogant discursive formation called
"modernity" than about mere technical mistakes.

In demonstrating a uniquely Japanese dialectic called *wakan,* "Japanese/

Chinese," by means of which the subjective identity of Japan has been installed, Pollack manipulates the master metaphor, an old trope repeatedly used in Western studies of the Far East for nearly a century, of "a frog from the bottom of its well, who would define its world almost exclusively in terms of its walls."[5] Until the mid-nineteenth century, China was Japan's walls in opposition to which Japan's existence was defined. The United States, Pollack adds, has recently taken over that role. Just as Japan previously defined itself as China's other, so today it defines itself as America's other. In both cases, Japan is self-parasitic in one sense and relational in another. Putting aside the problem of whether or not every possible form of subjective identity is parasitic and relational, he proceeds to display many "scientific facts" that, without exception, testify to a distinctive gap between the Chinese and Japanese languages. And he begins more detailed descriptions of a uniquely Japanese culture "with the simple and very modern-sounding premise that culture and language reflect and are informed by the same structures."[6] Yet, based on this premise, or on one of the implications of this premise, that both culture and language must be able to be isolated as unitary systems in order for these unities to "reflect and to be informed by the same structures," the gap between China and Japan at the level or representation is inscribed upon and merged with the difference between the two at the level of the real.

In linguistics, some systematic unity of regularities has to be posited as a necessary presupposition in order to analyze and organize so-called empirical information. What constitutes the possibility of linguistics as a systematic and formal corpus of knowledge is this positing of language unity, which should never be confused with the actual substance of a language. But the systematic unity of a language does not exist in various linguistic activities as "the spine exists in the body of the mammal."[7] Hence, it is misleading to say that linguistics discovers and identifies the unity of a particular local or national language after the examination of data. On the contrary, the positing of such a particular language unity is the necessary condition for the possibility of language research. The nature of language unities such as Japanese or Chinese is basically discursive.

This is to say that a language unity cannot be represented as a circumscribed space or closure. The metaphor of "a frog in the well" is not necessarily irrelevant; it is rather accurate and extremely persuasive in the context of contemporary Japan, where the outside world seems to be a mere image projected on the walls erected by national mass media. However, if this metaphor is linked to a typical epistemological cliché of cultural solipsism, all these unities would be reified, and this is what happens with Pollack. In part this results from his inability to maintain the difference between a category of analysis and an object of analysis. But, more important, this seems to be a consequence of the general lack of theoretical critique about modern discourse.

For instance, the three unities of Japanese language, Japanese culture, and the Japanese nation are repeatedly used almost interchangeably. As if obediently following the models of Japanese historiography (*kôkoku shikan*) or more recent discourse on Japanese uniqueness (*nihonjin-ron*), Pollack projects the stereotypical image of contemporary Japan into its middle ages and antiquity. In order to stress how different the Japanese are from the Chinese, and to demonstrate the dialectic interaction of the two nations, he frequently resorts to the kind of circular argument in which Japanese culture is identified by referring to the identity of Japanese language; Japanese is then identified by referring to the national identity of the people; and, finally, the Japanese people are identified by their cultural and linguistic heritage. He is not aware that this series of tautologies is a feature of a historically specific discursive formation. What Pollack does not see is that there is no logical ground on which the three categories correspond to each other in their referents. As I argued elsewhere, it is only in recent history that the putative unity of Japanese culture was established.[8] An object of discourse called culture belongs to recent times. For Pollack, these three unities are transhistorical universals: *The Fracture of Meaning* most specifically endorses cultural essentialism. His argument amounts to the task of determining Japan as a particularity, whose sense of identity is always dependent on the other. Needless to say, this other is a universal one in contrast to which Japanese particularism is rendered even more conspicuous. By extension, this determination of Japan implies that Japan has been from the outset a "natural" community, has never constituted itself as a "modern" nation.

Pollack argues that, despite the evident linguistic heterogeneity between China and Japan, the Japanese adapted Chinese writing, which generated an endless anxiety over their own identity:

> It would no more have occurred to the Chinese, for example, than it would to us to find a "problem" in the adequacy of their own script to represent their thoughts. And yet our investigation begins precisely with the problem of the adoption of the Chinese script in Japan's "first" text, a problem that will become paradigmatic for all that follows.[9]

Japanese uniqueness, he asserts, is best manifested in the fact that Japan had to borrow a foreign script. Plainly, the title of his book, *The Fracture of*

Meaning, comes from this understanding. But the reader will be caught by surprise when reading the following: "Clearly, the notion of a 'fracture' of the semiotic field of culture is not unique to Japan; nor is modern semiotics, after all, a subject particularly associated with Japan."[10] Evidently, Pollack did not mean to say, "It would no more have occurred to the Chinese, for example, than it would to us to find a 'problem' in the adequacy of their own script to represent their thoughts." Of course, he did not *mean* it, for, after all, the meaning is fractured not solely for the Japanese, but for us all. But does not the pretense of not admitting that the script is not adequate to thought lead to the formation of an ethnocentric closure? Does not the recognition of the meaning's fracture purport that, because not only writing but also speech is exterior and inadequate to thought, the script is always foreign and that it, therefore, pierces the imagined closure of ethnic, cultural, and language unity? Does not Derrida say that, when one speaks or writes, one is always external to one's putative identities?

In order to criticize Japanese particularism and possibly what Pollack thought of as Japanese cultural essentialism, he had to construct an image of Japan that would never adopt and include others. This is to say that he first had to create an object he could later bash. But, in this process, he mistakenly defined this peculiar object in terms of his own cultural essentialism. As a result, cultural essentialism has been accepted as the basic vocabulary belonging to the subject who studies rather than as an attribute of the object studied.

This kind of inversion repeatedly occurs in Pollack's book. When the overall methodological construction of this work is examined, one cannot help but notice another inversion. In the Introduction, Pollack states: "I am concerned with the Japanese interpretations of what they saw as essentially "Chinese," rather than our own interpretations or those of the Chinese themselves."[11] In accordance with the metaphor of "a frog in the well," these three fields, or three wells, form a hermeneutic horizon, as Pollack asserts the hermeneutic nature of his study. However, he says in the conclusion: "I am concerned here with a dialectical process . . . so that this study becomes more than anything else a hermeneutics of Japanese culture, a study of the ways in which the Japanese interpretation of themselves and their culture evolved over time."[12] Here the Japanese field is chosen, and he says he is concerned only with the dialectic of the Chinese and the Japanese seen from the viewpoint of the Japanese, so "neither China nor even the idea of China was necessarily involved in its operation."[13] He deals with China only insofar as it is represented by the Japanese.

What he is unable to comprehend is the fact, without reference to which the metaphor of the frog in the well would not work, that the frog can never see its own well on the walls. For the frog, the totality of the well can never be visible. Therefore, it would never know that it is confined to a tiny space; it is not aware that what it believes to be the entire universe is merely a small well. In order to know that its universe is merely a well, the image of the well must be projected on the walls. Thus, for the frog (Japanese) the totality of the well (Japan) is basically invisible and has to be recognized only as a representation projected on the walls. If China is dealt with only as a representation, Japan should be dealt with in exactly the same fashion. Furthermore, if the Japanese do not have some representation of Japan and their confinement or subjection to it, they could not even recognize that they are Japanese; they would not be able to identify themselves with Japan. As China is simply imaginary for the Japanese, so Japan is also imaginary for them. If Pollack wishes to talk about the synthesis of China and the Japanese culture, he must first talk about the synthesis of Japan in the Japanese culture. There should be as much dialectic between the Japanese and Japan as between the Japanese and China. Of course, his cultural essentialism is totally blind to the problem of subjectivity.

One of the ironic implications of this metaphor is that no one can confidently claim to be free from the fate of the frog. The frog believes that there is no other and different world.outside its small world; so its knowledge of its small world is supposed to be universally valid everywhere. But how can the world of those who laugh at the frog be guaranteed not to be another well? The haughty and self-confident smile on their faces will freeze as soon as this question is posed. After all, is the Japan Pollack describes any different from the China the Japanese imagined on the walls of their well?

In a sense, *The Fracture of Meaning* is haunted by a sense of insecurity that seemingly stems from an implicit knowledge that somebody might ask this question anytime. What has been undertaken to repress this sense of insecurity is the setting up of an enunciative position from which the author speaks in universal terms—a ubiquitous and transcendent stance from which he views things. It is arranged to appear natural that Pollack's words are automatically registered as metalanguage. His language posits the *us* with whom he wished to speak, and his *we*, the speaking subject of this metalanguage, coincides with the West, and the United States in particular. Thus, once more, the West assumes its universality and ubiquity in the midst of its particularity. Pollack's argument presupposes that the opposition of theory (universal) and the object of theory (particular) corresponds to that of the West and Japan.

A privileged object of discourse called Japan is thus constituted in order to show *us* the supposedly concrete instance of particularism, in contrast to which *our* universalism is ascertained. Japan is defined as a specific and unitary particularity in universal terms: Japan's uniqueness and identity are provided insofar as Japan stands out as a particular object in the field of the West. Only when it is integrated into Western universalism does it gain its own identity as a particularity. In other words, Japan becomes endowed with and aware of its own "self" only when it is recognized by the West. It is no accident that the discourse on Japanese uniqueness (*nihonjin-ron*) mentions innumerable cases of Japan's difference from the West, thereby defining Japan's identity in terms of deviations from the West. Its insistence on Japan's peculiarity and difference from the West embodies a nagging urge to see the self from the viewpoint of the other. But this is nothing but the positing of Japan's identity in Western terms, which in return establishes the centrality of the West as the universal point of reference. This is why, despite the gestures of criticizing Japanese exclusivism and ethnocentricity, Pollack in fact eagerly embraces and endorses the Japanese particularism and racism so evident in *nihonjin-ron*. As a matter of fact, his entire argument would collapse without this open acceptance of particularism.

Contrary to what has been advertised by both sides, universalism and particularism reinforce and supplement each other; they are never in real conflict; they need each other and have to seek to form a symmetrical, mutually supporting relationship by every means in order to avoid a dialogic encounter that would necessarily jeopardize their reputedly secure and harmonized monologic worlds. Universalism and particularism endorse each other's defect in order to conceal their own; they are intimately tied to each other in their complicity. In this respect, a particularism such as nationalism can never be a serious critique of universalism, for it is an accomplice thereof.

Still, the relationship between the West and the non-West seems to follow the old and familiar formula of master/slave. During the 1930s, when "the times after the modern" (*gendai*), somewhat similar to our postmodernity, were extensively examined, one of the issues that some Japanese intellectuals problematized was the West and the non-West relationship itself. In offering a diagnosis of the times, many, including the young philosophers of the Kyoto school such as Kôyama Iwao and Kôsaka Masaaki, singled out as the most significant index the rapport between the Western (European) and the non-Western (non-European) worlds. A fundamental change, they observed, had taken place in the world since the late nineteenth and the early twentieth centuries. Until the late nineteenth century, history seemed to have moved linearly toward the further unification of the world. The entire globe was entirely organized according to the singular framework that ultimately would allow for only one center. History appeared to be an unending process of unification and centralization, with Europe at the center. Hence, it was understandable and partially inevitable to conceive of history simply as the process of Westernization (Europeanization). In this historical scheme, the entire world was viewed from the top, and was thought of as being Western in the sense that the rest of the world was being taken to be that which was doomed to be Westernized. Essentially, as is best represented by Hegelian historicism, "the history of the world was European history."[14]

However, toward the late nineteenth century, Kôyama claims, the non-Western world began to move toward its independence and to form a world of its own. As a consequence of this transformation, what had hitherto been taken for the entire world was revealed to be a merely modern (*kindai*) world, a world among many worlds. This possibility for historical cognition and praxis, informed by the fundamental historical transformation of the world, was then called "World History." In this "World History," it was assumed that historical changes simply could not be comprehended without reference to the already established spatial categories: climate, geography, race, nation, culture, and so on. Only within the framework set up by those categories was it possible to understand historical developments and make sense out of various changes that were to be incorporated into a larger unit of narrative. What this simple but undeniable recognition pointed to was that history was not only temporal or chronological but also spatial and relational. The condition for the possibility of conceiving of history as a linear and evolutionary series of incidents lay in its not as yet thematized relation to other histories, other *coexisting* temporalities. Whereas monistic history (*ichigenteki rekishi*) did not know its implicit reliance on other histories and thought itself autonomous and total, "world" history conceived of itself as the spatial relations of histories. In world history, therefore, one could not think of history exclusively in those terms that referred back only to that same history: monistic history could not deal with the world as it was apprehended in world history since the world is primarily a sphere of heterogeneity and others. To what extent Kôyama's world history was capable of facing heterogeneity and others, and whether or not world history would ever be able to be exposed to them in their heterogeneity and otherness, will be examined later.

But I should note that this notion of otherness and heterogeneity was always defined in terms of differences among or between nations, cultures, and histories, as if there had been no differences and heterogeneity within one nation, culture, and history. For Kôyama, heterogeneity and otherness were at most moments of *international* differences.

An oblivion of spatial predicates, which reveals itself as the truth of monistic history at the emergence of world history, comes from certain historical conditions. Unless the historical and cultural world is seriously challenged and influenced by another, it will never reach an awareness that its own world can never be directly equated with the world at large, and would continue to fantasize about itself as being the representative and representation of totality. Eurocentric history is one of the most typical cases of this: for it, the world does not exist. But Kôyama also adds Japanese national history to the list. Japanese national history is another example of monistic history in which, in spite of the fact that Japan has been challenged and influenced by other histories and cultures, it has yet to arrive at the knowledge that history resides in those interactions with others, because of its island situation (*shimaguni-teki jôken*).

What Kôyama brought into awareness is the fact that the very identity of a history is constituted by its interdependence with other histories, things other than itself. Precisely because monistic history does not recognize the conditions for the possibility of its own identity, it naively expands specific values indefinitely and continues to insist on the universal validity of those values: it misunderstands and misconstrues the moment according to which the necessity to claim its universality and the insistence on its identity are simultaneously inaugurated. Thus the moment of otherness is deliberately transformed in order to maintain its putative centrality as the initiator of the universal and the commensurability of universal and particular values. This no doubt amounts to the annihilation of the Other in its otherness. Probably the mission that monistic history believes itself to take charge of is best summarized in the following statement: "They are just like us." Of course, it has to be remembered, this statement is definitely distinct from another statement—"We are just like them"—in which the centrality of *us* is not ensured; that is, the inferiority in the power of *us* is instituted instead of the superiority, but these form a *supplementary* pair.

Monistic history has worked in the service of a certain historically specific domination, a form of domination that has not ceased to be turbulent in its effect even today. However, Kôyama saw and tried to seize a turning point in the development of monistic history. He insisted that another history, world history, which recognizes other histories, was about to emerge, and this emergence should mark a fundamental change in the relationship between the subject of history and its others; it should indicate that the monistic history in which others were refused their own recognition was no longer possible. In this new history, the plurality of histories and the interaction among them would be the principle. Hence, spatial terms of necessity would be incorporated into a history that would have to be construed as a synthesis of time and space, and internationalized.

What Kôyama advocated may sound like a genuinely pluralistic history as opposed to a linear singular one, and, if one were to believe all that has been said, this transition from monistic history to world history should mark a radical historical change leading to a different power arrangement in which cultural, national, and historical particularities are fully expressed. All the cultural worlds would then be mediated not by what Kôsaka Masaaki called the "ontological universals" (*yû-teki fuhen*) but by the *mu* universals (*mu-teki fuhen*).[15] And if this should be the case, one would then envisage the beyond of modern times, the other side of the historical break that would allow one to identify the limits of the modern discourse—in short, a genuine postmodernity.

In this context, it is noteworthy that, for Kôyama as well as Kôsaka, the unity of the subject of history, of pluralistic history, is unequivocally equated with that of the nation-state. Yet they stress that the nation-state does not immediately correspond to a race (*jinshu*) or folk (*minzoku*). The state for them is a being-for-itself that is opposed to other states, and, in this regard, it exists in the "world." The state, therefore, is not likened to other "entities" such as race, nation, clan, or family precisely because it has to be mediated by its relationships with other states and consequently be self-reflective—that is, a subject. On the other hand, the nation designates a community rooted in nature, a community where people are born and die. The bondage that keeps its members together is that of blood, procreation, and land, and is natural in the sense that the tie between mother and child is natural.

Kôyama issues a warning disclaimer here: the nation as a natural community can never be the subject of history because it is not mediated by universals. The natural community (Kôsaka refers to it as "substratum" [*kitai*]) is not a subject in itself, for it has yet to be rationalized. The natural community must be represented by the state; only through the state, the natural community is identified as the *nation for itself*. And only through this representation to itself does the nation become historical and generate its own culture, a historical world of its own. At this stage, a nation forms a history or historical world of its own with the state as its subject.

While rejecting Hegelian philosophy as an extension of monistic history, Kôyama rigorously follows Hegelian construction. Accepting all the "modern" premises, Kôyama attempts to change merely their historical view. By introducing pluralistic world history and thereby claiming to go beyond modernity (kindai), he endorses almost everything the Japanese state has acquired under the name of modernization. The critique of the West and of the modern expressed in his critique of monistic history seems to disclose the fact that the whole rhetoric of antimodernity is in fact a cover for the unprincipled endorsement of anything modern when Kôsaka and Kôyama deal with the issues on which the critique of the West is most urgent—the issues related to the Sino-Japanese relations during the 1930s and early 1940s.

In a roundtable talk held in November 1941, Kôsaka, Kôyama, and others refer to the relationship between historical development and the morality of a nation.[16]

> KÔYAMA: The subject [shutai] of moral energy should be in the nation [kokumin]. . . . The nation is the key to every problem. Moral energy has nothing to do with individual or personal ethics, or the purity of blood. Both culturally and politically the nation is the center of moral energy.
> KÔSAKA: That is right. The folk [minzoku] in itself is meaningless. When the folks gain subjectivity [shutaisei], they necessarily turn into a national folk [kokka-teki minzoku]. The folks without subjectivity or self-determination [jiko gentei], that is, the folks that have not transformed themselves into a nation [kokumin], are powerless. For instance, a folk like the Ainu could not gain independence, and has eventually been absorbed into other folks [that has been transformed into] a nation. I wonder if the Jews would follow the same fate. I think the Subject of World History must be a national folk in this sense.[17]

One can hardly discern any difference between this understanding of modern subjectivity and that of the Hegelian dialectic. The modern nation must be an embodiment of the will (jiko-genteisei); that is, the subject of the nation is, at any time, self-determination (the determination of the self as such) and the determining self (the self that determines itself). And the modern nation must externalize itself in order to be aware of itself and to realize its will. Hence, it is, without exception, a nation representing itself in the state; it is the synthesis of folks (irrational) and the state (rational).

The nation is the reason concretized in an individuality (*kobetsusei* = folk), so that the nation cannot coincide with the folk immediately. In order for the folk to transform itself into the nation, the folk must be negatively mediated by other folks; that is, the stronger folk must conquer and subjugate weaker folks in order to form the nation.[18]

The fragility of their antimodern rhetoric becomes all the more apparent when the pluralistic world history is discussed in the context of the contemporary historical situation. In another roundtable talk titled "Tôakyôeiken no rinrisei to rekishisei" (Ethics and Historicality of the Greater East Asian Coprosperity Sphere"), held about three months after the previous one and with the same participants, they directly relate the issue of history to the Sino-Japanese relationship.[19]

> KÔSAKA: The Sino-Japanese war [*shina jihen*] involves many things and is extremely complex. But the final factor that determines the outcome should be the question "Which morality is superior, the Japanese or Chinese one?" Of course, political and cultural maneuvers are very important. Yet our moral attitude toward the Chinese is even more important, perhaps. We should consider measures like this: we should send many of our morally excellent people over there to show our moral energy so that the people over there would be persuaded to convince themselves [of our moral superiority]. The Sino-Japanese war is also a war of morality. Now that we have entered the Great Asian War, the war is much larger in scale now, namely, a war between the Oriental morality and the Occidental morality. Let me put it differently, the question is which morality will play a more important role in World History in the future.[20]

It is amazing that they could still talk not only about the Japanese nation's morality but also about its superiority over the Chinese at that stage. Imagining the national atmosphere around the time these utterances were made, one would rather refrain from asking whether or not Kôsaka was joking. Nevertheless, it is at least worth noting that the relationship between the Japanese and Chinese moralities is put in a sort of dialectic. Kôsaka seems confident that the superiority of Japanese morality would eventually be proven, as if the whole thing had been guaranteed by Japanese military superiority.

For Kôsaka, historical processes involve a series of inevitable conflicts in which the morality of one nation is judged against that of another. Thus the incident in China (the Sino-Japanese war) is a moral war, and the war over the Pacific is also a war that will decide the moral superiority of the

East or the West in view of the ultimate morality of the totality—that is, all of humanity. In this sense, history as he conceives of it is the history of moral development toward the establishment of morality for humanity, toward the ultimate emancipation of humankind. Despite repeated denunciation of the term "humanism," Kôsaka is never able to resist the temptation to justify the status quo in terms of humanism. In other words, his critique of humanism and modernity is, in fact, a thinly disguised celebration thereof.

Apart from the incredible conceit expressed in this passage, there is a theoretical formation that clearly contradicts the premises of *pluralistic* world history. To imagine the relationship between China and Japan in terms of the war of Chinese and Japanese moralities is to posit a dialectic relationship between the two moralities. This means that, in the optimistic imagination, Japanese morality will eventually prove its universality as well as the particularity of Chinese morality. This would necessarily be a process in which particularities would be subjugated to the domination of a universality. Kôyama said, "[The Chinese] have a subjective sense of their Sinocentrism but do not have an objective consciousness of 'the World.' . . . Although there is morality in China, there is moral energy in Japan."[21]

What we see here is the ugliest aspect of universalism, and it should not be forgotten that this is, after all, the reality of Kôyama's "pluralism." Not only was a Japanese victory over China presumed and unquestioned, but Japanese moral superiority was also assumed; the temporary military superiority of Japan (which, after all, was faked by the national mass media) was thought to guarantee the right to speak condescendingly. If this dialectic movement between universalistic and particularistic moralities had proceeded as it was imagined, it would eventually have eliminated the pluralistic coexistence of many histories and traditions passionately advocated in the critique of *monistic history*. Within the scheme of the universalism-particularism pair, the plural subjects will gradually be organized as many particularities subjected to a single center of universalism.

How, then, can one possibly avoid the detested *monistic history?* For world history would be no different from the history of progress toward the complete dominion by one center. Kôyama and Kôsaka thought they were entitled to accuse the Chinese for their lack of a world-historical sense, for their insolence, and finally for their particularism; they felt entitled to do so because they thought they were speaking from the position of universalism.

Pluralistic world history proves itself to be another version of monistic history. I do not know how one could possibly avoid this conclusion when the subjects of world history are equated with nations. How can one put forward an effective critique of modernity when one affirms and extols national identity as the sole base for historical praxis? These thinkers' critique of modernity is at best some guise of anti-imperialism under which Japanese modernity (including the inevitable consequences of its expansionist impulse) is openly endorsed. What annoyed them in monistic history is not the fact that many people were suppressed and deprived of a sense of self-respect because of its Eurocentric arrangement. What they were opposed to was the fact that, in that Eurocentric arrangement of the world, the *putative* unity of the Japanese happened to be excluded from the center. They wanted to change the world so that the Japanese would occupy the position of the center and of the subject that determines other particularities in its own universal terms. In order to achieve this goal, they would approve anything Western on the condition that it conformed to the structure of the modern nation-state. Far from being an anti-Western determination, what motivated them was the will to pursue the path of modernization. Insofar as centralization and homogenization are part and parcel of modernization, their philosophy of world history paradoxically illustrates the inevitability of war by showing the impossibility of coexistence *outside* of the West. Even in its particularism, Japan was already implicated in the ubiquitous West, so that neither historically nor geopolitically could Japan be seen as *outside* of the West. This means that, in order to criticize the West in relation to Japan, one has necessarily to begin with a critique of Japan. Likewise, the critique of Japan necessarily entails the radical critique of the West. Insofar as one tries to speak from the position of *us*, the putative unity of either the West or Japan, one would never be able to escape the domination of the universalism-particularism pair: one would never be effective in criticism, no matter how radical a posture one might put on.

After Japan's defeat in 1945, Takeuchi Yoshimi was one of those few intellectuals who engaged themselves in the serious examination of Japanese morality in relation to China, and openly admitted that the war Japan had just lost was a war between Chinese and Japanese moralities. He brilliantly demonstrated the inevitability of Japan's defeat on both socioeconomic and moral grounds. However, Takeuchi was also one of the few who refused to ignore a certain legitimacy in what incited many, including the philosophers of world history, to a rhetoric of *pluralism*, despite the fact that, during the war, he was among those who despised and rejected the idea of a "Greater East Asian Coprosperity Sphere" advocated by the philosophers of world history. By every means he tried to sustain an intellectual concern about the problem of Western domination, which, of course, did not disappear with Japan's defeat.

In a manner similar to Kôyama's definition of monistic history, Takeuchi draws attention to the involuntary nature of modernity for the non-West. Here, too, the term "modernity" must signify not only a temporal or chronological, but also a spatial, concept in the sense that the significance of modernity for the non-West would never be grasped unless it is apprehended in the non-West's spatial relationship to the West. Modernity for the Orient, according to Takeuchi, is primarily its subjugation to the West's political, military, and economic control. The modern Orient was born only when it was invaded, defeated, and exploited by the West; that is, only when the Orient became an object for the West did it enter modern times. The truth of modernity for the non-West, therefore, is its reaction to the West; Takeuchi insists that it must be so precisely because of the way modernity is shaped with regard to the problematic concerning the subjective identity of the West:

> Modernity is the self-recognition of Europe, the recognition of Europe's modern self as distinct from her feudal self, a recognition rendered possible only in a specific historical process in which Europe liberated itself from the feudalistic (with her liberation being marked by the emergence of free capital in the economy, or the establishment of the modern personality as an independent and equal individual in human relations). Europe is possible only in this history, and inversely it can be said that history is possible only in Europe. For history is not an empty form of time. It consists in an eternal instance at which one struggles to overcome difficulties in order thereby to be one's own self. Without this, the self would be lost; history would be lost.[22]

The West (Europe) cannot be the West unless it continually strives to transform itself; positively the West is not, but only reflectively it is.

> Her [Europe] capital desires to expand her market; the missionaries are committed in the mandate to expand the kingdom of heaven. Through ceaseless tension, the Europeans endeavor to be their own selves. This ceaseless effort to be their own selves makes it impossible for them to remain what they are in themselves. They must take a risk of losing themselves in order to be their own selves.[23]

The idea of progress or historicism would be unintelligible without reference to this continual search for the self, a ceaseless process of self-recentering.

Inevitably, the self-liberation of the West resulted in its invasion of the

Orient. In invading the Orient, "[Europe] encountered the heterogeneous, posited herself in opposition to it." At the same time, Europe's invasion gave rise to capitalism in the Orient. No doubt, the establishment of capitalism there was taken as a consequence of the West's survival expansion, and it was thought to testify to progress in the history of the world and the triumph of reason. Of course, the Orient reacted to the West's expansion and put up resistance to it. Yet in this very resistance it was integrated into the dominion of the West and served, as a moment, toward the completion of Eurocentric and monistic world history. In this scheme, the Orient was to play the role of self-consciousness that had failed in the continual dialectic reaffirmation and recentering of the West as a self-consciousness that was certain of itself; it also served as an object necessitated in the formation of the West as a knowing subject. Thus the Orient was expected to offer an endless series of strange and different things whereby the familiarity of *our* things was implicitly affirmed. The knowledge of Oriental things was shaped after the existing power relation between the West and its other-object, and, as shown in Edward Said's *Orientalism*, it continued to affirm and solidify that relation. But we must not forget that the Orient thus known cannot be represented to itself; it can be represented only to the West.

On the one hand, the West is delimited, opposed to that which is alien to it; it needs its other for its identity. On the other hand, the West is ubiquitous and invisible as it is assumed to be the condition of the possibility for the universal validity of knowledge. Only in a discursive formation called modernity is universality possible as essentially Western universality. But, Takeuchi says, "The Orient resists." He reiterates the term "resistance."

The Orient resists; it disturbs the West's dominion. It is important to note that the modernization of the Orient was prompted by this resistance. Here, Takeuchi stresses that if the Orient had not resisted it would never have been modernized. Accordingly, the modernization of the Orient should not be thought of as a mere imitation of Western things, although there have been cases in which the will to resist was very weak, as in Japan's modernization. As is amply shown by the fact that the Orient had to modernize and adopt things from the West in order to resist it, the modernization of the Orient attests to an advance or success for the West, and, therefore, it is always Westernization or Europeanization. So it necessarily appears that, even in its resistance, the Orient is subjugated to the mode of representation dominated by the West. Its attempt to resist the West is doomed to fail; the Orient cannot occupy the position of a subject. Is it possible, then, to define the Orient as that which can never be a subject?

Neither the West nor the Orient are immediately referents. The unity of the West is totally dependent on the manner in which resistance is dealt with in the gathering together of its subjective identity. At this juncture, Takeuchi's explanation of the term "resistance" seems to begin to oscillate between two different readings.

Meanwhile, Takeuchi points out, the Orient does not connote any internal commonality among the names subsumed under it; it ranges from regions in the Middle East to those in the Far East. One can hardly find anything religious, linguistic, or cultural that is common among those varied areas. The Orient is neither a cultural, religious, or linguistic unity, nor a unified world. The principle of its identity lies outside itself; what endows it with some vague sense of identity is that the Orient is that which is excluded and objectified by the West in the service of its historical progress. From the outset, the Orient is a shadow of the West. If the West did not exist, the Orient would not exist either. According to Takeuchi, this is the primary definition of modernity. For the non-West, modernity means, above all, the state of being deprived of its own subjectivity. Does the non-West, then, have to acquire its own subjectivity? His answer harbors the kind of ambiguity characteristic of his entire discourse. "For there is no resistance, that is, there is no wish to maintain the self (the self itself does not exist). The absence of resistance means that Japan is not Oriental. But at the same time, the absence of the self-maintenance wish (no self) means that Japan is not European. This is to say, Japan is nothing."[24]

Takeuchi says "Japan is nothing." But is Japan really nebulous and amorphous without any inclination toward self-recentering? Because Japan does not wish to be itself, to posit itself anew, he argues, it fails to be itself and also fails to be like the West. His denunciation of contemporary Japan makes it seem as if Japan had not had any representation of itself, or a self that was not concretized in various institutions: as if there had not been any state that imposed the sense of a nation on those living in the region; as if those living in the region did not identify themselves with the nation; as if the nation called Japan had existed for thousands of years merely as a natural community.

Japan is a modern nation. Precisely in their effort to sustain themselves, people in Japanese territories have organized themselves as a nation and represented themselves in the state of that nation. How could a nation without a sense of identity possibly launch a war that lasted for more than fifteen years, resulting in an amazing amount of human and economic wreckage? It seems that Takeuchi is caught in the historico-geopolitical pairing of the premodern and the modern, according to which, since the West is modern, Japan should be premodern, or at least nonmodern. Instead of analyzing the pairing of the West and the non-West excluded by the West, Takeuchi assumes the validity of this pairing in talking about Japan. But his analytical device collapses upon the object of its analysis.

This sort of misapprehension seems to derive from Takeuchi's conviction that, in order to counteract the West's aggression, the non-West must form nations. Then what is heterogeneous to the West can be organized into a kind of monolithic *resistance* against the West, but within the nation homogeneity must predominate. Without constructing what Hegel called the "universal homogenous sphere," the nation would be impossible. Thus, whether one likes it or not, the modernization process in the formation of the entire nation should entail the elimination of heterogeneity within. Exactly the same type of relationship as that between the West and the non-West will be reproduced between the nation as a whole and heterogeneous elements in it. In this context, the nation is always represented by the state so that it is a subject to which its members are subject, whereas heterogeneous elements remain deprived of their subjectivity so that they are not subject to the subject.

Insofar as he never loses faith in the universal emancipation of mankind, Takeuchi is certainly a modernist. Therefore, he believes that monistic world history is, after all things are considered, an inevitability and that, consequently, the universal emancipation will be realized not by the West but by the Orient. In history, he says, the true subject is the Orient. In the meantime, we must endure the elimination of heterogeneity in order to construct the nation, the subject of history. It is misleading to say that Takeuchi is antimodern; he rejects only limited aspects of modernization.

On the other hand, one can detect a thread suggesting a different reading of his term "resistance." For the Orient, resistance is supposed never to contribute to the formation of its subjective identity. In other words, resistance is not negation by means of which a subject is posited in opposition to what it negates. Hence, resistance has to be likened to negativity, as distinct from negation, which continues to disturb a putative stasis in which the subject is made to be adequate to itself. Here, Takeuchi is concerned with something fundamental to the whole problem of modernity and the West.

I do not know what resistance is. I cannot logically pursue the meaning of resistance. . . . I dread the rationalist belief that everything can be brought into presence. I am afraid of the pressure of an irrational will that underlies the rationalistic belief. And to me that seems to be [the essence of] Europe. [Until recently] I have noticed that I have been haunted by this feeling of fear. When I realized that many thinkers and writers in Japan, except for a few poets, did not feel what I felt and were not afraid of rationalism, and when I noticed that what they had produced in the name of rationalism— including materialism—did not look like rationalism, I felt insecure. Then I came across Lu Xun. I saw Lu Xun enduring this kind of fear all by himself. . . . If I were asked "What is resistance?" the only answer I have is "It is what you find in Lu Xun."[25]

Resistance comes from a deeply rooted fear of the will to represent everything, the will essential for modern subjectivity. Lu Xun exemplifies a desperate effort to resist subjectivity, to resist subjection to subjectivity, and finally to resist subjection to the subject.

For Lu Xun, it is impossible to assume an observational and indifferent attitude, that is, the attitude of humanism. For the fool [Lu Xun himself] would never be able to save the slave as humanism naively hopes. . . . The slave is a slave precisely because he seeks to be saved. Hence, when he is awakened, he will be put in the state of "no road to follow," of "the most painful moment in life." He will have to experience the state of self-awareness that he is a slave. And he has to endure the fear. As soon as he gives in and begs for help, he will lose the self-awareness of his own slave status. In other words, the state of "no road to follow" is the awakened state, so if he still believes that there is a road to march on, he must be dreaming.

And he continues:

The slave must refuse his slave identity, but at the same time, he must refuse the dream of liberation as well. He must be a slave with the acutest sense of his miserable status, and remain in the "most painful awakened state in his life." He must remain in the state that, because there is no road to follow, he rejects a wish to be someone other than what he is. This is the meaning of despair that exists in Lu Xun and that makes Lu Xun possible. . . . There is no room for humanism here.[26]

Above all, resistance here is that which disturbs the possible representational relationship between the self and its image. It is something that resists the formation of those identities that subject people to various institutions. Yet this does not liberate them; this does not lead to emancipation because people are often subject to what they fear most through the words of emancipation. Possibly one should leave them in their sleep rather than "cry aloud to wake a few of the lighter sleepers, making those unfortunate few suffer the agony of irrevocable death." But if one is determined to be awake, one must at least resist one's hope to go beyond. What enabled Takeuchi to criticize modernity seems to come from this sense of resistance, although Takeuchi is so deeply committed to the values of modernity. This is what separated him from those who naively imagine the possibility of overcoming the modern. By the same gesture of emancipation, they all fall into the trap set up by modernity. As Takeuchi has given up an emancipatory ideology, he can be all the more effectively critical of modernity despite his commitment to certain modern values.

The sense of uncertainty that the term "postmodernity" provokes may indicate the gradual spreading of this resistance. I think I understand the term "play" best when I, unjustifiably perhaps, associate it with what Takeuchi saw in Lu Xun.[27] Only at this stage one could talk about hope, but rather hesitantly, just as Lu Xun did in his short story "My Old Home."

> The access of hope made me suddenly afraid. When Jun-tu had asked for the incense burner and candlesticks I had laughed up my sleeve at him, to think he was still worshipping idols and would never put them out of his mind. Yet what I now called hope was no more than an idol I had created myself. The only difference was that what he desired was close at hand, while what I desired was less easily realized.
>
> As I dozed, a stretch of jade-green seashore spread itself before my eyes, and above a round golden moon hung from a deep blue sky. I thought: hope cannot be said to exist, nor can it be said not to exist. It is just like roads across the earth. For actually the earth had no roads to begin with, but when many men pass one way, a road is made.[28]

6

Death and Poetic Language in Postwar Japan[1]

Some works of poetry interfere with history rather than preserve and record it. Often the writing or reading of poetry constitutes a historical practice in terms of which the general conception of historical experience itself is altered. The case in point here is Japanese poetry produced within the few decades after Japan's defeat in the Fifteen-Year War (the Second World War).

It has been claimed that much of postwar Japanese poetry was prompted by the experience of death and destruction during the war, and that it was, in one way or another, a deferred response to it. It has also been claimed that it pertained to some psychology of guilt that not only the poets but also many of the writers of this generation shared, and that obviously derived from the fact that they survived the war and left behind their loved ones and those they had themselves killed in the past. We cannot help recognizing some undeniable reality in these accounts about postwar poetry. But, insofar as one neglects to inquire into the internal process of the production of poetic texts, one would certainly fail to take note that postwar poetry has constituted a kind of historical practice and that it was at least an attempted interference with history, even if it may be said to be an aborted one.

By no means can postwar poetry be regarded as an eyewitness account of a traumatic experience the poets encountered during the war, although the literary works normally classified under this name (*sengo shi*—postwar poetry) contain many seeming references to this collective experience. Instead, it should be argued, the war as a collective historical experience was a product of various discursive activities that followed the defeat. We must remember that there is always an unsurpassable gap between an experience as one lived through it and its account as it is narrated and memorized. Hence the war as a collective historical event was produced in such a manner that an event, which is made up of a series of statements in a certain historical narrative, could be identified with an experience that was supposed or imagined to precede the actual production of such a narrative. What was at issue in the postwar poetry was the very relationship between what is conventionally understood as history, itself a discursively constituted sphere, and a kind of experience that eludes fixation in words and appears irrevocably lost.

Here a paradoxical situation inevitably arises; at its face value, the discourse on that historical event seems preceded by the event itself, so that the event that is represented in discourse may be apprehended as some kind of entity that should exist independently of its oral or written inscription. However, if we should ever be able to talk about an experience prior to discursive operation and to its representation in discourse, we would have to conceive of it as something similar to the Kantian thing-in-itself or the absolute exterior. Only in this sense would we possibly be able to comprehend on what ground we are justified to say that historical experience precedes its narrative account.

What distinguishes some poetry written immediately after the war from many of the contemporary literary and nonliterary works resides in this concern for the paradoxical nature of the relationship between history and discourse. This chapter is a preliminary attempt to elucidate how this concern was structurally integrated into the poetic works usually associated with a group of poets known as "Arechi" or "The Waste Land."

As many have already suggested in a variety of ways, the statement "I am dead" seems to permeate the works by the Arechi poets. It is of no surprise that the poets simply could not evade the vision of their own death in the production of their texts because the fifteen years of mass killings in the Asian continent, the Pacific, and finally Japan proper did not allow them to bypass the accumulated memories of decaying corpses and ruins. Not only those professionally involved in literature but also the Japanese people in general—"the Japanese people," of course, being an extremely ambivalent and unstable term for reasons of its historical contingencies, particularly in the geopolitical and historical conditions of the period immediately following the defeat on August 15, 1945—it seems, could hardly contain their impulse to narrate and reiterate almost indefinitely what they thought they had witnessed, undergone, and eventually learned during the war years. But by so doing, we must note, they also produced historical schemes without reference to which their presence in postwar Japanese society could not be ascertained. Undoubtedly, these historical schemes were frequently in conflict with one another and competed for the hegemonic dominance over the others; that is, their continued talk about the past, like many historical narratives, was essentially presentist and directed toward the constitution of their collective present rather than toward past occurrences themselves. No matter whether or not it was intentional, the production of historical narrative was a necessary procedure for a collectivity to resume its disrupted continuity, even if it narrated the rebirth of Japan or of Japan's defeat as the moment of historical discontinuity. The sense of the historical present, and of collective contemporeity, had to be constructed. However, as always, the sense of contemporaneity was an imaginary one: one does not live in it, but one will be persuaded to believe that one has lived it.

A human being may have faced severe hunger, fear, or desolation during the war, yet in the final analysis it can only be said that he or she experienced it alone. Experience in its most traumatic intensity cannot be lived collectively as we know it from observing the burning silence of those victims of atrocities. The task of representing it as a collective event has to be assigned to a historical narrative in which traumatic experience is universalized and integrated into the regimes of collective representations. Of course, through this process of universalization the experience must lose its primordial intensity and be transformed into its substitute, that is, its representation. Simultaneously, the individual who has experienced it is universalized and transformed into a subject of historical narrative. The process of universalization, as Jacques Lacan has shown, is also a process in which the subject is split.

If, however, historical experience is of such intensity that it erodes the very system of collective representations in terms of which historical narrative is generated, it would then be destined to remain silent and unrepresentable. Just as the experience of the dead cannot be represented since, as Emmanuel Levinas pointed out, history is always written by historiographers who are necessarily survivors, historical experience of such gravity must likewise be left mute and buried.[2]

Hence, we find a strange aura, an intense silence, in the midst of pervasive discussion of the dead in postwar Japanese poetry. It is as if some literary works had been prompted by a sober cognizance that words would never reach the core of the past experience; it seems that they aspired to affirm a self-contradictory thesis that the possibility of poetic discourse depends on the knowledge that this is impossible. Or, put differently, their attempt was to represent what was by definition unrepresentable. No doubt, this situation can be best summarized by the statement "I am dead."

By showing the rupture between the "I" who is enunciating this statement (the subject of enunciation) and the "I" who is posited by the existence of this statement (the subject of the enunciated), this elucidates a fundamental but necessary contradiction inherent in language use; in order for an enunciation to bring about signification, the subject of enunciation must be erased, lost and dead, and transform itself into a universalized and therefore anonymous "I."[3] This is to say that the statement "I am dead" explains, in a dramatized form, the essence of speech in general.

Accordingly, by pretending to enunciate from the position of the dead, which is nowhere, the poets tried to bring into language what they believed was unrepresentable. Yet it is worth reminding ourselves that death had been a focal point of literary production even before the defeat, and that literature's obsessive concern for death is nothing new. Any collectivity possesses cultural devices by which death is rendered representable. During the war the tropic vocabulary of traditional Japanese poetry was very effective in aestheticizing death. As Yoshimoto Takaaki argued in his article on the poets of the Shiki group, mass killings in modern warfare were likened to ritualistic death in terms of classic poetic tropes.[4] Similarly, the image of nature was extensively utilized to make death representable. Nature, as it was evoked in the works of the wartime poets, refers to a system of isotopies in which various words are linked to one another to form a vocabulary of imageries. The postwar poets were strongly opposed to this system of isotopies precisely because it helped form a specific type of subjectivity. In the passage Awazu Norio quoted from his autobiographical essay, Miyoshi Tatsuji, a poet affiliated with the Shiki group, said, "I accepted the beauty of nature before feeling the fear of death." Awazu argues:

> The fact that the acceptance of the beauty of nature preceded the fear of death should suggest the essential form of Miyoshi Tatsuji's spirit. His development (as a poet) thereafter was a rapid process of maturity toward this form. It was a process in which the fear of death, an endless movement of the inner life that could bring about the collapse of life's order, was tamed

and reorganized into a static world of beautiful nature. Here is a significant reason for which poetry for him could never be a penetrating, critical
movement against the external world; for, the a priori acceptance of natural
beauty, a complete world, invites the acceptance of the external world as
another complete world.[5]

What was achieved by this system of information of isotopies was the
concealment of the gap that always exists between collective aesthetic
imagination and the fact of individual death, and the positioning of the individual within the system of collective representations. The fear of death
was thereby refracted and transformed into a desire for a subjective position within collective representations. In other words, the fear of death
was translated into a wish to be remembered and worshiped by collectivity. It is important to note in this context that the kind of collectivity that
the aesthetic imagination was to serve was defined neither by medieval
clan nor archaic kin but by a modern nation-state. Death was thus represented as a meaningful death, but because this meaning can be given only
within the system of collective representations, it can only be a meaning
for the nation, that is, a meaningful death for the nation. Moreover, death
thus universalized was understood to mean an end to itself. Death was no
longer an accident, an unintelligible occurrence, that takes place in the
process of an action aimed at realizing some value other than death.[6]
Hence, so-called traditional poetic language continually appealed to the
image of death as the privileged moment at which the split between one's
life as an individual and one's identity as a subject of the nation would be
ultimately sutured and healed; through the universalization of death, the
so-called wartime poetry fabricated a fiction that one could finally identify
oneself with the nation by dying.

Perhaps the power of such poetic imagination derives from a widely
shared assumption that the vocabulary of poetic tropes is inherent in the
collective life of the Japanese. What many wartime poets refused to see,
however, was that any collective identity is posterior to the formation of
discourse that posits such an identity and presents the collectivity as "already and always being there." It is because of the nature of discourse that
what is represented appears to be anterior to its formation. But this does
not mean that the represented, such as collective identity, must exist prior
to the act of representation in actual temporal sequence.

For wartime poets, therefore, the collective identity was a substance
that existed independent of its representation. In many respects, the same
situation continued after the defeat. Insofar as one believed that discourse

on the war experience was, purely and simply, the past experience itself, one would never have been aware of its ideological implications. It might not be unnecessary to repeat the truism that the manipulation of the past is indisposable for the domination of the present. Hence, what was at issue in the kind of postwar poetry that concerns us here was, above all, how to create a poetic language capable of revealing those ideological implications. Naturally, the image of death incorporated into the wartime poets' works was very different from that of so-called traditional poetry. This problematic guides us to the following inquiries: How did these poets define their enunciative position in postwar society? Or, more specifically, how did they think they could avoid receiving uncritically a reserved position from which an author was to speak?

When Ayukawa Nobuo, an Arechi poet, had to resume his life after the defeat, he had to first concern himself with the problem of how the past could be evoked to generate a critical perspective that had not hitherto existed:

> tatoeba kiri ya
> arayuru kaidan no ashioto no naka kara
> yuigon shikkônin ga bonyari to sugata o arawasu
> —kore ga subete no hajimari de aru[7]

From the mist, for instance, or from the footsteps at every stairway, emerges an obscure figure of a testamentary executor—with this everything begins.

It is only in the capacity of a testamentary executor for a dead friend M that the poet barely justifies reentering postwar Japan, where he had not expected a place, a position, reserved for him. He assumed, and continues to assume, that a social position to be occupied by him, and his right to inclusion in the society, have long been canceled. Yet, without notice, he returned there much to his own embarrassment. He should not be there and his presence should not be accepted according to the rules of a supposedly renewed society. For some who returned from battlefields, their presence in postwar Japan seemed to demand an explanation, if not an apology, by which to redefine their existence and traumatic past, since there were, or should have been, no terms available in which their past and their existence in the present could at the same time be reconciled. In other words, they demanded that the defeat be made to signify such a threshold that they could only see a disjunctive alternative between Japan before its de-

feat and after ("kage ni wa nezumi no ashi hodo no ashi mo nai / kataashi
o kako ni, kataashi o mirai ni kakeru ashi ga nai" [The shadow has no feet,
no feet even as small as a rat's / no feet with one in the past and one in the
future]).[8] To affirm the present, thereby approving their survival and existence after the war, should have meant the denial of their past and life up
until August 15, 1945. At least they wished to believe so; they wished to
believe that Japanese society, as well as they themselves, could completely
change at that historical juncture.

However, under the new leadership, the same collectivity continued to
affirm its identity. It appeared that, despite mass publicity over the birth of
a new nation and a new age, the past was integrated into the present without causing much fundamental disruption to the system of collective representations. The past was apprehended in more or less the same manner.
Obviously, in their assessment, neither the change of leadership nor the
introduction of liberal ideology could constitute a historical discontinuity. Some, including the Arechi poets, observed that the purge of military
and political leaders and the alteration of political organization were not
enough: the fundamental change of "national consciousness," as some called
it, was absolutely necessary. Hence, on the part of the poets, what was
needed in order to create a critical perspective was the maintenance of the
sense of historical discontinuity. If such a historical discontinuity had not
actually taken place, then they had to sustain the fiction that it had occurred
and continue to write based on this fiction. Therefore, they had to reject
any enunciative position given in the existing system of representations
with which the poets would certainly feel familiarized. They refused to take
up a subjective position in the postwar society, not because they wished to
adhere to an old one but because what might have appeared to be a new
one was in fact no different than the old. This determination to refuse
underlies the following stanza by Tamura Ryūichi, another Arechi poet:

> wareware wa itoshii mono o korosanakereba naranai
> kore was shisha o yomigaeraseru tada hitotsu no michi de ari
> wareware wa sono michi o yukanakereba naranai[9]

We have to kill all those we are familiar with / this is the only road to the
revival of the dead / We must go on this road.

It was, then, imperative to deny any seductive gesture that would reduce the individuality of the poet as a radical Other to an other, an individual subject, who was accommodated within the continuing system of

collective representations. But as long as the poet works with language, this seems to be an impossible task since the utterance of words, when it forms a signification, necessarily posits him as a subject. Would he have to remain silent in order to guard his Otherness? The "solution" was the incorporation of death into poetic texts, not as an object of representation but as a structure or as a limit. This does not mean that the poet regarded himself merely as a testamentary executor, an agent who speaks on behalf of the dead. Allegedly, death here designates an absence, a strange presence of a void, in the present world. In this respect, it should be more accurate to say that the testamentary executor was determined to guard the silence of the dead rather than their words. What he was assigned to is not the task of monitoring whether the words of the dead will be properly observed and executed; instead, he was to announce to the present world that their will would never be comprehended; death must remain unintelligible and inaccessible; the dead ought not to be able to be integrated into the existing system of collective representations. In his characterization of postwar Japanese poetry, Ehara Tsurao refers to this fact from a different angle. The transformation of poetry, he says, reflects the historical process of the decomposition of collective consciousness.

> Fiction synthesizes the fragmented sense of everyday life [*danpen ni bunretsu shita seikatsu jikkan*] into some collectively shared whole, but such a synthesis is doomed to collapse, with the arrival of a new reality in everyday life. . . . it is inevitable that (poetic) sensitivity resists and tries to be freed from such an imposed fiction, and expresses its denial of a forged collective sympathy [*gisei teki kyôkan*] in many nonconformist ways.[10]

At first, poetry must gainsay the presumption that all experience is articulable and therefore can be comprehended collectively. Without any doubt, what Ehara calls "forged collective sympathy" arises from the necessity to sustain the authenticity of the system of collective representations in which whatever experience there may be presumably can be communicated. It presupposes that every experience can be tamed and shared: rupture, incommensurability, and conflict must be concealed. I must stress that it is not merely a question of whether the system of collective representations is in fact capable of dealing with every possible experience: it is primarily a matter of whether it is believed to be capable of doing that. Only when such an unfounded belief is challenged can poetry, as Ehara understands it, come into view. Therefore, the possibility of postwar poetry is closely linked to the poet's ability to resist the fiction of collective sympathy that inevitably reinforces that belief, since the "forged collective sympathy" is too often generated not by concrete incident but by its fantasies. Sympathy thus generated is completely closed up in the system of collective representations, and it is a representation of representation without any reference to the outside of the system. One can hardly imagine an occasion when such a sympathy calls in question and alters the existing system fundamentally.

For many of the postwar poets, the only *road* leading to the real experience, a sort of experience referring to the outside of the system, was to be found in their obsessive concern for the dead. However, it is also worth noting that, in their gesture of guarding the silence of the dead, the poets did not and could not identify themselves with the dead. Despite their pretense of speaking from the position of the dead, many times they pulled back from the temptation to fall into the trap of regarding themselves, without irony, as dead. Nakagiri Masao writes:

> shi ni tsuite hito ni kataru na/kemuri no gotoku kiesaru
> kotoba o kataru na/shi o omae wa mirukoto ga dekinai/sono toki
> soko ni aru mono wa hai ni suginai[11]

Do not speak to people about death / Do not speak words that disappear like smoke / You cannot look at death / When (you think you look at death), what you find there are ashes only.

For it is precisely the nature of death that one can never merge in the dead. Only on the condition that the dead be rendered a subject could one possibly identify with them. Because the dead is dead, it can never be a subject. In other words, the poet refuses to accept any fantasy in which the dead could be given a position within society, and integrated into the representation of its imagined whole.

Thus death means the very possibility of the outside or exteriority of a given system of collective representations because it is unrepresentable and untamable. At the same time, it refers to some site of realness, although it is never explicitly designated.

Many writers of postwar Japan attempted to reach this nonexisting site. Undoubtedly, I think, what was at stake in this almost self-defeating project was less the concern for their past than the concern for the future, a concern for the possibility of changing the existing system.

When placed among the works of postwar Japanese-language poetry, the statement "I am dead" brings to light the site of ambivalence toward which the voices of these poets seem to converge. On the one hand, the poets as individuals refused to merge in the dead, and thereby resisted the seductive lure of communion fantasy. In this sense, they knew too well that they were irredeemably separated from the dead. On the other hand, they sought to find a position that could be more or less identified with that of the dead. In such works as *1940 nendai. Natsu* (The 1940s. Summer) by Tamura Ryûichi, the wish to obtain the enunciative position of the dead reaches an almost unbearable intensity:

"ore wa mada ikite iru
shinda no wa ore no keiken na no da"
"ore no heya wa tozasarete iru shikashi
ore no kioku no isu to
ore no gen'ei no mado o
anata wa hitei dekiya shinai"
. . . .
wareware wa wareware no shinda keiken o maisô suru
wareware wa wareware no fushô shita gen'ei no sosei o yumemiru
. . . .
watashi wa kore ijô kizutsuku koto wa naideshô naznara
kizutsuku koto tada sono tame ni watashi no sonzai wa atta no dakara
watashi wa mô taoreru koto mo nai deshô nazette
hametsu suru koto sore ga watashi no yui'itsu no shudai na no dakara

"I am still alive. / It is my experience that died." / "My room is locked up. But / how can you deny a chair of my memory and / a window of my illusion" / . . . / We bury our own dead experience. / We dream of the resurrection of our own wounded illusion. / . . . / I will not be wounded anymore because / I have existed solely for the sake of being wounded / I will not fall down any more because / to perish is my only raison d'être.[12]

Here, as well as in many of Tamura's works, we find an unusually explicit use of pronouns—*wareware* (we), *ore* (I), *anata* (you), and so on. It is evident that the series of pronominal oppositions *wareware—ore, ore—anata, ore—watashi*, and so on, further articulates the relationships of the dead and the living. (The *ore—watashi* opposition is particularly important in that, while indicating a certain gender differentiation, it also alludes to an opposition of two civilizations, namely, Europe and Japan.) We can see from this example that the opposition of the dead and the living has to be articulated in more than one dimension. As is shown by the line "*wareware* wa *wareware* no shinda keiken o maisô suru" (We bury our own dead experience), this multiple articulation of the dead—the living opposition is expressed by the somewhat redundant use of pronouns and consequently by what may be termed "schizophrenic effect." The kind of expression in which *I* is separated from my experience or in which *I* watches *myself* bury *my own body* is repeatedly utilized. In addition, attention must be drawn to another aspect of this poem: the use of quotation marks articulates a different enunciative position. We cannot overlook the fact that *ore* appears only in quoted sentences. In this work, it is important to note that the *ore—wareware* opposition more or less coincides with the quoted—unquoted opposition.

These findings suggest that, at least at the level of syntax, the poet continually shifts his enunciative position, as a result of which he cannot have a single unified voice. What is remarkable about this poetic strategy is that the poet never addresses himself to the readership in a straightforward manner. Even in the poem "Hosoi sen" (Narrow line),[13] in which we may find a fairly simple and almost symmetrical opposition *kimi—boku*, the last stanza ("kimi wa gekitetsu o hiku! / boku wa kotoba no naka de shinu" [You pull the trigger! / I die in language.]) reverses the supposed stable composition *kimi-boku*. Since it is not in the external world but in language ("kotoba no naka de") that I die, death arrives not in that which is represented but in the very medium of representation. Accordingly, the opposition of *you* and *I* cannot be located at the level of that which is represented. In this respect, death arrives at the moment when the presumed correspondence between the represented and representation collapses. This means, by way of extension, that the pronominal oppositions, utilized in much postwar poetry, do not necessarily denote the human relations implied in the modes of address as we normally understand them.

Moreover, the very possibility of speaking from the position of the dead is given rise to by the fact that the poet does not have an identifiable enunciative position. The constant shift from one pronoun to another is the place from which his voice comes; the very fact that the poet is "schizophrenic," separated from himself, divided in himself, enables him to speak from the position of the dead. Therefore, the poet is a difference, a sliding move, between various positions referred to by pronouns rather than by a fixed identity constituted in the network of pronouns.

Perhaps this is best exemplified by the stylistic quality we often ascribe to some works of postwar poetry. Wittingly ignoring the wealth of rhetorical devices available in traditional Japanese poetry, some poets adhere to a stiff style that stresses the declarativeness of utterances. This is especially explicit in the early works of Tamura, many of which consist virtually of a series of declarative statements. In one of these works, "Maboroshi o miru hito" (Seer), for example, each stanza ends abruptly, thereby creating a vivid sense of the completion of signification. In such forms of sentence ending, utterances are presented as being finished and completed. On the one hand, a declarative ending constitutes the poet's gesture of refusal, a refusal to entertain any objection or agreement, as if the utterance had been terminated and the case closed. Probably this is a privilege to which only the dead are ultimately entitled: the dead are the ones at whom absolutely no objection can be directed, because they cannot and would not listen to it. On the other hand, a declarative ending engenders the sense of detachment in which those sentences are presented as objective and dehumanized, in the same way statements are put in a logic textbook or legal codes. In this kind of discourse, the speaker is universalized to such an extent that the one speaking is equated with a logician stripped of all attributes but his logical rationality in the case of the logic textbook, or to an abstract subject, the ultimate legal subject of the state, in the case of legal codes. Since it belongs to poetic texts, the declarative ending never reaches such extreme generality in Tamura's works. However, the sense of detachment remains prominent. The retrogressively imagined existence of the poet, or the subject of enunciation, seems erased from the textual surface of those works. The subject of the enunciated, whose presence is indicated by pronouns such as *ore* and *wareware*, appears unrelated to the poet in flesh and blood. Emotive and affective features often associated with the process of enunciation are carefully whittled down, although I do not claim that those works evoke no emotional response in the readership. Inevitably, we are solicited by this rupture, between the subjects of enunciation and the enunciated, to imagine a firm determination on the part of the poet never to submit himself to the temptation of autobiographical anecdotes. As many have remarked, it is precisely because of this quality that Tamura's works are said to carry the air of "transcendence."

Above all, the tendency to exclude the subject of enunciation also signifies an endeavor to reject the dependence of a poetic discourse on referents. By denouncing the somewhat elusive merger between the subjects of enunciation and the enunciated, which often happens in Japanese poetry, the poet expels the subject of enunciation to the blank space outside language. This is, of course, an attempt to discern what can be talked about from what cannot, and eventually to locate the source of the poet's voice outside the former: the poet speaks from outside language, or more specifically, outside the system of collective representations. Doubtless, this is also an answer to the impossible demand requiring the poet to be a testamentary executor who is to guard not the word, but the silence of the dead.

It is well known in literary criticism, as well as literature, that one's immediate and vivid impression turns pale as soon as it is enunciated and inscribed. In postwar Japanese poetry, it seems, the poets resumed writing after the defeat by abandoning any expectation that the past experience could be rendered as it was actually experienced. Instead, they produced works in which their own existence and past experience are presented as an absence, as a glaring void beyond the limits of the language. Thus, they gave an expression to their historical experience, encompassing both the past and the present, Japan at war and Japan after the defeat, the dead and the living. In their minds, however, these pairs form disjunctive alternatives in which the one ought to be rejected in favor of the other. Yet the incorporation of the disjunctive alternative as a whole was accomplished precisely because its equivalent can be found in the structure of enunciation. This is to say that poets utilized the disjunctive alternative intrinsic in enunciation, the radical rupture between the subjects of enunciation and the enunciated, in order to accommodate conflicting pairs in their poetic discourse. In the most straightforward manner, postwar poetry succeeded in embodying the essential negativity inherent in modern subjectivity insofar as the modern subject is structured around the principle of the undecidability of its self-identity.

According to the logic of postwar poetry, therefore, it was an ethical imperative to maintain the radical discontinuity that history itself imposed on poets in the form of the disjunctive alternative, and which they replaced by the radical rupture inherent in the process of enunciation. In other words, postwar poetry began with the recognition that neither the dead nor the subject of enunciation could return and be reconciled with the living, and the subject of the enunciated, respectively.

> watashi no shitai o chi ni nekasu na
> omaetachi no shi wa
> chi ni yasumu koto ga dekinai
> watashi no shitai wa
> ritsukan no naka ni osamete
> chokuritsu saseyo[14]

Do not lay down my corpse on the ground / Your death / can never rest on the ground / You must put / my corpse in a standing coffin. / Keep me standing straight.

Besides the carefully delineated oppositions of pronouns that I have already discussed, it is Tamura who most expressively postulates the radical discontinuity because of which the experience of the past could never be appropriated by and grafted onto the present. It is, indeed, a poetic strategy with the function of maintaining the past in such a way that it would continually objectify, estrange, and criticize the society in which the poets lived. For them, "chijô ni wa wareware no kuni ga nai / chijô ni wa wareware no shi ni atai suru kuni ga nai" (On earth, there is no country for us. / On earth, there is no country worthy of our death). One would overlook one of the most striking merits of this poem if these two lines are understood to express merely a disillusionment incurred by the defeat of the country. Just think of the opposite of the second line: "On earth, there is a country worthy of our death." This statement elucidates in its most primitive form the sentiment on which patriotism and the romantic notion of wars are based. Yet, the poet here is neither concerned with a criticism of patriotism nor with the denunciation of wars. The statement "On earth, there is a country worthy of our death" implies a certain form of discourse in which the dead, as the absolutely Other, are tamed and transformed into the concept of death. In order to say "one dies *for* the country," the fact of one's death must be substituted for the concept of death. At the same time, an individual who dies must be turned into a subject whose identity is constituted within the system of collective representations. Unless these conditions are met, how can we make sense out of "for" in "dying for the country"? Just as wartime poetry did, this statement idealizes death and turns it into an end in itself. For this very reason, we always find some romanticism about death in any patriotism. Before being a matter of politics in the narrow sense of the term, patriotism is, first and foremost, a matter of collective representations.

Hence, an inner consistency in postwar poetry is revealed when we relate that form of poetry to the issue of collective representations. The poet attempts to attack the *forged collective sympathy* that would never be there but for a blind faith in the system of collective representations. What is in question here should be all the more evident: one cannot talk about the experience of collective death; death always lies outside collectivity—it always constitutes the exterior. And patriotism pertains to the very device of displacement in terms of which the radical Otherness, the absolute exterior, of death is concealed and forgotten.

The hegemonic authenticity of collective representations, which would otherwise appear all-inclusive, natural, and transparent, is delimited and relativized by death. In the sense that it designates and demonstrates the fundamental inadequacy of the system, we can say that death is a critical experience, provided that it is never called an experience.

Death is crucial in two senses. First, it marks an ambivalent limit of collective representations. Yet we should not confuse this limit with the border dividing the inside and the outside of a collectivity. Any system of collective representations is fully equipped with devices that render the outside of a collectivity representable. In any system, its outside is always and already represented as an other, a symmetrical and reflective opposite to the self that sustains the putative representability of the self, and not as an Other, not as the otherness in the sense of an exteriority that cannot be captured in the synchronic systematicity of representability. In this regard, the outside and the boundary are harmoniously accommodated in the system, and do not necessarily jeopardize the assumed authenticity of collective representations. What we have called the absolute exterior can be spotted even within a collectivity when the totality of it is envisioned spatially. The exterior is neither a referent nor the outside of a group of referents. It reveals itself when an incommunicable phenomenon strikes us. We then become aware that the existing system of representations is not adequate, nor as reliable as we are led to believe. Its limit is exposed and the system of collective representations can be said to be *in crisis*. Thus, death is capable of bringing forth a *critical* situation when it is not masked.

Second, death is critical in the sense that it elucidates the fundamental mechanism of the working of collective representations. The splitting of the subjects of enunciation and the enunciated, which also implies the death of the subject, is the fundamental principle without which one cannot posit oneself as a subject, as I have argued. Thus death elucidates the following two issues at the same time: in order for the system of collective representations to work at all, it inevitably introduces the split and excludes the subject of enunciation from its representation, on the one hand, which means that one can never fully identify oneself with a subject position defined in the system. On the other hand, the very authenticity of that system depends on the imagined correspondence between the subjects of enunciation and the enunciated, which is supposed to be an adequate one. But this sense of adequacy can only be sustained as long as the loss, disappearance, and death that necessarily occur in enunciation are concealed. It is for this reason that, unless death is concealed and displaced, the system of collective representations cannot claim its authenticity.

What postwar Japanese poetry has achieved, or tried to achieve, is the incorporation of these two aspects of death into poetic language so as to create a critical perspective. It is not aimed at changing any particular political institution. Yet it constitutes a social action or historical praxis precisely because it is designed to change the system of collective representations that underlies all the political and social transactions. If what we conventionally call political action is constituted in terms of circulations of economic, social, and cultural values within the existing channels of social exchange, this kind of historical praxis can hardly be subsumed under the title of the political: it should be called apolitical.[15]

Only when it is understood as an attempt to change the conditions for political action can we see its historicality. By virtue of the fact that it cannot be apprehended in conventional historical terms, it is a historical praxis/practice par excellence. To appreciate this point, one only need refer to Hegelian history, in which the dead are in the final analysis a historical nutrition that necessarily is consumed and preserved in the process of progress. The situation does not basically change in other forms of chronological history, no matter how explicitly historians claim to be free from the idea of progress.[16] No matter how solemnly and respectfully the dead are worshiped by the nation, they are historical nutrients serving the spirit as long as they do not lead us to a historical praxis beyond the economic rationality of the existing system.

This, I think, is what the presence of the texts by postwar Japanese poets forces us to face.

Notes

FOREWORD

1 Naoki Sakai, *Voices of the Past: The Status of Language in Eighteenth-Century Japanese Discourse* (Ithaca, N.Y., and London: Cornell University Press, 1991), pp. 104–5.

2 I am adapting here from Ann Curthoys and Stephen Muecke, "Australia, for Example," in Wayne Hudson and David Carter, eds., *The Republicanism Debate* (Kensington: New South Wales University Press, 1993), pp. 177–200, adapting in turn from Giorgio Agamben, *The Coming Community*, trans. Michael Hardt (Minneapolis: University of Minnesota Press, 1993), pp. 9–11.

3 Gilles Deleuze and Félix Guattari, *A Thousand Plateaus: Capitalism and Schizophrenia*, trans. Brian Massumi (Minneapolis: University of Minnesota Press, 1987), pp. 327–50.

4 Sakai, *Voices of the Past*, p. 101.

5 For example, David Harvey writes in this way of opacity throughout *The Condition of Postmodernity: An Inquiry into the Origins of Cultural Change* (Oxford: Blackwell, 1989).

6 Eve Kosofsky Sedgwick, *Epistemology of the Closet* (Berkeley and Los Angeles: University of California Press, 1990), p. 100.

7 Robert Hughes, *Culture of Complaint: The Fraying of America* (New York and Oxford: Oxford University Press, 1993).

8 Ibid., p. 96.

9 *Voices of the Past*, p. 106.

INTRODUCTION

1 Naoki Sakai, *Voices of the Past: The Status of Language in Eighteenth-Century Japanese Discourse* (Ithaca, N.Y.: Cornell University Press, 1991). All Japanese names appear with the surname followed by the first name.

2 In his brilliant work on Joesph Jacotot (*The Ignorant Schoolmaster*, trans. Kristin Ross [Stanford, Calif.: Stanford University Press, 1991]), an exiled schoolteacher who taught in French to Flemish students who knew no French during the age to which

nowadays we often ascribe the emergence of the nation-states, Jacques Rancière argues that what brings people together is not aggregation. On the contrary, "One can say, if one likes, that truth brings together. But what brings *people* together, what unites them, is nonaggregation. Let's rid ourselves of the representation of the social cement that hardened the thinking minds of the postrevolutionary age. People are united because they are people, that is to say, *distant* beings. Language does not unite them. On the contrary, it is the arbitrariness of language that makes them try to communicate by forcing them to translate—but also puts them in a community of intelligence" (p. 58; emphasis in the original).

3 See Jacques Derrida's argument in his well-known article on psychoanalysis and Poe's *The Purloined Letter*: "The remaining structure of the letter is that—contrary to what the Seminar says in its last words ('what the "purloined letter," that is, the not delivered letter means is that a letter always arrives at its destination.')—a letter can always not arrive at its destination. Its 'materiality' and 'topology' are due to its divisibility, its always possible partition" ("Le Facteur de la Vérité," in *The Post Card*, trans. Alan Bass [Chicago: University of Chicago Press, 1987], pp. 443–44). It is because the message can always *not arrive* that addressing is possible.

4 Jean-Luc Nancy, *The Inoperative Community*, trans. Peter Connor, Lisa Garbus, Michael Holland, and Simona Sawhney (Minneapolis: University of Minnesota Press, 1991), p. 4.

5 "To grasp the genuine relationship between an original and a translation requires an investigation analogous to the argumentation by which a critique of cognition would have to prove the impossibility of an image theory. There it is a matter of showing that in cognition there could be no objectivity, not even a claim to it, if it dealt with images of reality; here it can be demonstrated that no translation would be possible if in the ultimate essence it strove for likeness to the original" (Walter Benjamin, "The Task of the Translator," in *Illuminations*, trans. Harry Zohn [New York: Schocken Books, 1969], p. 73).

6 For an elucidation of the disparity between the two radically differing registers of "community" and "communication," see the following: "It is a community in that Bataille immediately communicates to me the pain and the pleasure that result from the impossibility of communicating anything at all without touching the limit where all meaning [*sens*] spills out of itself, like a simple ink stain on a word, on the word 'meaning.'

"This spilling and this ink are the ruin of theories of 'communication,' of the conventional chatter that attempts to promote reasonable exchange and serves only to obscure violence, betrayal, and lies, leaving no possibility of measuring oneself against powerful follies. But the reality of community, where nothing is shared without also being removed from this kind of 'communication,' has already, always, revealed the vanity of such discourses. They communicate only the postulation of the communication of a 'meaning,' and of the meaning of 'communication.' Bataille, beyond and sometimes apart from what he says, communicates community itself—that is, naked existence, naked writing, and the silent, haunting referral of the one to the other, which makes us share meaning's nakedness: neither gods nor thoughts, but the *us* that is imperceptibly and insuperably *exscribed*" (Jean-Luc Nancy, "Exscription," in *The Birth to Presence*, trans. Brian Holmes et al. [Stanford, Calif.: Stanford University Press, 1993], pp. 319–20; emphasis in the original).

7 "To write, and to read, is to be exposed, to expose oneself, to this not-having (to this non-knowledge) and thus to 'exscription.' The exscribed is exscribed from the very first word, not as an 'inexpressible' or as an 'uninscribable' but, on the contrary, as writing's opening, within itself, to itself, to its own inscription as the infinite discharge of meaning—in all the senses in which we must understand the expression" (ibid., p. 338).

8 In order to fail, we must work. When we do not address, we cannot even fail to communicate. Only in the work, therefore, can we fail. Thus, says Jean-Luc Nancy, "What is exposed in the work, or through the works, begins and ends infinitely within and beyond the work—within and beyond the operative concentration of the work: there where what we have called up to now men, gods, and animals are themselves exposed to one another through an exposition that lies at the heart of the work and that gives us the work at the same time as it dissolves its concentration, and through which the work is offered up to the infinite communication of community" ("Literary Communism," in *The Inoperative Community*, p. 73).

9 Rancière, *The Ignorant Schoolmaster*, p. 64.

10 With regard to the limits of the theories of translation, Jacques Derrida poses the following questions: "Let us note one of the limits of the theories of translation. They treat passages from one language to another too much and do not adequately consider the possibility for languages to be implicated into more than two [*à plus de deux*] in one text. How do you translate a text written in plural languages at the same time? How do you 'render' the effect of plurality? And if we translate by plural languages at the same time, will we call it translation?" ("Des tours de Babel," in *Psyché* [Paris: Galilée, 1987], pp. 207–8; emphasis in the original).

11 Roman Jakobson, "On Linguistic Aspects of Translation," in *Selected Writings*, vol. 2 (The Hague and Paris: Mouton, 1971), p. 261. As I have argued, there is no reason why translation must be understood to be interlingual translation (Sakai, *Voices of the Past*, pp. 211–39). To use Jakobson's terminology, the distinction between intralingual and interlingual translations cannot be sustained unless the economy of transmutation is captured in a specific regime of intersemiotic (or intertextual) correlation, that is, in a regime I call phonocentrism. Where there is no phonocentrism, intralingual and interlingual translations can hardly be distinguished.

12 For discussion of framing and subjectivity, see Sakai, *Voices of the Past*, pp. 113–207.

13 Émile Benveniste, *Problems in General Linguistics*, trans. Mary Elizabeth Meek (Coral Gables: University of Florida Press, 1971), p. 224.

14 This phrase with an apparent resonance with modern mathematics is from Nishida Kitarô (1870–1945). In conceptualizing social praxis and self-awareness (*jikaku*), Nishida appealed to the mathematical formulation of discontinuity. Following the tradition of modern philosophy since Leibniz and Kant, he conceived of the formation of the practical subject after the model of differential calculus but at the singular point of discontinuity. Therefore, for Nishida, as his later formulation clearly shows, the constitution of the subject in ethical action is also the poiesis or making of the social formation. "Hirenzoku no renzoku" (or continuity of discontinuity) thus suggests the possibility of conceptualizing the constitution of the subject at the site of the incommensurate in the social. See "Genjitsu no sekai no ronri-teki kôzô" or "the logical structure of the real world" (1934), in *Nishida Kitarô Zenshû*, vol. 7 (Tokyo: Iwanami Shoten, 1965) pp. 217–304, and "Sekai no jiko dôitsu to renzoku" or "the self-identity of the world and continuity" (1935), in ibid., vol. 8, pp. 7–106.

15 The split cannot be contained only in the cases of translation, for, as Briankle Chang suggests, the putative unities of the addresser and the addressee can hardly be sustained because the addresser himself is split and multiple, as is figuratively illustrated by the Plato-Socrates doublet in Derrida's "Envoi" in *The Post Card* (pp. 1–256). With regard to communication in general, Chang argues, "Because both delivery and signing are haunted by the same structural threat of the message's nonarrival or *a*destination, the paradox of the signature also invades communication. Communication occurs only insofar as the delivery of the message *may* fail; that is, communication takes place only to the extent that there is a separation between the sender and receiver, and this separation, this distance, this *spacing*, creates the possibility for the message *not* to arrive" (Briankle G. Chang, *Deconstructing Communication* [Minneapolis: University of Minnesota Press, 1996], p. 216).

16 Putting forth a different conception of continuity in discontinuity, Tanabe Hajime, who like his mentor Nishida based his argument on insights from modern mathematics, insisted that social formation in general is infinitely divisible and that a society cannot be conceived of as a homogeneous and harmonious unity. On the contrary, a society always contains an infinite number of societies, and every society consists of discontinuities and conflicts. What unites a society into one is not naturally given. Even an ethnic society, he argued, is not a given unity. Whether racial, ethnic, or national, no identity is naturally given and every identity has to be socially constructed through the dialectic process of negativity. See *"Shakai sonzai no ronri"* or "the logic of social beings," in *Tanabe Hajime Zenshū*, vol. 6 (Tokyo: Chikuma Shobo, 1963), pp. 51–168, and *"Shu no ronri to sekai zushiki"* or "the logic of the species and the schema 'world,'"* in ibid., pp. 299–397.

It is important to keep in mind that Nishida and Tanabe both offered philosophical formulas by which to undermine the validity of ethnic nationalism and to legitimate the unity of the Japanese Empire against the implicit threat of anticolonial ethnic separatism. I am most critical of the philosophical discourses of Nishida Kitarô and Tanabe Hajime, two champions of what is usually referred to as the Kyoto School of Philosophy. But my critique of their philosophical formation is not premised on an assumption that their philosophy was primarily concerned with the justification of Japanese ethnic and cultural nationalism. On the contrary, I characterize theirs primarily as a universalistic philosophy of an imperial nationalism, and only secondarily as an ethnic nationalism in the sense that every universalism that does not denounce imperialism is inherently ethnocentric.

17 For example, Willard V. O. Quine's hypothesis of the radical translation, from which all the help of the interpreter is excluded, suffers from this retrospectivism. If there is no help of the interpreter, is it possible to recognize "a language of a hitherto untouched people"? See Willard V. O. Quine, *Word and Object* (Cambridge: MIT Press, 1960), pp. 26–80.

18 For a more detailed discussion about "feeling" and difference, see chapter 4, note 7. And for the poetic aspect of "feeling," see Gilles Deleuze, *Difference and Repetition*, trans. Paul Patton (New York: Columbia University Press, 1994), pp. 291ff.

19 Here let me draw attention to the notions of representation, concept, difference without concept, and conceptual difference, according to Gilles Deleuze. "The relation of a concept to its object under this double aspect, in the form that it assumes in this memory and this self-consciousness, is called representation" (ibid., p. 11).

". . . every determination is conceptual in the last instance, or actually belongs to the comprehension of a concept"(ibid., p. 12). "In so far as it serves as a determination, a predicate must remain fixed in the concept while becoming something else in the thing (animal becomes something other in man and in horse; humanity something other in Peter and in Paul). This is why the comprehension of the concept is infinite; having become other in the thing, the predicate is like the object of another predicate in the concept. But this is also why each determination remains general or defines a resemblance, to the extent that it remains fixed in the concept and applicable by right to an infinity of things" (ibid.). "Thus, the principle of difference understood as difference in the concept does not oppose but, on the contrary, allows the greatest space possible for the apprehension of resemblances. Even from the point of view of conundrums, the question "What difference is there?" may always be transformed into: "What resemblance is there?" But above all, in classification, the determination of species implies and supposes a continual evaluation of resemblances" (ibid.). "Repetition thus appears as difference without a concept, repetition which escapes indefinitely continued conceptual difference" (ibid., p. 13).

CHAPTER 1: DISTINGUISHING LITERATURE AND THE
WORK OF TRANSLATION: THERESA HAK KYUNG CHA'S *DICTÉE*
AND REPETITION WITHOUT RETURN

1 Originally delivered on August 26, 1996, at the thirteenth congress of the International Comparative Literature Association in Tokyo. This article was translated into Japanese by Onoda Toshiya and Matsui Miho and published in *Shisô*, no. 859 (January 1996): 250–78.

2 Perhaps, one of the best representations of the International World can be found in the idea of the pluralistic "World History" (*tagenteki sekaishi*) put forth by Japanese philosophers during the 1930s. Literature as a discipline is in complicity with the International World, as James Snead succinctly demonstrated: "We are familiar enough with the practice whereby literary history or literary canons stand in for a notion of national spirit or character. . . . This tendency would valorize particular national authors not just to the extent that they speak for themselves or for their 'race', but also to the extent that that they speak for 'mankind'. Authors such as Homer, Dante, Rabelais, Cervantes, Shakespeare, and Goethe are often seen as 'consummate geniuses' of a given national spirit, or 'founding fathers' of their respective national literatures, yet ultimately attract even greater interest because they seem in some way to have embodied 'universal truths'" ("European Pedigrees/African Contagions," in *Nation and Narration*, ed. Homi K. Bhabha [London and New York: Routledge, 1990], p. 233). In a similar vein, I discuss the codependency of the particular (the national) and the universal (the international or imperialist) in reference to the pluralistic World History in chapter 5 of this volume.

3 Leonard Forster, *The Poet's Tongues: Multilingualism in Literature* (Cambridge: Cambridge University Press, 1970); Chinua Achebe, *A Man of the People* (London: William Heinemann, 1966).

4 Although I have translated this term into "topos" in the past, I have decided to translate the term *basho*, coined by Nishida Kitarô (1870–1945), into "khoraic place." Borrowing from Plato's "khora" and Aristotelian "hypokeimenon," Nishida attempted to introduce this term *basho* to explicate the construction of subjectivity in judg-

ment, consciousness, will, and praxis. *Basho* is explained as the "plane of predicative determination" on or against which the subject, or *shugo* in the sense of propositional subject, is posited. Therefore, *basho* is that which enables judgment (in which onto- logical determination in the combination of subject-predicate takes place), will (in which the agent of ethical action is problematized), and historical praxis (in which the agent of historical manufacture of institutions such as national subjectivity is problematized), but which remains unthematized (not molded into a subject). See Nishida Kitarô, *Nishida Kitarô Zenshû*, (Tokyo: Iwanami Shoten, 1965), vol. 4: *Hataraku mono kara miru mono e*; vol. 5: *Ippansha no jikakuteki taikei*; vol. 6: *Mu no jikakuteki gentei*. Nishida's dialectic is distinct from Hegel's because of its critique of sub- jectivism (*sugoshugi*), which views the subject as the agent of historical change and also as the locus of logic and knowledge in general. Nishida proposes predicativism (*jutsugoshugi*), which locates the agent of judgment, will, and praxis at the predicate. Nevertheless, as it can be seen from the initial definition of *basho*, which also implied "hypokeimenon" (sub-jectum), Nishida's dialectic had never severed its alliance with the obsession with the subject. His exposition of *basho* seemed to remain as- similationist, particularly in its optimistic assumption about the state's ability con- tinuously to manufacture the Japanese subject out of the heterogeneous. It is exactly such an optimistic—optimistic from the viewpoint of the imperialist administrators and *senbukôsakuin* (colonial public-relations officials), but pessimistic from the view- point of the colonized—that *Dictée* seems to decompose.

5 The problematic exception is Chinese literature in Japanese academia. But, until the 1930s, Chinese literature did not include works by modern Chinese writers. It is important to note that the study of modern Chinese literature immediately led to the inquiry about the role of Japanese imperialism in China.

6 See Naoki Sakai, *Voices of the Past: The Status of Language in Eighteenth-Century Japanese Discourse* (Ithaca, N.Y.: Cornell University Press, 1991), pp. 208–319.

7 Suzuki Akira, *Hanareya gakkun*, in *Nihon shisô taikei*, vol. 51 (Tokyo: Iwanami Shoten, 1971), pp. 361–405.

8 Ibid., p. 387.

9 "After all, *bungaku* is the residence of the Way. One who has familiarized oneself with the Way which resides in *bungaku* through the learning of *bungaku* is called the man of the Way. And one who has installed in one's own body the ability to practice the Way is called a man of virtue" (ibid., p. 373).

10 See Nishida Kitarô, "*Poieshisu to purakushisu* [Poiesis and praxis]" (originally published in *Shisô*, no. 223 [December 1940]; reprinted in *Nishida Kitarô Zenshû*, vol. 10, pp. 124–76 [Tokyo: Iwanami Shoten, 1965]). Two different Japanese translations of the term "subject" are *shukan* and *shutai*. I adopted the adjectival form of the latter, "*shutai-teki.*" "One may automatically assume that poiesis or technology is immediately *shukan-teki* [subjective in the epistemological sense]. But . . . what may appear simply techno- logical, such as the building of a house, is possible only upon the relevant historical substratum, whereas what may appear unrelated to technology, such as language, must in fact be constituted technologically. It goes without saying that society can- not exist without language. Hence, our dialogue or conversation here and now is al- ready a historical manufacturing act [*rekishi-teki keisei sayô*], and it therefore is a matter of technology. . . . Technology requires dexterity. Dexterity means the historical formation of the individual's habits. However, the habits are not formed by the indi-

vidual's subjective [*shukan-teki*] act: they are formed as historical manufacturing acts. Otherwise, we would never be able to manufacture anything by those habits. Our habits, therefore, are the habits of the historical world" (*Nishida Kitarô Zenshû*, vol. 10, p. 135). "Praxis in its proper sense means a human being's acting with a human being as the ultimate objective of his or her action. It is also an act by which the self becomes itself. In praxis our self is effected; in praxis the self is born. Therefore, praxis can be regarded as a poiesis in which our self is manufactured" (ibid., p. 142). The difference between *shukan* and *shutai* lies in the fact that *shukan* is merely the subject of knowing, whereas *shutai* is invariably the agent of praxis who also manufactures itself for itself. Thus, subjective or *shutai-teki* technology is the kind of technology by which the subject manufactures itself through praxis. This is why I claim that both *bungaku* and translation are subjective or *shutai-teki* technologies par excellence.

11 In *Dictée*, no explanation can be found of this photograph, but it is fairly well known in Japan and Korea that these characters were discovered on the wall of a building at Toyosu Coal Mine in northern Kyushu. They were believed to be inscribed there during the Fifteen-Year Asian-Pacific War by those workers involuntarily recruited from Korea by the Japanese government. Recently, however, some doubt has been cast about their historical credibility.

12 Theresa Hak Kyung Cha, *Dictée* (New York: Tanam Press, 1982), pp. 8–9. In the original, "francais" in the phrase "Traduire en francais" does not have a cedilla (ç).

13 Ibid., p. 13.

14 J. L. Austin, *How to Do Things with Words* (Cambridge: Harvard University Press, 1962), p. 95.

15 Ibid.

16 Cha, *Dictée*, p. 81.

17 Ibid., p. 1.

18 John R. Searle, *Speech Acts* (Cambridge: Cambridge University Press, 1969), p. 74.

19 It is important not to reduce the difference between what one says and what one means to say immediately to the generality of the so-called deconstruction that is inherent in any textuality, although it is not difficult to show that the inside and the outside of the sphere of what Searle takes to be the property and propriety of English language are always contaminating each other.

20 Cha, *Dictée*, pp. 61–75. Particularly important are the illustrations on page 74.

21 Ibid., p. 69.

22 See Sakai, *Voices of the Past*, pp. 106–11 and 134–38, for more detailed discussions of the problematics of framing and the body of enunciation.

23 Theresa Hak Kyung Cha's ethnic identity has often been picked up as a cue to some reductionism.

24 Here I follow the classical use of the term "schema." A foreign language that we do not know can be subsumed under what Kant called an "object in the idea." According to Kant, "There is a great difference between something being given to my reason as an object absolutely, or merely as an object in the idea. In the former case our concepts are employed to determine the object; in the latter case there is in fact only a schema for which no object, not even a hypothetical one, is directly given, and which only enables us to represent to ourselves other objects in an indirect manner, namely in their systematic unity, by means of their relation to this idea" (Immanuel Kant, *Critique of Pure Reason*, trans. Norman Kemp Smith [New York: St.

Martin's Press, 1929], p. 550 [A670, B698]). "The idea is thus really only heuristic, not an ostensive concept. It does not show us how an object is constituted, but how, under its guidance, we should seek to determine the constitution and connection of the objects of experience" (ibid., p. 551 [A671, B699]).

In his reading of Heidegger (*Zushiki "jikan" kara zushiki "sekai" e* [From the schema "time" to the schema "world"], in *Testugaku Kenkyû*, no. 200 [1932], and *Shu no ronri to zushiki sekai* [The logic of species and schema-world], in *Tetsugaku Kenkyû*, nos. 235, 236, and 237 [1935]), Tanabe Hajime attempted to introduce the term "schema-world." For the development of philosophical argument about the schematism and "schema-world" during the 1930s, see my article "Subject and Substratum: On Specific Identity and Cultural Difference in Japanese Imperial Nationalism," in *Positions* (forthcoming).

25 This is what is suggested by Homi K. Bhabha's use of the "analytic of cultural differ- ence.": "The analytic of cultural difference intervenes to transform the scenario of articulation—not simply to disturb the rationale of discrimination. It changes the position of enunciation and the relations of address within it; not only what is said but from where it is said; not simply the logic of articulation but the topos of enun- ciation" (Bhabha, "DissemiNation," in *Nation and Narration*, p. 312).

26 In the first of the two historical fronts, subjective technology was aimed at manu- facturing patriotic subjects for the Great Japanese Empire, or "Emperor's babies" who would wittingly misrecognize the emperor as their mother or wet-nurse figure, out of the population in the Korean peninsula. To say that *Dictée* somewhat undoes this technology, it is necessary to risk a certain anachronism, an anachronism pro- duced by the historical delay between the implementation of this subjective tech- nology prior to 1945 and its unexpected consequence, that is, the birth of Theresa Hak Kyung Cha as a writer in exile. In this chapter, I am concerned with an anachro- nistic contextualization in which the historical consequence criticizes the condi- tions of its origin retrospectively.

27 The term "unwork" is borrowed from Jean-Luc Nancy's *désœuvrement* in *The Inoper- ative Community*, trans. Peter Connor, Lisa Garbus, Michael Holland, and Simona Sawhney (Minneapolis: University of Minnesota Press, 1991).

28 As to the scapegoating violence spurted by the marginal's excessive identification with the mainstream and the penetrating critique of such a violence, see John Okada, *No No Boy* (San Francisco: Combined Asian American Resources Project, 1976).

29 See Philippe Lacoue-Labarthe, *Typography*, trans. Christopher Fynsk (Cambridge: Harvard University Press, 1989), pp. 139–207.

30 Cha, *Dictée*, p. 45.

31 Ibid.

32 Ibid.

33 Bhabha, "DissemiNation."

34 For example: "Immaterial now, and formless, having surrendered to dissolution limb by limb, all parts that compose a body. Liquid and marrow once swelled the muscle and bone, blood made freely the passages through innumerable entries, all give will- ingly to exile. From the introit, preparation is made for communion when the in- habitation should occur, of this body, by the other body, the larger body.

"Stands now, empty column of artery, of vein, fixed in stone. Void of wing. Void of hands, feet. It continues. This way. It should, with nothing to alter or break the full- ness, nothing exterior to impose upon the plenitude of this void" (Cha, *Dictée*, p. 161).

35 Ibid., p. 37. It should be mentioned that this is a retrospective imagining, from the viewpoint of one who missed the opportunity of dying "in time," of the death one could have died. But it is because of the retrospective time inherent in this imagining, which is almost always accompanied by some sense of guilt as well as the yearning for assimilation into the whole, that one's own death can be thematized as a sacrificial devotion that is believed to serve to integrate a part (an individual) into the whole (the nation). It is also important to note that the idealization of patriotic death as celebrated here is counterposed by the following: "The 'enemy.' One's enemy. Enemy nation. Entire nation against the other entire nation. One people exulting the suffering institutionalized on another. The enemy becomes abstract. The nation the enemy the name becomes larger than its own identity. Larger than its own measure. Larger than its own properties. Larger people than its own signification. For this people. For the people who is their enemy. For the people who is their ruler's subject and their ruler's victory.

"Japan has become the sign. The alphabet. The vocabulary. To this enemy people. The meaning is the instrument, memory that pricks the skin, stabs the flesh, the volume of blood, the physical substance blood as measure, that rests as record, as document. Of this enemy people" (p. 32). The nation of the colonizers is not merely the people's enemy. The profound injury of colonialism can be detected in the fact that, even after independence, people's life is prescribed by the legacy of the enemy. "Japan has become the sign. The alphabet. The vocabulary." The enemy nation is no longer external, but it has been internalized by the people themselves, so that the abhorrence of their enemy will in due time return to haunt them in the form of self-hatred. For this reason, one cannot help abhorring the enemy people all the more. Colonialism never ends with the retreat of the colonizers.

36 Ibid., p. 161.

CHAPTER 2: THE PROBLEM OF "JAPANESE THOUGHT": THE FORMATION OF "JAPAN" AND THE SCHEMA OF COFIGURATION

1 The original version of this article was written in Japanese for the second volume of *Iwanami Kôza: Shakai Kagaku no Hôhô* (Iwanami lecture series: methods of social sciences), ed. Yamanouchi Yasushi et al. (Tokyo: Iwanami Shoten, 1993), pp. 1–37.

2 Kaji Nobuyuki, *Chûgoku kenkyû kara mita nihon shisôshi kenkyû* (The study of the history of Japanese thought from the viewpoint of Chinese studies); (Tokyo: Yoshikawa Kôbunkan, 1985), p. 1.

3 Watsuji Tetsurô (1889–1960), *Zoku Nihon Seishin-shi Kenkyû*, in *Watsuji Tetsurô Zenshû*, vol. 4 (Tokyo: Iwanami Shoten, 1965), p. 281 (original in 1935). Watsuji equates the Japanese spirit thus identified with the subject of the Japanese ethnos or nation (*minzoku*). See pp. 298–301.

4 Ibid., p. 282.

5 In philosophical discourse in the 1930s in Japan, the difference between the Japanese national *subject* and the *ethnic community* as the Japanese nation was often discussed in terms of the difference between *subject* (*shutai*) and *substratum* (*kitai*). The subject can never come into being unless the substratum is self-reflectively negated, that is, rationalized. As will be seen when I come back to this point in discussing Tanabe Hajime's "Schema 'World,'" self-reflective negation whereby an ethnic community or communities constitutes a nation should be mediated by a certain schematism. It

is worth while noting that, unlike Tanabe, Watsuji completely obliterates this distinction. As we will see later, Maruyama deliberately follows this dialectic process of negation/self-reflection from an ethnic community to a nation.

6 Tsuda Sôkichi (1873–1961), *Nihon Shisô Keisei no Katei* (The process of the formation of Japanese thought), in *Tsuda Sôkichi Zenshû*, vol. 21 (Tokyo: Iwanami Shoten, 1965), p. 151 (original in 1934).

7 Tosaka Jun (1900–45): "*Ketsuron o arakajime kateishiteokukoto wa mottomo guainoî ronpô da* [The most convenient argument in which the conclusion is the supposition from the outset]," in *Nihon ideologî-ron* (Tokyo: Iwanami Shoten, 1977), p. 27 (original in 1935). Tosaka's critique bases itself on the distinction between "the system of categories for actuality [*genjitsuteki na hanchû soshiki*]" and "the system of categories for interpretation [*kaishakuyô no hanchû soshiki*]." He understands hermeneutics rather too narrowly, and did not pay attention to the poietic function of interpretation. It seems that his critique of hermeneutics is inadequate in this respect.

8 Tsuda, *Nihon Shisô Keisei no Katei*, p. 157.

9 In a lucid and extremely perceptive analysis of a similar situation in the case of Chinese modernity, Rey Chow argues: "The identification with an ethnic or 'national' history, and the pain and pleasure that this involves, cannot be understood simply in terms of 'nativism.' The spectator is not simply ethnic but *ethnicized*: the recognition of her 'Chineseness' is already part of the process of cross-cultural interpellation that is at work in the larger realm of modern history" (*Woman and Chinese Modernity: The Politics of Reading between West and East* [Minneapolis: University of Minnesota Press, 1991], p. 25). "The point must be emphasized, especially from the position of those that are feminized and ethnicized: these identificatory acts are the sites of productive relations that should be reread with the appropriate degree of complexity. This complexity lies not only in the identification with the ethnic culture, but also in the strong sense of complicity with the 'dismembering' process that structure those imaginings in the first place. For instance, the Chinese person obsessed with China emotionally is not necessarily one that would dress and live in a 'Chinese' manner, as any superficial acquaintance with 'Westernized' Chinese would reveal. Unlike what Oriental things still are to many Europeans and Americans, 'Western things' to a Chinese person are never merely dispensable embellishments; their presence has for the past century represented the necessity of fundamental adaptation and acceptance. It is the permanence of imprints left by the contact with the West that should be remembered even in an ethnic culture's obsession with 'itself'" (p. 27; emphasis in the original).

10 "*Waga kokumin shisô*" is part of the title of a famous history by Tsuda Sôkichi, *Bungaku ni arawaretaru waga kokumin shisô no kenkyû* (Study of our national thought as expressed in literature); my emphasis.

11 In his rather sympathetic critique of Heidegger's *Kant and the Problem of Metaphysics*, Tanabe Hajime (1885–62) attempted to replace the schema of "time" with that of "the world" that he adopted from Minkowski ("Zushiki 'jikan' kara zushiki 'sekai' e" [From the schema "time" to the schema "world"], *Tanabe Hajime Zenshû*, vol. 6 [Tokyo: Chikuma Shobô, 1963], pp. 1–49 [original in 1932]) as a preliminary step toward his own philosophy of practice, which would eventually be called "the logic of species" (*shu no ronri*). Although Tanabe enthusiastically endorsed Heidegger's project to read Kant's first critique as a laying of the ground for metaphysics, he stressed

that the Heideggerian project did not pay due attention to the social aspect of historicity. Let me summarize his critique of Heidegger's Kant book as follows: (1) Heidegger failed to take into account the mutual contamination and mutual negation of the forms of inner sense and outer sense and the social dimension of the schematism that should mediate not only sensibility and spontaneity but also the other and the self. (2) The transcendence of *Dasein* must also be grasped as a transcendence to the "other." Hence, Kantian empirico-transcendental doubling of the subject must be understood in terms of the two moments, temporality and spatiality. When the subject is able to negate itself in its praxis, it can represent itself through the schema of time. But when it cannot *freely* negate itself, it has to represent itself through the schema of space. And time and space are mediated in what Tanabe calls "the Schema world," in which time and space are sythesized by mutually negating each other. Therefore, if social and historical conditions do not allow the subject to transcend itself through its essential freedom, it would be forced to represent itself in spatial terms. Thus, as a result of the spatial schematism, the subject must also be understood *spatially* as doubling of the self and the other as opposing particularities that assume the synthesis of the self and the other by the self as universality. In other words, the subject is not merely an ekstatic movement of the self to its self: the self-affection must also be a consequence of the othering of the self through spatial schematism when its essential negativity—that is, freedom—is repressed, because the subject can come into being through the othering and externalization of its corporeality or its *substratum* (*kitai*). (3) Therefore, the schema that mediates sensible intuition and conceptual spontaneity must be neither time nor space but the world in which time and space are mutually negated and mediated.

Such a viewpoint would indeed lead to the issue of spatialization of historical time. In "From the schema 'time' to the schema 'world,'" Tanabe did not discuss the international dimension of the schema "world," but in "*Shu no ronri to sekai zushiki*" (The logic of the species and the schema "world") (*Tanabe Hajime Zenshû*, vol. 6, pp. 169–264), which he published three years later, he already discussed the subject in terms of the nation-state.

12 See Martin Heidegger, *Kant and the Problem of Metaphysics*, trans. Richard Taft (Bloomington: Indiana University Press, 1990), pp. 60–76 (original in 1929). Of course, Heidegger does not discuss translation in this book, and Kantian schematism concerns itself with the subsumption of the manifold of senses under the pure concept of understanding.

13 This is what is implied by Tanabe's "schema world," in which time and space are mutually negated and thereby *mediated*. Tanabe explains the mutual negation of time and space with regard to his concept of the species as follows: "So, by the spatiality of the species, which suppresses its temporality and keeps its mobility at minimum level, I mean, in short, that the past represses the future and arrests its movement. Thus, as room for absolute negativity of the present diminishes, temporality disappears as well" ("*ronri no shakai sonzairon-teki kôzô*," in *Tanabe Hajime Zenshû*, vol. 6 [Tokyo: Chikuma Shobô, 1963], p. 361).

14 Immanuel Kant, *Critique of Pure Reason*, trans. Norman Kemp Smith (New York: St. Martin's Press, 1929), p. 550.

15 Ibid., p. 552.

16 See note 14 above.

17 The Japanese original of this article was published as a chapter for the second vol-
ume of the series titled "Methods of Social Sciences" for a general readership in
Japan interested in the recent developments of social sciences, mainly in North
America, Europe, China, and Japan.

18 For more discussion on the emergence of the regime of bilateral international translation and the birth of Japanese language as a regulative idea, see Naoki Sakai, *Voices
of the Past: The Status of Language in Eighteenth-Century Japanese Discourse* (Ithaca, N.Y.:
Cornell University Press, 1991).

19 The motto is attributed to Fukuzawa Yukichi (1834–1901). In his *"Datsu-A ron"*
(1885), he argued that Japan had to flee the constraints of Asian societies and join
the Western powers.

20 For the term "subjective technology," see chapter 1, note 10.

21 For the term "narcissism of the West," see Robert Young, *White Mythologies: Writing
History and the West* (London and New York: Routledge, 1990).

22 Maruyama Masao, *Studies in the Intellectual History of Tokugawa Japan*, trans. Mikiso
Hane (Tokyo and Princeton, N.J.: University of Tokyo Press, 1974) (original in
1952), p. 323. The essays contained in this book were published separately between
1940 and 1944.

23 Ibid.

24 Ibid.

25 First, let me note that, since the late 1940s, Maruyama Masao has been known as
one of the most astute critics of the prewar Japanese emperor system for his analysis
of what he termed the Emperorist Fascism (*Ten'nô-sei fashizumu*) of Japan. Yet, Parts I
and II of *Studies in the Intellectual History of Tokugawa Japan* can be read as an elaborate
justification of the prewar Japanese emperor system. Second, as far as Maruyama's
argument in Parts I and II is concerned, the formation of the modern national subject does not theoretically require that the nation be based on the unitary unity of
an ethnos. In this respect, it is possible to read Part III as a later addition that testifies to the change in Maruyama's political stance from a political theorist of multiethnic nationalism to a liberal ideologue of monoethnic nationalism.

26 Ibid., p. 84.

27 Ibid., p. 89, emphasis in the original; translation slightly modified.

28 Ibid., p. 92.

29 The formula underlying Maruyama's interpretation of Ogyû Sorai's postulate of the
Sages might be clarified by reference to Tanabe's dialectic of the self and the other.
Tanabe argued: "The 'I' is the ego [*jiga*] but it is also a self-negating unity that simultaneously sublates both the 'you' as another ego (*taga*) and the self. Of course, the 'I'
is an individual I [*kobetstu-teki naru ware*], and unless it is individualized, the 'I' cannot
be universal. However, the individualized 'I' is also an ego. It follows that the ego is
an ego only in relation to another ego. Where there is no other ego, the ego cannot
be posited. By the way, in actuality the other ego is a 'you' who coexists outside and
in opposition to the ego. This external relation [between the ego and the other ego]
is nothing but the primordial meaning of space. The unity of the 'I' contains the
'non-I' [*higa*] as the negative principle, and through the 'non-I' the unity of the 'I' is
mediated by the split between the ego and the other ego. But this split is a moment
without which the 'I' can never be individualized. . . . Therefore, the 'I' is an ego, yet
is not merely an ego. To be an ego means to mediate another ego and sublate it at

the same time. Thus, because the 'I' is at the same time a particular and a universal, the 'I' is individualized" (Tanabe, "From the schema 'time' to the schema 'world,'" pp. 27–28). Tanabe's discussion owes much to Nishida Kitarô's work; see Nishida Kitarô, "Ware to nanji" ("I" and "you"), in Nishida Kitarô Zenshû, vol. 6 (Tokyo: Iwanami Shoten, 1965), pp. 341–427 (original in 1932). One important difference between Tanabe and Maruyama in their respective appropriations of Hegel: Tanabe followed Hegel in that, by sublating the other, the subject as "I" eventually becomes universal, whereas universality is primarily ascribed to the other in the case of Maruyama.

30 Maruyama, Studies in the Intellectual History of Tokugawa Japan, p. 95.

31 See Sakai, Voices of the Past, pp. 211–79.

32 Maruyama Masao: "Chûsei to hangyaku" (Loyalty and rebellion), in Chûsei to hangyaku (Tokyo: Chikuma Shobô, 1992), p. 77 (original in 1960).

33 Maruyama, Studies in the Intellectual History of Tokugawa Japan, p. 323.

34 Quoted by Maruyama, Chûsei to Hangyaku, p. 44.

35 Maruyama, Studies in the Intellectual History of Tokugawa Japan, p. 241.

36 Ibid., pp. 206–73.

37 Maruyama Masao, Thought and Behaviour in Modern Japanese Politics, ed. Ivan Morris (Oxford: Oxford University Press, 1969) (original in 1946–49).

38 Jean-Luc Nancy, The Experience of Freedom, trans. Bridget McDonald (Stanford, Calif.: Stanford University Press, 1993), p. 22; emphasis in the original.

39 Maruyama Masao, "Kindai nihon ni okeru kokka risei no mondai" (The problem of state-reason in modern Japan), in Chûsei to hangyaku, p. 205 (original in 1949); emphasis in the original.

40 Ibid., p. 204. I want to stress that Maruyama's argument centers around the subject matter of "schema."

CHAPTER 3: RETURN TO THE WEST/RETURN TO THE EAST: WATSUJI TETSURÔ'S ANTHROPOLOGY AND DISCUSSIONS OF AUTHENTICITY

1 This essay contains presentations delivered at two conferences in March 1990 at the State University of New York at Binghamton and at Cornell University. Some parts of it were also presented at the Association for Asian Studies annual meeting in April 1990, and finally at the symposium "Representation of the Other: Japan and the United States" held in May and June at the University of California Humanities Research Institute. Portions of this essay appeared under the same title in Boundary 2, vol. 18, no. 3 (fall 1991), special issue "Japan in the World" edited by Masao Miyoshi. The present essay is the original of "Return to the West / Return to the East: Watsuji Tetsurô's Anthropology and the Emperor System" ("Seiyô e no kaiki/Tôyô e no kaiki— Watsuji Tetsurô no ningengaku to ten'nôsei"), which was published in a Japanese translation in Shisô, no. 797 (Tokyo: Iwanami Shoten, November 1990). I would like to express my gratitude to the discussants of my papers, Professor Christopher Fynsk (at Binghamton) and Professor Dominick LaCapra (at Cornell), for their comments.

2 T. J. Clarke, "Olympia's Choice," in The Painting of Modern Life (Princeton, N.J.: Princeton University Press, 1984), pp. 74–146.

3 For a discussion of collective psychology and subjectivity, see Mikkel Borch-Jacobson, The Freudian Subject, trans. C. Porter (Stanford, Calif.: Stanford University Press, 1988), pp. 146–237. For the image of maternal emperor and the mechanism of sympathy,

see Kanô Mikiyo, "'Ômigokoro' to 'haha gokoro,' 'Yasukuni no haha' wo umida-sumono" ("The emperor's mercy" and "Mother's heart"—that which gives rise to "the mothers of the Yasukuni Shrine"), in *Josei to Ten'nôsei* (Women and the emperor system) (Tokyo: Shisô no Kagakusha, 1979).

4 See: Martin Heidegger, *Being and Time*, trans. J. Macquarrie and E. Robinson (New York: Harper and Row, 1962), Part I, chapter 29, pp. 172–79. Miki's argument, how-ever, seems to be based on a much earlier version of *Dasein* analysis than what we find in *Being and Time*.

5 *Rinrigaku* was published as part of the series *Tetsugaku Kôza* (Tokyo: Iwanami Shoten, 1931). Watsuji published *Rinrigaku* many times throughout his life, each time radi-cally modified from the previous version. I have not obtained all the original ver-sions of the *Ethics* yet. I have only the 1931 version of *Rinrigaku or Ethics* (I call this version A), the postwar reproduction of the 1934 version of *Ningen no gaku to shiteno rinrigaku or Ethics as the Study of the Human Being* (B), the postwar reproduction of the 1937 version of *Rinrigaku (jô) or Ethics (I)*(C), the postwar reproduction of the 1942 version of *Rinrigaku (chu) or Ethics (II)*(D), which contains the list of parts rewritten in the postwar publication, and the 1949 version of *Rinrigaku (ge) or Ethics (III)*(E).

6 *Rinrigaku* (A), p. 4. The quote is ascribed to the translation by Miki Kiyoshi of *The Ger-man Ideology* (Tokyo: Iwanami Shoten, 1930) (or *The German Ideology* [Moscow: Progress Publishers, 1964], p. 618). In this translation, Miki Kiyoshi explicitly identified the use of the term "subject" (*shutai*). In *Voices of the Past*, I have explained the variety of Japanese renderings of the term "subject" and their philosophical implications.

7 For the term "equipment," see Heidegger, *Being and Time*, p. 97.

8 See "The Community of Two People and Sexual Love" in section 2, chapter 3 of *Ethics (I) or Rinrigaku (jô)* ([C], pp. 336–82). Probably in this part, Watsuji is most "modern" and "liberal." After examining sociological and ethnographic publications (G. Simmel, E. Durkheim, B. Bauch, B. Malinowski, T. Hobhouse, J. K. Folsom, T. Toda, L. H. Morgan, etc.), he argues that the prevailing view of family in primi-tive societies by Social Darwinists such as Spencer and Morgan was based on the confusion of sexual relation and kinship, and that, in creating social relations, the sexual relation is the foundation of intimacy, and primary in relation to kinship. From this viewpoint, Watsuji claimed that, in spite of the diversity of familial forms at the level of kinship, the monogamous sexual relation was universal and that the primary definition of community had to be defined in terms of the sexual union of one man and one woman. The romantic view of marriage was internalized into Watsuji's ethics to this extent.

9 I tentatively render the term *jikaku* as "self-awareness." "Apperception," "self-consciousness," and "self-recognition" are also possible English equivalents since *jikaku* could be equated with the uses of equivalent terms by Kant, Fichte, Hegel, Bergson, Nishida Kitarô, and Heidegger. The Japanese compound *jikaku* itself, which was also a common word in colloquial conversation, was registered and has been discussed extensively as a philosophical term since the turn of the century. One aspect of *jikaku* that cannot be ignored is that it is concerned with the unity of the self but that its unity is primarily given as the unity of the will. This is most clearly manifest in Nishida Kitarô's works in the late 1910s and early 1920s in which he sought for the conception of apperception not in cognition but in the modality of possibility.

10 *Rinrigaku* (A), p. 7.

11 It goes without saying that the entire project of *The Study of the Human Being as Ethics* is overshadowed by Heidegger's *Kant and the Problem of Metaphysics*, although actual references to Heidegger's Kant book do not appear until the 1937 version of Watsuji's *Ethics*. However, already in 1932, Tanabe Hajime's essay *Zushiki "jikan" kara zushiki "sekai" e* (From the schema "time" to the schema "world" [in *Tetsugaku Kenkyū*, vol. 200, 1932]) attempted a radical critique and appropriation of Heidegger's Kant book in order to offer an idea of schematism based on the mutual negation and mediation of time and space.

12 See Watsuji's article "Jinkaku to Jinruisei," originally published in *Tetsugaku Kenkyū* from 1931 until 1932, and as a monograph in 1938. In this paper, I refer to the 1938 version, which was reproduced in *Watsuji Tetsurō Zenshū* (Tokyo: Iwanami Shoten, 1965), pp. 317–476.

13 Immanuel Kant, *Critique of Pure Reason*, trans. Norman Kemp Smith (1965), (New York: St. Martin's Press, 1929), pp. 331–32 (B404).

14 In fact, Watsuji simply borrowed this use of *mu* from Nishida Kitarō. But Nishida too formulated this term in his reading of Kant with regard to the problem of consciousness—in the context of the critique of consciousness and, in particular, of Husserlian phenomenology. However, in spite of the identity of the term *mu*, Nishida and Watsuji employ this philosopheme in very different contexts, and the essentializing or substantializing tendency of Watsuji is very obvious in this case too. As I will show, despite his etymological examination of the Chinese and Japanese words for "being," Watsuji's anthropology could never dislodge itself from the ontology of subjectivity or what Nishida called *ronri-teki shugoshugi* (logical subjectivism). For Nishida's use of it, see "Mu no jikaku-teki gentei" (The apperceptional determination of *mu*), in *Nishida Kitarō Zenshū*, vol. 6 (Tokyo: Iwanami Shoten, 1965).

15 Sakabe Megumi, *Perusona no shigaku* (Tokyo: Iwanami Shoten, 1989), pp. 121–46.

16 The issue of schematism here seems to be concerned with the question of spatiality as opposed to temporality, which was asked by many around that time. Undeniably, it was connected to Heidegger's Kant book. Together with Tanabe Hajime and others, Watsuji saw in Heidegger's discussion an unjustifiable privileging of temporality over spatiality—a privileging that Watsuji construed as symptomatic of Heidegger's "individualistic" tendency and the asocial character of his philosophy.

17 Kant, *Critique of Pure Reason*, p. 341 (A362).

18 Later, Watsuji also accused Heidegger of an "individualistic" tendency and of neglecting the "being-with." In view of Heidegger's notion of the "being-with," I find it very difficult to apprehend Watsuji's critique. Watsuji summarized the Heideggerian argument in terms of individualism. However, he failed to take into consideration the wide variety of positions the term "individualism" could connote, and neglected the fact that it was impossible to ascribe to Heidegger a naive form of individualism in which the self of an individual person was granted the status of an enduring substance. Already operating at this stage in his career is a facile culturalist/ civilizationist dichotomy of individualist West and collectivist East, because of which Watsuji would be adored as the symbolic thinker of the stereotypical Japanese particularism by the postwar Japan experts—particularly in the history of Japanese religions—in the United States. As I will show, it seems to me that this blindness prevented Watsuji from perceiving how akin, in its social and political consequences,

his anthropology was to the kind of individualism he detested and objected to so much.

19 *Rinrigaku* (A), p. 9.

20 Many Japanese terms are made up of Chinese compounds that can be disassembled into unit characters. However, the phonetic units associated with Chinese characters do not remain identical when the characters are pronounced independently or in combination with other characters. Furthermore, depending on the syntactical and semantic context in which a particular character is put, the same grapheme may correspond to different phonetic units. Semantically, the Chinese character may be taken to be univocal in Japanese uses. But phonetically it is, in principle, multivocal. The pronunciations in parentheses are other phonetic choices for the same characters.

21 Sakabe Megumi, *Watsuji Tetsurô* (Tokyo: Iwanami Shoten, 1986), particularly chapter 2, pp. 53–94. Sakabe also notes the undeniably humanistic tendency of Watsuji's philosophy, which seems to derive partly from his theoretical laxity: "Although Watsuji was under the influence of Nishida philosophy in the formative stage of his ethics, he narrowly delimited Nishida's 'plane of transcendental predicate' or the 'khoraic place of *mu*' as the 'human being.' And he heedlessly construed the field of the 'human being' according not to the mutually penetrating—connotative, analogical, chiasmic—logic of what is called the 'weak structure' in mathematics but to the extensive logic of the 'strong structure' in which totality is conceived of as the sum of mutually exclusive individuals" (p. 94). Sakabe suggests the direction in which the critique of Watsuji's anthropology is to be carried out: "Let me briefly talk about an ideal format for ethics or philosophy. A sort of systems theory (indicated by such terms as 'reduction' and 'constitution') that was adopted in *Ethics as the Study of the Human Being* and *Ethics* must be supplemented by historical destruction—or, one might say, 'deconstruction.' A circular narrative form, something like *Kidentai* [an ancient Chinese historiographic narrative format adopted in Ssu Ma-chien's *History*, for instance], which, unlike Hegel's 'system,' does not close up, suggests many possibilities" (p. 237).

22 Watsuji differentiated many communities that the same individual simultaneously belongs to, from the family, the neighborhood, through the nation, to the state. However, these communities are hierarchically organized with the state encompassing all the other smaller communities.

23 In Watsuji's work, there exist fragments that suggest the possibility of conceiving of social relations not in terms of intersubjectivity but as a series of deferrals. A case in point is his article "Men to Persona" (*Watsuji Tetsurô Zenshû*, vol. 17) on the mask and personality. In this article, he seems to escape from the substantialization of the person and understands the person as a mask without the original self behind it, that is, as a mask masking another mask. However, this comprehension of person and social relationality is incompatible with his conceptualization of *aidagara* in terms of intersubjectity in his anthropology of subjectivity.

24 *Rinrigaku* (A), pp. 91–92; *wake* (and *wakatte*) is to divide, to distinguish, and so on (*wakatte* from *wakaru* is to comprehend, to agree; *wake* and *wakaru* are supposed to share the same etymological root). I translate it as "to articulate" here.

25 *Rinrigaku* (A), pp. 84–90; also *Ningen no gaku to shiteno rinrigaku* (B), in *Watsuji Tetsurô Zenshû*, vol. 9, pp. 28–34.

26 The relation of the emperor to his subject was very frequently presented in terms of "one who looks after the baby" and the "baby who is looked after" in the regimen of

the national identification called *Isshi Dōjin*, which was promoted by the prewar Japanese state. It goes without saying that the "looking" or "seeing" constituted the central locus of the prewar emperor system as well.

27 It seems undeniable that the issue of individuality in Watsuji's *Ethics* was closely connected with the problematic of *tenkō* or conversion. Needless to say, the confession was the public format in which the *tenkō* of a political prisoner arrested under the Public Security Maintenance Law was announced.

28 Louis Althusser, "Ideology and the Ideological State Apparatuses," in *Lenin and Philosophy and Other Essays*, trans. Ben Brewster (New York: Monthly Review Press, 1971), p. 171.

29 Ibid., p. 173. This issue of subjectivity played an important role in Watsuji's postwar discussion of the emperor system. See *The Problems of Modernity and the Japanese Emperor System*, ed. Naoki Sakai and Tak Fujitani (forthcoming from M. E. Sharpe). Indeed, it does not directly follow that the subject criticized by Althusser is the essence of the emperor system; for Watsuji's anthropology poses itself primarily as the state ethics in which the subject is equated to the state, and the state can by no means be identified with the emperor system.

30 *Fūdo*, in *Watsuji Tetsurō Zenshū*, vol. 8, pp. 1–256 (English translation: *Climate and Culture*, trans. Geoffrey Bownas [Tokyo: Japanese Ministry of Education, 1961]). First published in a series of articles for the monthly *Shisō* (1928–34). Published as a monograph in 1935 by the Iwanami Shoten Publishers. This is perhaps the best example of Watsuji's attempt to "spatialize" Heideggerian hermeneutics. See chapter 4 in this volume for a discussion of this book.

31 Watsuji's understanding of internationalism goes as follows: "It is senseless to think of scientists as individuals disregarding their role for the nation." "Those who most militantly attack the national delimitation of scholarship are Jewish scholars. But, in their attack, they most vehemently express their own national limits. The particularity of the Jews, unlike any other nations, consists in their ability to leave their own land, and, therefore, exist *dispersed* among other national groups. In other words, the ethnic-national [*minzoku-teki*] being of the Jews lies in the fact of being among other national groups. In this respect, the Jews are not *exclusionist*; but, precisely because of this, they are especially *exclusionist*. What is referred to as the transnational cooperation of scholarship is synonymous with Jewish national cooperation" (originally in *Rinrigaku* (*chū*) (D), in *Watsuji Tetsurō Zenshū*, vol. 10, p. 557). (Here, *minzoku*, which I rendered "nation" or "ethnic-national" can also be race and the German *Volk* in some cases.) It goes without saying that Watsuji's comprehension of the Jews is not only naive but also a fairly straightforward manifestation of stereotyping, as is prominent in European and North American Christianity, which underlies cultural essentialism. This type of xenophobic fear can also be detected in Watsuji's description of the Asian, notably the Chinese, in his *Fūdo* (as I will examine in the next chapter) or *Climate and Culture*, pp. 119–33. Yet, it should be noted that this concept of *minzoku* serves as a cornerstone for Watsuji's idea of global scientific cooperation.

32 Perhaps the most sophisticated expression of the anxiety over the fate of Europe can be found in Paul Valéry, "The Crisis of the Mind," in *Collected Works of Paul Valéry*, vol. 10, trans. Denise Folliot and Jackson Matthews (New York: Pantheon Books, 1956), pp. 23–36.

33 On this account, to my knowledge and to this day, Jacques Derrida's Introduction to Husserl's *Origin of Geometry* remains the most penetrating critique of such a restorationist logic, of the "return to the West." However, it is also important to note that Derrida seems to have yielded to such a temptation to return in a recent publication, *Un autre cap* (Paris: Éditions de Minuit, 1991).

34 See Philippe Lacoue-Labarthe, *Typography*, trans. Christopher Fynsk (Cambridge: Harvard University Press, 1989); Mikkel Borch-Jacobson, *The Freudian Subject*, trans. Catherine Porter (Stanford, Calif.: Stanford University Press, 1988); and, as an essay that bridges these two books, Philippe Lacoue-Labarthe, "Le dernier philosophe: Œdipe comme figure," in *L'imitation des modernes* (Paris: Galilée, 1986). There are innumerable cases of the violent manifestation of disavowed mimetic identification— the most famous of which include the cases of Takamura Kôtarô (poet and sculptor), Miyoshi Tatsuji (poet and French literature specialist), and Hagiwara Sakutarô (poet)—in which the admirers of European culture turned into its detesters overnight. Although his transition came much more gradually, Watsuji should be classified in this group of admirers of European culture who had repressed their critique of various aspects of European society until the last moment. During the war, Watsuji devoted many pages to the description and denunciation of Western, particularly Anglo-American, racism, which cannot simply be dismissed even today. (See *Nihon no Shindô*, in *Watsuji Tetsurô Zenshû*, vol. 14, pp. 295–312, and *Amerika no kokuminsei*, in *Watsuji Tetsurô Zenshû*, vol. 17.) But his critique was enunciated with the understanding of his own situation, where there was absolutely no possibility of reaching the intended audience of his critique. Given these conditions, I can see little critical effect in Watsuji's critique of Western racism; in the absence of those to whom his critical words should be addressed, such a critique merely functions as a declaration of exclusionist loyalty to the community on the part of the author; it would amount to an act of communal self-indulgence. At the same time, we must take into consideration that, even prior to the war, there were scarcely means of communication whereby the critique of aspects of the Western societies, including their racism against the Asians and so on, could be conveyed to the very audience who ought to listen to such a critique. The existing international power structure, including the configuration of the international mass media, did not allow for a critical voice coming from the non-West to question the self-legitimating discourse in Western Europe in which the image of the West was constituted. The West constructed its identity primarily as a closure, and did not hesitate to use its political and military superiority in order to sustain that closure.

35 This explains Watsuji's generally positive attitude toward Durkheim in his *Ethics* (*I*) (*C*). This side of his *Ethics* will be emphasized—by Watsuji himself—in his postwar writings on the emperor system.

36 Takahashi Tetsuya, "Kaiki no hô to kyôdôtai," in *Gendai Shisô*, vols. 17–19 (Tokyo: Seito-sha, September 1989). Takahashi persuasively shows linkages between Watsuji and Heidegger, but he does not seem to pay enough attention, perhaps because of the limitation in length of the article, to internal errancy in Heidegger. See Christopher Fynsk, *Heidegger—Thought and Historicity* (Ithaca, N.Y.: Cornell University Press, 1986).

37 Originally in *Rinrigaku (chu)* (D), but in the postwar edition this part was rewritten. See Appendix, *Watsuji Tetsurô Zenshû*, vol. 11, p. 422. It is important to stress that

Watsuji's conception of negativity is devoid of temporality and, accordingly, differs significantly from Tanabe Hajime's or Heidegger's.

38 For the simultaneity of the historico-social, see: William Haver, "The Body of This Death: Alterity in Nishida-Philosophy and Post-Marxism," Ph.D. dissertation, University of Chicago, 1987.

39 See Jean-Luc Nancy, *The Inoperative Community*, trans. Peter Connor, Lisa Garbus, Michael Holland, and Simona Sawhney (Minneapolis: University of Minnesota Press, 1991).

40 This is exactly the case with the Japanese Romantics (*Nihon Roman-ha*), and particularly their postwar remnant, Mishima Yukio. For him, death was primarily this mechanism of insulation. It is no accident that the aggressive resoluteness to his own death and nostalgic yearning for integration into the aestheticized image of a "people" were united in his literary discourse. See Mishima Yukio, "Death in Midsummer," trans. Edward G. Seidensticker, in *Death in Midsummer and Other Stories* (New York: New Directions, 1966), pp. 1–29.

41 As to Watsuji's explanation of the state ethics, see *Watsuji Tetsurô Zenshû*, vol. 11, pp. 425–30, and *Benshôhô-teki shingaku to kokka no rinri* (Dialectic theology and the ethics of the state), Z–9, pp. 443–60.

42 With regard to cohistorizing and Being-with-Others, see Heidegger, *Being and Time*, pp. 436–38.

43 Jean-Luc Nancy argues: "If the *I* cannot say that it is dead, if the *I* disappears in effect in *its* death, in that death that is precisely what is most proper to it and most inalienably its own, it is because the *I* is something other than a subject. All of Heidegger's research into 'being-for (or toward)-death' was nothing other than an attempt to state this: *I* is not—*am* not—a subject. (Although, when it came to the question of community as such, the same Heidegger also went astray with his vision of a people and a destiny conceived at least in part as a subject" [Nancy, *The Inoperative Community*, p. 14]). I will discuss the problematic of death again in chapter 6.

44 Ibid., p. 12.

45 "This is why political or collective enterprises dominated by a will to absolute immanence have as their truth the truth of death. Immanence, communal fusion, contains no other logic than that of the suicide of the community that is governed by it. Thus the logic of Nazi Germany was not only that of the extermination of the other, of the subhuman deemed exterior to the communion of blood and soil, but also, effectively, the logic of sacrifice aimed at all those in the 'Aryan' community who did not satisfy the criteria of *pure* immanence, so much so that—it being obviously impossible to set a limit on such criteria—the suicide of the German nation itself might have represented a plausible extrapolation of the process" (ibid.) See also Philippe Lacoue-Labarthe, *Heidegger, Art and Politics*, trans. Chris Turner (Oxford: Basil Blackwell, 1990).

46 "Kokumin tôgô no shôchô," in *Watsuji Tetsurô Zenshû*, vol. 14, p. 339.

47 Ibid., p. 341.

48 Ibid.

49 Ibid., p. 340.

50 Ibid., p. 341.

51 Ibid., p. 367.

52 Ibid., pp. 345–46.

53 Philippe Lacoue-Labarthe says: "The essential organicity of the political is in reality infra-political, if not indeed infra-social (in the sense of *Gesellschaft*). It is the organicity of the community: the *Gemeinschaft*, or as Heidegger says in his commentary upon the *Republic*, the *Gemeinwesen*. Consequently, it is the organicity of the people, the *Volkstum*, which our concept of 'nation,' restored to the original meaning, renders reasonably well, in so far as it indicates a natural or 'physical' determination of the community which can only be accomplished and revealed to that community by a *technê*—if not indeed by *technê* itself, by art, beginning with language (with the community's language). If *technê* can be defined as the surplus of *physis*, through which *physis* 'deciphers' and presents itself—and if, therefore, *technê* can be said to be *apophantic* in the Aristotelo-Heideggerian sense of the term—political organicity is the surplus necessary for a nation to present and recognize itself. And such is the political function of art" (Lacoue-Labarthe, *Typography*, p. 69). Already in *Gendai nihon no shisô* (Contemporary Japanese thought) (Tokyo: Iwanami Shoten, 1956), Kuno Osamu and Tsurumi Shunsuke described the emperor system as follows: "In his *Civilization of the Renaissance in Italy*, the historian Burckhardt talked about the state as a work of art. The Meiji state that Itô [the first prime minister in the Meiji state] created with the Meiji emperor at its center is such a work of art. It is because the materials used by Ito and others to construct it dazzle us so much that we fail to see it as such: as an excellent work of art, it appears to be a natural product, and Itô worked hard to make it appear that way" (pp. 126–27). "However, the role of the emperor was not limited to that of the pope: the emperor was not merely the legate in this world of God, but also the son of God and the living God. The *ten'nô* was not merely the emperor/pope, but also had to play the role of Jesus, son of God, in the national religion" (p. 128). "Japanese polity was a system in which, inheriting absolute authority from the ancestors, the emperor ruled the consciousness of the nation as well as its behavior. In this sense, the emperor was the absolute Subject [*shutai*], and, from the emperor's point of view, the nation was an object. Equality among the Japanese nation was, at best, equality for an object. . . . The ingenuity of Ito consists in the fact that he attempted to recover subjectivity for the nation without changing these conditions" (pp. 128–29).

54 *Watsuji Tetsurô Zenshû*, vol. 10, p. 587, and vol. 14, p. 337.

55 See especially *Ethics (III) (E)*, *Watsuji Tetsurô Zenshû*, vol. 11, pp. 1–414.

56 *Ethics (II) (D)*, *Watsuji Tetsurô Zenshû*, vol. 11, pp. 421–22.

57 See "Nihonbunka no jûsôsei, Zoku nihonseishin-shi kenkyû" (The study of the history of Japanese spirit) (1935), in *Watsuji Tetsurô Zenshû*, vol. 4, pp. 273–551, especially pp. 314–21.

58 Watsuji grounds the concept of the national community (*kokumin kyôdôtai*) on the ethnos (*minzoku*) and the ethnos (*minzoku*) on the commonality of language. "What is the scope of the commonality of language? We call it *minzoku*. Throughout all of history, there is no ethnos-nation (*minzoku*) whose primary characteristics is not given the commonality of language: the only exception is the Jews. But, even for the Jews, what expresses their ethnic unity is the sacred text in Hebrew" (*Watsuji Tetsurô Zenshû*, vol. 11, p. 533). Watsuji does not distinguish the commonality of language from the unity of national language.

59 *Watsuji Tetsurô Zenshû*, vol. 14, pp. 340–41.

CHAPTER 4: SUBJECT AND/OR *SHUTAI* AND
THE INSCRIPTION OF CULTURAL DIFFERENCE

1 This chapter was originally a speech titled "The Analytic of Cultural Difference and
the Interior Called Japan," delivered at the conference "Theory and Asian Studies"
on May 17, 1992, at the Center for Asian and Pacific Studies, University of Oregon.
The translation of an early version of this paper was published in *Jôkyô*, vol. II–3,
no.10 (Tokyo: Jôkyô Shuppan-sha, 1992).

2 Pierre Bourdieu, *The Logic of Practice*, trans. Richard Nice (Stanford, Calif.: Stanford
University Press, 1990), p. 31. Bourdieu problematizes the distinction between
theory and practice: "Because theory—the word itself says so—is a spectacle, which
can only be understood from a viewpoint away from the stage on which the action
is played out, the distance lies perhaps not so much where it is usually looked for,
in the distance between cultural traditions, as in the gulf between two relations to
the world, one theoretical, the other practical" (p. 14). I propose to use the term
"theory" in a manner explicitly different from Bourdieu's.

3 See Tokieda Motoki, *Kokugogaku genron* (Tokyo: Iwanami Shoten, 1941).

4 See Homi K. Bhabha, "Postcolonial Authority and Postmodern Guilt," in *Cultural
Studies*, ed. Lawrence Grossberg, Cary Nelson, and Paula A. Treichler (New York:
Routledge, 1992), p. 59. For a remarkable elucidation concerning simultaneity as
distinct from synchronicity and repetition (*Hanpuku*) in the alterity of the other, see
William Haver, "The Body of This Death: Alterity in Nishida-Philosophy and Post-
Marxism," Ph.D. dissertation, University of Chicago, 1987.

5 Nishida Kitarô formulated the term *shutai* in his reading of Kant. In the early 1920s
he published a series of articles in which he elaborated on the issues of subjectivity
in judgment, self-awareness (*jikaku*), and will. Later, as his focus shifted from *the
subject who wills* to *the subject of action*, Nishida had to deal with the radical difference
between the epistemic subject (*shukan*) and the agent of practice (*shutai*). Whereas
shukan posits itself in relation to the object of its own representation and, therefore,
can be understood as the transcendental ego that accompanies every representation, *shutai* cannot be thought of as an entity because practice is essentially social.
Shutai exists only insofar as it is in exposition (exposed and opposed simultaneously)
to other *shutai*; that is, any relation between *shutais* cannot be reduced to that of the
ego and a representation in its consciousness. In other words, in social and practical
relations, one cannot encounter an other singular being or *kobutsu* as an object of
representation; one can encounter an other only in the otherness of the other. (See
Nishida Kitarô Zenshû, vol. 6 [Tokyo: Iwanami Shoten, 1965], pp. 341–427.) However,
it is important to stress that, in the final analysis, Nishida seems to have failed to differentiate *shutai* from "subject" mainly thanks to a religious tendency because of
which he could not resist the temptation of dissolving antagonism into holistic harmony, singularity into some totalizing universalism and speculative humanism. This
is why I propose a translation *shutai* in contradistinction to Nishida's or Watsuji's.

6 Jonathan Crary, *Techniques of the Observer* (Cambridge: MIT Press, 1990).

7 In Sung neo-Confucianism, "feeling" or *jô* (*qing* in Beijinghua), such as compassion,
shame, humility, and propriety, is defined as the externalization of "human nature" or
sei (*xing*) for "'Human nature' is the 'principle' or *li* of the 'mind' or *shin* (*xin*). 'Feeling' is
the movement of 'human nature.' The mind is that to which both 'human nature' and
'feeling' are subject." And "human nature," "feeling," and "mind" are further explained

as follows: "'Human nature' is anterior to movement. 'Feeling' is already in movement. 'Mind' is capable of encompassing both the being-already-in-movement and the being-anterior-to-movement." Thus "feeling" is determined as "that which moves." As long as the ontological priority of human nature or principle is guaranteed, "feeling" is an externalization or the expression of universally shared "human nature" so that "feeling" is from the outset an intersubjective occurrence. However, when the ontological priority of "human nature" and "principle" is denied (this happened in certain versions of Confucianism in the seventeenth and eighteenth centuries, notably in some articles by Itô Jinsai), the determination of "feeling" as the being-already-in-movement takes on a radically different significance. When "human nature" is understood to be a set of categories based on historically mutable social habits, "feeling" is stripped of its a priori communal immanence. Instead, as opposed to "human nature" as the synchronic systematicity of social habits and as categories of thought that warrant the intelligibility of "feeling" in terms of "human nature," "feeling" would be a "movement" that cannot be arrested within the synchronic spatiality of human nature. Then "feeling" must be inexplicable. But, as Itô Jinsai claimed, "feeling" should be thought precisely as "movement" that eludes the arrest of the static principle. In other words, "feeling" should be able to be thought in its inexplicability. Thus "feeling" is given as difference in the sense in which Deleuze discusses it. "Thought must think difference, that absolutely different from thought which nevertheless gives it thought, gives to be thought" (Gilles Deleuze, *Difference and Repetition*, trans. Paul Patton [New York: Columbia University Press, 1994], p. 227). "It is not surprising that, strictly speaking, difference should be 'inexplicable.' Difference is explicated, but in systems in which it tends to be cancelled; this means only that difference is essentially implicated, that its being is implication. For difference, to be explicated is to be cancelled or to dispel the inequality which constitutes it" (p. 228). It is in this question of implication that the notion of "feeling" shows itself to be affiliated with the problematic of the sensible. "[Plato means that] sensible qualities or relations are not in themselves separable from a contrariety, or even a contradiction, in the subject to which they are attributed. However, while the contrary-sensible or contrariety in the quality may constitute sensible being par excellence, they by no means constitute the being *of* the sensible. It is difference in intensity, not contrariety in quality, which constitutes the being 'of' the sensible. Qualitative contrariety is only the reflection of the intense, a reflection which betrays it by explicating it in extensity. It is intensity or difference in intensity which constitutes the peculiar limit of sensibility. As such, it has the paradoxical character of that limit: it is the imperceptible, that which cannot be sensed because it is always covered by a quality which alienates or contradicts it, always distributed within an extensity which inverts and cancels it. In another sense, it is that which can only be sensed or that which defines the transcendent exercise of sensibility, because it gives to be sensed, thereby awakening memory and forcing thought" (pp. 236–37).

As we saw in chapter 3, Watsuji's ethics assumes an ontological priority similar to that presumed in the neo-Confucian concept of human nature. Neo-Confucian human nature is an essence whose determination is given in terms of what Watsuji calls *aidagara* or the relationality of subjective positions. In his *Ethics*, Watsuji tried to eliminate "feeling" as the sensible and build his ethical philosophy entirely on the intersubjectivity of sympathy.

8 See Jean-Luc Nancy, "Literary Communism," in *The Inoperative Community*, trans. Peter Connor, Lisa Garbus, Michael Holland, and Simona Sawhney (Minneapolis: University of Minnesota Press, 1991): "If community is 'posited before production,' it is not in the form of a common being that would preexist works and would still have to be set to work in them, but as a being *in* common of the singular being. This means that the articulation from which community is formed and in which it is shared is not an organic articulation (although Marx can find no other way to describe it). This articulation is doubtless essential to singular beings: these latter are what they are to the extent that they are articulated upon one another, to the extent that they are spread out and shared along lines of force, of cleavage, of twisting, of chance, whose network makes up their being-in-common. This condition means, moreover, that these singular beings are ends for one another" (p. 75). Of course, translation is such an instance of articulation.

9 Ernesto Laclau and Chantal Mouffe, *Hegemony and Socialist Strategy* (London and New York: Verso, 1985). See also Jean-Luc Nancy's explanation of the term "articulation" in note 8.

10 Ibid., p. 94.

11 Ibid., p. 96; emphasis in the original.

12 Ibid., p. 111; emphasis in the original.

13 Ibid., p. 96; emphasis in the original.

14 Ibid., p. 113; emphasis in the original.

15 Ibid., p. 115.

16 Mary Louise Pratt, *Imperial Eyes—Travel Writing and Transculturation* (London and New York: Routledge, 1992). Pratt uses the term "contact zone" to refer to "the space of colonial encounters, the space in which peoples geographically and historically separated come into contact with each other and establish ongoing relations, usually involving conditions of coercion, radical inequality, and intractable conflict" (p. 6).

17 Bhabha, "Postcolonial Authority and Postmodern Guilt," p. 58.

18 Ibid., p. 59.

19 Gilles Deleuze, *Bergsonism*, trans. Hugh Tomlinson and Barbara Habberjam (New York: Zone Books, 1988), p. 38.

20 See Henri Bergson, *Time and Free Will*, trans. F. L. Pogson (London: George Allen and Company, 1913), pp. 75–139.

21 The following passage is suggestive in understanding why it is necessary to differentiate between *shutai* and subject-*shukan* in order to put forth the articulatory function of the enunciation of cultural difference, as distinct from the representation of cultural difference in cultural essentialism: "Freedom is the relation of the concrete self to the act which it performs. This relation is indefinable, just because we *are* free. For we can analyse a thing, but not a process; we can break up extensity, but not duration. Or, if we persist in analysing it, we unconsciously transform the process into a thing and duration into extensity. By the very fact of breaking up concrete time we set out its moments in homogeneous space; in place of the doing we put the already done; and, as we have begun by, so to speak, stereotyping the activity of the self, we see spontaneity settle down into inertia and freedom into necessity. Thus, any positive definition of freedom will ensure the victory of determinism. . . . every demand for explanation in regard to freedom comes back, without our suspecting it, to the following question: 'Can time be adequately represented by space?' To which we an-

swer: Yes, if you are dealing with time flown; No, if you speak of time flowing. Now, the free act takes place in time which is flowing and not in time which has already flown" (ibid., pp. 219–22).

22 According to Nishida, Bergsonian temporality excludes the social definition of *shutai*; for *shutai* acquires its own contradictory and caesural identity (*mujun-teki jikodôitsu*) in its essential opposition to other *shutai*, whereas Bergsonian temporality lacks such a social and spatial dimension. Nishida believed that Bergson did not take into account the social and expositional nature of *shutai*. See, for instance, "Keijijôgaku josetsu" (Introduction to metaphysics) (originally published in 1933), in *Nishida Kitarô Zenshû*, vol. 7 (Tokyo: Iwanami Shoten, 1965), pp. 5–84. In his stress on the importance of space, Nishida did not conceptualize the distinction between the iterative, interrogative space and the space of synchronicity, although on so many occasions his argument did center around these heterogeneous conceptions of space.

23 See Robert Young, *White Mythologies: Writing History and the West* (London and New York: Routledge, 1990).

24 Bourdieu, *The Logic of Practice*, p. 34.

25 Kang Sangjung, "Shôwa no shûen to gendai nihon no shinshô chiri = rekishi— kyokasho no naka no chôsen wo chûshin to shite," *Shisô* (December 1988).

26 Readers might notice that the term "homosociality" is used here in order to designate a field of critical investigation that is somewhat different from Eve Sedgwick's in her monumental book *Between Men* (New York: Columbia University Press, 1985). My emphasis is not so much on the construction of male bonding and sexual homogeneity through the homophobic disavowal of homoeroticism and the misogynist appropriation of women as on the construction of national, ethnic, and cultural homogeneity through the spectacularization of the outsiders. Yet, I do not want to neglect the fact that a certain gender differentiation is powerfully operating in the construction of national, ethnic, and cultural homogeneity. The identity of the West, for instance, cannot be critically understood unless we take into account gender politics, which is always copresent in the construction of the West.

27 This question was posed in the proposal for the "Theory and Asian Studies" conference at the University of Oregon. This chapter originated as a response to the question concerning universalism and particularism in theories and Asian Studies.

28 Homi K. Bhabha, "The Commitment to Theory," *New Formations*, no. 5 (summer 1988): 16.

29 Catherine Hall, "Missionary Stories," in *Cultural Studies*, pp. 240–76. Hall demonstrates one of the instances where complicity between universalism and racism is unequivocally manifest.

30 Deleuze, *Difference and Repetition*, pp. 140–41.

31 See Chandra Talpade Mohanty, "Under Western Eyes: Feminism Scholarship and Colonial Discourses," *Boundary* 2, 12–3/13–1. Cited by Young, *White Mythologies*, p. 162.

32 Watsuji Tetsurô, *Climate and Culture*, trans. Geoffrey Bownas (Tokyo: Japanese Ministry of Education, 1961), p. 25.

33 Ibid., p. 38.

34 Ibid.

35 Ernesto Laclau explains freedom and subjectivity in relation to dislocation as follows: "the subject is partially self-determined. However, as this self-determination is not the expression of what the subject already is but the result of its lack of being in-

stead, self-determination can only proceed through processes of identification. . . . Dislocation is the source of freedom. But this is not the freedom of a subject with a positive identity—in which case it would just be a structural locus; rather it is merely the freedom of a structural fault which can only construct an identity through acts of identification" ("New Reflections on the Revolution of Our Time," in *New Reflections on the Revolution of Our Time* [London and New York: Verso, 1990], p. 60).

36 See Watsuji Tetsurô, *Kokoku no tsuma e* (To my wife in my home country) (Tokyo: Kadokawa Shoten, 1965).

37 According to Furukawa Tetsushi's *kaisetsu* or afterword to *Watsuji Tetsurô Zenshû*, vol. 17 (Tokyo: Iwanami Shoten, 1963), p. 483: "Amerika no kokuminsei" was first published in the October issue of *Shisô*, 1937. (Recently, I had a chance to meet Yonetani Masafumi, who edited the addendum to *Watsuji Tetsurô Zenshû*. These additional volumes contain articles and manuscripts that were not included in the original *Zenshû*. Some of them, it seems, were intentionally withdrawn from the initial publication of *Zenshû*. Yonetani confirmed that Furukawa Tetsushi's account of "Amerika no kokuminsei" was a mistake and that it was written after the Pacific war broke out. Under the light of this new information, I had to reformulate my reading of it. It is even less plausible to attribute any critical intention to Watsuji's writing of this article than I had previously thought.)

38 *Watsuji Tetsurô Zenshû*, vol. 8 (Tokyo: Iwanami Shoten, 1962), p. 232; emphasis in the original.

39 "Amerika no kokuminsei," pp. 456–57.

40 Ibid., p. 464.

41 Ibid., p. 466; emphasis in the original.

42 Homi K. Bhabha, "DissemiNation," in *Nation and Narration*, ed. Homi K. Bhabha (London and New York: Routledge, 1990), p. 310.

43 In *Watsuji Tetsurô Zenshû*, vol. 4 (Tokyo: Iwanami Shoten, 1962). Originally published as a serial article in *Shisô*, in April, May, and June 1932.

44 Ibid.

45 Étienne Balibar, "Racism and Nationalism," in *Race, Nation, Class* (London and New York: Verso, 1991), p. 43.

46 *Watsuji Tetsurô Zenshû*, vol. 4, pp. 252–53.

47 Ibid., p. 255.

48 Preface to the 1944 edition of *Climate and Culture*, reproduced in *Watsuji Tetsurô Zenshû*, vol. 8, p. 3. Perhaps more interestingly, Watsuji also gave a reason why the chapter on China had to be rewritten: "Since I put down those observations, the Chinese situation has changed. Most conspicuous is the decline of the Chinese mercantile force in the South Sea. This has also served to alter the situation for military industries in Japan proper. Even if we take into account those rapid changes—the Manchurian incident, the Shanghai incident, the dispute between Japan and China at the League of Nations, the changing economic situation, the global acceptance of the Japanese currency, panics in China, and so on—for several years, I do not think my observations about the Chinese character were greatly misleading" (ibid., p. 256). Watsuji's fear of transnational capital is closely related to his stance with regard to economic policies. According to Yonetani Masafumi, since the 1920s Watsuji consistently advocated National Socialist economic policies. See Yonetani Masafumi, "Watsuji rinrigaku to jûgo nen sensôki

no nihon" (Watsuji's *Ethics* and Japan during the Fifteen-Year War), *Jôkyô* (September 1992).

49 *Watsuji Tetsurô Zenshû*, vol. 8, p. 125.

50 Maeda Ai, "Shanghai 1925," in *Toshikûkan no naka no bungaku* (Tokyo: Chikuma Shobô, 1982), pp. 365–401. For economic development and politics, see Sherman Cochran, *Big Business in China* (Cambridge: Harvard University Press, 1980), pp. 171–200; Nakamura Naosuke, *Kindai Nihon mengyô to chûgoku* (Tokyo: University of Tokyo Press, 1982); Peter Duus, "Zaikabô: Japanese Cotton Mills in China, 1895–1937," in *The Japanese Informal Empire in China, 1895–1937* (Princeton, N.J.: Princeton University Press, 1989), pp. 314–29; Banno Junji, "Japanese Industrialists and Merchants and the Anti-Japanese Boycotts in China, 1919–1928," in *The Japanese Informal Empire in China, 1895–1937*.

51 Maeda, "Shanghai 1925," p. 371.

52 Mao Dun, *Rainbow*, trans. Madeleine Zelin (Berkeley: University of California Press, 1992).The last two chapters of this unfinished novel are particularly concerned with the same historical developments and the transformation of characters' consciousness brought about by those developments as is Yokomitsu's *Shanghai*. These two authors approached the turbulent encounter of the Chinese and the Japanese in Shanghai almost simultaneously from opposite sides.

53 Maeda, "Shanghai 1925," p. 394.

54 *Watsuji Tetsurô Zenshû*, vol. 8, p. 127.

55 Ibid.; emphasis in the original.

56 It is misleading to characterize Shanghai simply as a city under colonial control. For a historical development of Chinese participation in the city's administrative structure, see Tonoki Kei'ichi, *Shanghai* (Tokyo: Iwanami Shoten, 1942). It is important to note that, when Watsuji was in Shanghai in February 1927, many parks in the city were still off-limits to the local population. According to Tonoki, it was on June 1, 1928, one year and four months later, that all the public parks were open (pp. 134–35).

57 Ibid., p. 128.

58 In this respect, the most perceptive and powerful reading of Yokomitsu's *Shanghai* can be found in Kamei Hideo, *Shintai, kono fushiginaru mono* (Tokyo: Renga Shobô Shinsha, 1984), pp. 122–46.

59 This documentary film recorded Japanese military actions in Shanghai and was produced by Toho Company, and edited by Kamei Fumio. As part of the war effort, the film was made in collaboration with the Japanese army and navy ministries to document the Japanese victory in Shanghai. It is important to note, however, that the rules according to which the observing gaze was directed were frequently disrupted. For instance, certain shots were organized not from the perspective of the position of what the Japanese military would have liked, but, for instance, from the perspective of the Chinese refugees. Thus the specific mode of separation between the seer and the seen, without which the subjectivity of the observer could not be constructed, were constantly reversed and called into question. For an insightful discussion of the viewing and the construction of the enemy and "home" at war, see Morio Watanabe, "Image Projection at War: Construction and Deconstruction of the DOMUS through Films on World War II in the U.S. and Japan," Ph.D. dissertation, University of Wisconsin–Madison, 1992.

60 On this issue I learned a lot about the relationship between Yokomitsu Riichi and

Kobayashi Hideo from conversations with Maeda Ai in 1981. I would like belatedly to express my gratitude to him.

61 James Baldwin, *The Fire Next Time* (New York: Dial Press, 1963), p. 10.

62 *Watsuji Tetsurō Zenshū*, vol. 8, p. 255. Yet it is important to emphasize that the parallelism involving the Greeks and the Jews or the Greeks and the Romans had already been used so many times in writings about Asia that, in this respect, Watsuji was not innovative at all.

63 See, for example, *Ethics [II] (Rinrigaku [chū])*, in *Watsuji Tetsurō Zenshū*, vol. 11 (Tokyo: Iwanami Shoten, 1962), pp. 421–42.

64 *Watsuji Tetsurō Zenshū*, vol. 8, pp. 55–56.

65 Slavoj Zizek, *The Sublime Object of Ideology* (London and New York: Verso, 1989), p. 48.

66 Ibid., p. 125.

67 *Rinrigaku (jō)*, in *Watsuji Tetsurō Zenshū*, vol. 10, p. 128.

68 Zizek, *The Sublime Object of Ideology*, p. 127.

69 Ibid.

70 Ibid.

71 Ibid., pp. 127–28.

72 Ibid., p. 176.

73 Karel von Wolferen, *The Enigma of Japanese Power* (New York: Vintage Books, 1990).

74 Watsuji's *shutai* therefore maintains the empirico-transcendental structure of subjectivity despite his claim that it is essentially ethical, not epistemological. And he asserts that the practical agent is understood as the transcendental subject (= the whole) being immanent in the empirical subject (= the part) of an individual person. From this conception of the practical subject (*shutai*), Watsuji concludes that the subject of praxis is the whole, that is, the state immanent in an individual. In the case of Watsuji's *shutai*, it is no doubt appropriate to translate it as "the practical subject." See chapter 3 for more on this subject.

75 Crary, *Techniques of the Observer*.

76 John Stuart Mill, "Coleridge," in *Utilitarianism and Other Essays*, ed. Alan Ryan (London and New York: Penguin Books, 1987), pp. 195–96.

77 On the relationship between sympathy or compassion and modern emperor system, see chapter 3.

78 Bourdieu, *The Logic of Practice*, p. 31.

79 Pratt, *Imperial Eyes*, especially pp. 111–97.

80 *Japan 2000*, ed. Andrew J. Dougherty. Prepared by the Rochester Institute of Technology, February 1991.

CHAPTER 5: MODERNITY AND ITS CRITIQUE:
THE PROBLEM OF UNIVERSALISM AND PARTICULARISM

1 This chapter was originally delivered as a paper at the conference "Problems of Postmodernity" organized by J. Victor Koschmann and Naoki Sakai at Boston Sheraton Inn on April 12 and 13, 1987. Its Japanese translation apeared in the special issue "Nihon no posuto modan" of *Gendai Shisō*, vol. 15–15 (1987): 184–207. An English version was included in the "Postmodernism and Japan" issue of the *South Atlantic Quarterly*, ed. Masao Miyoshi and Harry D. Harootunian, vol. 87, no. 3 (summer 1988): 475–504.

2 Jürgen Habermas, *The Theory of Communicative Action*, vol. 1, trans. Thomas McCarthy (Boston: MIT Press, 1984), p. 44.

3 Ibid.

4 See Richard Rorty, "Habermas and Lyotard on Postmodernity," in *Habermas and Modernity*, ed. Richard J. Bernstein (Cambridge: MIT Press, 1985), p. 167.

5 David Pollack, *The Fracture of Meaning* (Princeton, N.J.: Princeton University Press, 1986), p. 4.

6 Ibid.

7 One could assert three points: the unity of language is very much like the Kantian "regulative idea" that makes the empirical study of language possible; the unity of language, therefore, is never given in "experience"; and, consequently, the idea of the universal essence of language would never be obtained through the induction of the accumulated empirical data on the increasing number of particular languages.

8 It is in the eighteenth century that the unities of Japanese culture, language, and ethnicity as they are conceived of today were brought into existence. In this sense, the Japanese were born in the eighteenth century.

9 Pollack, *The Fracture of Meaning*, p. 4.

10 Ibid., p. 16.

11 Ibid., pp. 3–4.

12 Ibid., p. 227.

13 Ibid.

14 Kôyama Iwao, "*Sekaishi no rinen*" (The idea of world history), *Shisô* (April–May 1940).

15 Kosaka Masaaki, *Rekishi-teki sekai* (Historical world) (1938), in *Kôsaka Masaaki chosakushu* (Complete works of Kôsaka Masaaki), vol. 1 (Tokyo: Risô-sha, 1964), pp. 176–217.

16 Kôsaka Masaaki, Suzuki Shigetaka, Kôyama Iwao, and Nishitani Keiji, "*Sekaishiteki tachiba to Nihon*" (The standpoint of world history and Japan), *Chûô Kôron* (January 1942).

17 Ibid., p. 185.

18 Kôsaka, *Rekishi-teki sekai*, p. 192.

19 Kôsaka Masaaki, Suzuki Shigetaka, Kôyama Iwao, and Nishitani Keiji, "*Tôakyôeiken no rinrisei to rekishisei*" (Ethics and historicality of the Greater East Asian Coprosperity Sphere), *Chûô Kôron* (April 1942).

20 Ibid., pp. 120–21.

21 Ibid., p. 129.

22 Takeuchi Yoshimi, "*Kindai towa nanika*" (What is modernity?) (1948), in *Takeuchi Yoshimi Zenshû* (Complete works of Takeuchi Yoshimi), vol. 4 (Tokyo: Chikuma Publishers, 1980), p. 130.

23 Ibid., p. 131.

24 Ibid.; emphasis added.

25 Ibid., p. 144.

26 Ibid., pp. 155–57.

27 See Jacques Derrida, *DissemiNation*, trans. Barbara Johnson (Chicago: University of Chicago Press, 1981), pp. 61–171.

28 Lu Xun, "My Old Home," in *Selected Stories of Lu Xun*, trans. Yang Hsien-ji and Gladya Yang (Peking: Foreign Languages Press, 1972), pp. 63–64.

CHAPTER 6: DEATH AND POETIC LANGUAGE IN POSTWAR JAPAN

1 This chapter was originally delivered at the International Symposium on Postwar Japan at Rikkyo University in Tokyo on December 17, 1985. Its Japanese translation by Ono Shûichi appeared in *Sengo Nihon no Seishinshi* (Spiritual history of postwar Japan), ed. Kamishima Jirô, Testuo Najita, and Maeda Ai (Tokyo: Iwanami Shoten, 1988), pp. 310–34.

2 See Emmanuel Levinas, *Totality and Infinity*, trans. Alphonso Lingis (The Hague: Mertinus Nijhoff, 1979).

3 For the elucidation of the relationship between the universalized "I" and the system of collective representations, see Jacques Lacan, *Le Séminaire 2: Le moi dans la théorie de Freud et dans la technique de la psychanalyse* (Paris: Éditions du Seuil, 1978), pp. 39–53, among other works of Lacan.

4 Yoshimoto Takaaki, "Shikiha no Honshitsu," in *Yoshimoto Takaaki Zenchosakushû*, vol. 5 (Tokyo: Keiso Shobo, 1970), pp. 119–35.

5 Awazu Norio, *Gendaishi Shi* (History of contemporary poetry) (Tokyo: Shicho-sha, 1972).

6 See Kasai Kiyoshi, *Teroru no Genshô-gaku* (Phenomenology of terror) (Tokyo: Sakuhin-sha, 1984), pp. 135–95.

7 Ayukawa Nobuo, *Ayukawa Nobuo Shishû* (Tokyo: Shicho-sha, 1968), p. 10.

8 Nakagiri Masao, *Nakagiri Masao Shishû 1945–1964* (Tokyo: Shicho-sha, 1964), p. 158.

9 Tamura Ryûichi, *Tamura Ryuichi Shishû* (Tokyo: Shicho-sha, 1968), p. 18.

10 Ehara Tsurao, *Shi no Bunmei Hihyôteki Seikakû* (Tokyo: Shicho-sha, 1966), p. 149.

11 Nakagiri, *Nakagiri Masao Shishû 1945–1964*.

12 Tamura Ryûichi, *Tamura Ryûichi Shishû 1 Yonsen no hi to yoru* (Tokyo: Shicho-sha, 1966), pp. 71–73.

13 The entire work is as follows:

> kimi wa itsumo hitori da
> namida o miseta koto no nai kimi no hitomi niwa
> nigai hikari no yô na mono ga atte
> boku wa suki de
>
> kimi no mômoku no imeji niwa
> kono yo wa kôryô to shita ryooba de ari
> kimi wa hitotsu no kokoro o taezu oitsumeru
> fuyu no hantaa da
>
> kimi wa kotoba o shinjinai
> arayuru kokoro o satsuriku shite kita kimi no
> ashiato niwa
> kyôfu e no fukai akogare ga atte
> boku wa tamaranaku naru
>
> kimi ga aruku hosoi sen niwa
> yuki no ue nimo chi no nioi ga tsuite ite
> donna na ni tôku e hanarete shimmatte mo
> boku niwa wakaru

kimi wa gekitetsu o hiku!
boku wa kotoba no naka de shinu

You are always alone. / Your eyes never show tears. / They have a bitter glim-
mer. / I like that. / To your blind vision, / the world is a barren hunting ground,
and / you a winter's hunter / forever stalking one heart. / You do not believe in
words. / In your footprints that murdered every heart / I read a thirst for fear. /
That is too much for me. / On the narrow line you walk along / a blood smell
hovers even in the snow. / However far apart you may be, / I can sense it. / You
pull the trigger! / I die in language. Translated by Takako *Shishu 1 Yonsen no hi to*
yoru

14 Tamura, *Tamura Ryûichi Shishû 1 Yonsen no hi to yoru*.
15 See Tamura Ryûichi, Seibu-en Shokan, in *Tamura Ryûichi Shishû 2 Kotoba no nai sekai*,
    pp. 32–35, in which the poet says:

> shi wa hyôgen o kaerunara ningen no tamashii nazuke gatai
> busshitsu hippai no rekishi nanoda
> ikanaru jôken
> ikanaru toki to baai to iedomo
> shi wa shudan towa naranu
> kimi machigaeruna

Poetry is, to use different expressions, man's soul, an unnamable material, a history of unavoidable defeats. / Under no condition, / at no time, or on no occasion / can poetry be a means. / Do not misunderstand it.

16 Emmanuel Levinas said, "History would not be the privileged plane where Being
    disengaged from the particularism of point of view (with which reflection would
    still be affected) is manifested. If it claims to integrate myself and the other within
    an impersonal spirit, this alleged integration is cruelty and injustice, that is, ignores
    the Other. History as a relationship between men ignores a position of the I before
    the other in which the other remains transcendent with respect to me. Though of
    myself I am not exterior to history, I do find in the Other a point that is absolute
    with regard to history—not by amalgamating with the Other, but in speaking with
    him. History is worked over by the ruptures of history, in which a judgement is
    borne upon it. When man truly approaches the Other he is uprooted from history"
    (*Totality and Infinity*, p. 52).

Index

Bodin, Jean, 150
body of enunciation, 30, 120, 150, 199n22. *See also shutai*
Borch-Jacobson, Mikkel, 205n3, 210n34
Bourdieu, Pierre, 118–19
bun, 28
bungaku, 22, 24, 38
Burckhardt, Jacob, 212n53

Caesar, Gaius Julius, 111
calligraphy, 10
Cha, Theresa Hak Kyung, 25, 28–31, 35–39
Chang, Briankle, 196n15
chiasm, 96
Chow, Rey, 202n9
civilizationism, 207n18
Clarke, T. J., 205n2
Cochran, Sherman, 218n50
cofiguration, 16, 20, 22, 24, 27, 34–35, 39, 52, 148
colonialism, 69, 149, 152
communion, 6, 10, 89, 101, 113–14, 116, 211n45
communism, 122
community
  ethnic, 43–44, 140, 201n5
  homogenized, 75
  national, 64, 98–100, 111–12, 115, 135, 140, 143, 147, 152, 212n58
  natural, 166, 173
  nonaggregate, 4, 7, 9, 14
confession, 92, 209n27
configuration of languages, 33–35, 38–39
consciousness, national, 65
conscription, universal, 98–99
continuity, historical, 179
Constitution, 103, 105, 115
corporatism, 143, 152
corporeality, 30, 36–37, 202n11
countertranslation, 7–8, 47
Crary, Jonathan, 121, 146
culturalism, 17, 63, 77, 79, 93, 95, 115, 143–44, 148, 207n18
culture, 79, 90, 108–12, 119, 129–30, 153–54
  ethnic, 10, 15, 17
  Indian, 130

Japanese, 42, 112, 147, 159–61
  national, 10, 15, 19, 63–64, 110, 143, 151

Dasein, 76, 83, 94
dead, the, 184–90, 192
death, 94–95, 98, 100–101, 115, 180–81, 185, 187, 189–91
decisionism, 65
defeat of Japanese Empire, 170, 178–82, 189–90
Deleuze, Gilles, 18, 128, 196nn18, 19; 213n7
Derrida, Jacques, 158, 161, 194n3, 195n10, 196n15, 210n33
desistance, 37–38
désœuvrement, 200n27. *See also* unwork
dialectic, 92
diaphora, 14–15
diaspora, 140, 148
difference, 196n18
  cultural, 119–25, 128–29, 136, 140, 143, 145, 148–49
  articulation of, 125–26, 138
  description of, 141
  enunciation of, 124, 215n21
  in repetition, 15
  without concept, 196n19
discipline, 40
discontinuity, 13–14
  continuity in, 13
  historical, 179, 183, 189
discourse (Benveniste's), 13
  (Foucault's), 13
  instance of, 53
  on Japanese uniqueness, 110, 150, 129, 163. *See also nihonjin-ron*
dislocation, 131, 216n35
durée, 123
Durkheim, Émile, 103, 206n8, 210n35
Duus, Peter, 218n50

East, 62, 79, 90–91, 95, 134, 140, 149, 207n18
economy, restricted, 75
Ehara, Tsurao, 184
Eight Corners of the World under One Roof. *See hakkô ichiu*

Eliot, Thomas Stearns, 91
emperor, 74, 88, 103, 105–7, 109–10, 112–15
  system, 72, 75–76, 102, 106–7, 115, 140,
    204n25, 208n26, 209n29, 210n35,
    212n53
Emperorist Fascism, 204n25
empire, 111
  Japanese, 65, 114
  loss of, 108, 114
emptiness. *See sunyata*
empirico-transcendental, 81, 83, 120,
  202n11
enemy people, 201n35
enunciation, 45, 47, 124, 180
  translational, 11, 54
Erigena, Don Scotus, 49
essentialism, cultural, 77, 79, 110,
  126–27, 151, 160–62, 207n31
ethics, 77–78
ethnicity, 50, 52
ethnocentricity, 30, 61, 118, 124, 156
ethnos. *See kokumin; minzoku*
  Japanese, 44
Eurocentrism, 50, 118, 126, 132, 158,
  172
Europeanization, 157, 164, 172
excription, 6–7, 194n6, 195n7
existentia, 87. *See also aru; Sein*
exposition, 97, 145, 148, 152, 213n5
exteriority, 7, 178, 190–91

Fanon, Franz, 123
feeling, 14, 121, 149, 196n18, 213n7
femininity, 73
Feuerbach, Ludwig, 78
Fichte, Johann Gottlieb, 150, 206n9
figure, 33–34
Folson, J. K., 206n8
Forster, Leonard, 20
Foucault, Michel, 40, 51, 74–75
framing, 11, 29–30, 195n12, 199n30
fraternity, national, 133, 135
Fukuzawa, Yukichi, 67, 204n19
Fynsk, Christopher, 210n36

Gemeinschaft, 60, 212n53
Gemeinwesen, 212n53

general will, 104–10, 114. *See also volonté
  générale*
"genre." *See* genus
genus, 14, 16
German Ideology, The, 78–79
Gesellschaft, 60, 212n53
good. *See yoshi*
Greater East Asian Coprosperity Sphere,
  168, 170
Greek, 140, 144
Guattari, Félix, 18

Habermas, Jürgen, 49, 155–56
Hagiwara, Sakutarô, 210n32
hakkô ichiu, 111
Hall, Catherine, 128
Hartmann, Nicolai, 96
Haver, William, 211n38, 213n4
Hegel, Georg Wilhelm Friedrich, 46, 55,
  90, 100, 132, 150, 164, 167, 174, 192,
  204n29, 206n9, 208n21
Heidegger, Martin, 54, 76–86, 90–100,
  199n24, 202n11, 207nn11, 16, 18;
  209n30, 210n37, 211nn42, 43; 212n53
Heracleitus, 49
Herder, Johann Gottfried von, 150
hermeneutics, 41, 76, 129, 209n30
Hippocrates, 150
Hirohito, Emperor, 72. *See also* Shôwa
  emperor
historical being, 76
historicality, 95, 100, 192
history. *See also* World History
  Japanese, 40, 45
  Japanese intellectual, 48
  monistic, 164–67, 169, 171–72
  national, 98, 156, 165
  of Japanese thought, 41, 44, 48–49, 52,
    60–68, 71
Hobhouse, T., 206n8
homosociality, 55, 127, 143, 145,
  147–48, 152, 216n26
human being, 76–78, 81, 83–84, 86, 87,
  96, 98, 113, 129, 142, 208n18. *See also*
  being-between; *ningen*
humanism, 78, 90, 93, 169, 174
Husserl, Edmund, 91, 207n14

hybridity, 61, 66–67, 71, 119, 139
hypokeimenon, 197n4

ichioku gyokusai (total suicidal death of one
hundred million), 101–2
idea, 50, 56, 62, 68
regulative, 56–60, 204n18, 219n7
ideal, 70
ideology, 23, 89, 90
illocution, 28
imitation, 68
imperialism, 18, 38, 133–35, 149, 152
Anglo-American, 19, 132–34
English-language, 19
Japanese, 37, 114
incommensurability, 10, 13–14, 54
indeterminacy, 93, 97
individualism, 88, 92–93, 97, 100, 113
individuum, 13, 98, 113
Inoue, Tetsujirô, 48
inscription, 5–6
interior called Japan, 145, 148
internationalism, 207n31
invention, 65, 67
Isshi Dôjin ("one who looks after the
baby"), 208n26
Itô, Hirofumi, 212n53
Itô, Jinsai, 214n7

Jakobson, Roman, 10, 16
Japanese way of reading Chinese. *See
wakun*
Jew, 111, 140–41, 143, 151, 209n31,
212n58
jikaku, 195n14, 206n9, 213n5. *See also* self-
awareness
sonzai, 80, 82
sonzai-ron, 80, 82

Kafka, Franz, 56
Kaji, Nobuyuki, 41
Kamei, Fumio, 139
Kamei, Hideo, 218n58
Kaneko, Mitsuharu, 136
Kang, Sangjung, 126
Kanô, Mikiyo, 205n3
kansatu-teki tachiba, 118

Kant, Immanuel, 32, 54, 56, 58, 81–83,
93, 95, 105, 150, 178, 199n24, 202n11,
203n12, 206n9, 213n5
Kasai, Kiyoshi, 221n6
khoraic place, 21, 197n4, 208n21. *See also
basho*
kitai, 64, 166, 202n11. *See also* substratum
Kiyô no gaku (Learning of Nagasaki Translators), 66
Kjellén, Rudolf, 150
Kobayashi, Hideo, 218n60
kobunji gaku (Learning of Ancient Text and
Words), 66
kobutsu, (singular being or individual
thing), 168, 213n5
kokumin, 45, 60–61, 109, 167. *See also* nation; *Volk*
Kôsaka, Masaaki, 163, 166–69
Kôyama, Iwao, 163–67, 169, 171
Kuki, Shûzô, 76
Kuno, Osamu, 212n53
Kyoto School of Philosophy, 163, 196n14

Lacan, Jacques, 88, 121, 141, 143, 179
Laclau, Ernesto, 115, 122, 131, 216n35
Lacoue-Labarthe, Philippe, 200n29,
210n34, 211n45, 212n53
language
ethnic, 15
foreign, 59
Japanese, 41, 160
national, 15–16, 19–20, 38, 151, 159,
212n58
Leibniz, Gottfried Wilhelm, 49
Levinas, Emmanuel, 97, 179, 222n16
literacy, 20
literature, 22–23, 25, 38, 109, 180. *See also
bungaku*
comparative, 22
Japanese, 40, 45
national, 41, 98
locution, 27
Logic of Species, 65
loyalty, 103
Lu, Xun, 175–76
Lukács, Georg, 76
Lyotard, Jean-François, 121

MacArthur, Douglas, 106
Maeda, Ai, 137, 218n60
Malinowski, Bronislaw, 206n8
Manet, Édouard, 73
Mao, Dun, 137, 148
Maruyama, Masao, 64–70, 201n5,
  204n29
Marx, Karl, 77–78, 84, 150, 215n8
Marxism, 76
mask, 208n23
materialism, 79
metalepsis, 47–48, 67
Miki, Kiyoshi, 76, 206nn4, 6
Mill, John Stuart, 117, 147
mimicry, 36
mimesis, 92
minzoku, 60–61, 91, 93, 110–11, 140,
  166–67, 209n31. *See also* nation; *Volk*
  kokka-teki (national folk), 167
Mishima, Yukio, 211n40
Miyoshi, Tatsuji, 180, 210n34
modality, enunciative, 51
modernity, 50, 60, 150, 153–56, 158,
  163–64, 167, 169, 170–74, 176
modernization, 167, 170, 172, 174
modernization theory, 156–57
Mohanty, Chandra Talpade, 216n31
Montesquieu, 150
morality, 167–68
Morgan, L. H., 206n8
mother tongue, 20–21, 28–31, 37–38
Mouffe, Chantal, 122
mu (nothingness), 82–83, 105, 141,
  207n14, 208n21
  mu-teki fuhen (*mu* universal), 166
multilingualism, 20–21, 23, 61, 66

Nakagiri, Masao, 185, 221n8
Nakai, Masakazu, 76
Nakamura, Naosuke, 218n50
Nancy, Jean-Luc, 5, 100–101, 122, 142,
  148, 194n6, 200n27, 211nn39, 43
nation, 16, 43–44, 60–61, 64–65, 67–68,
  74–75, 91, 93, 100–113, 129, 136, 145,
  151, 153, 164, 167–70, 173, 181–83,
  192, 212n53. *See also kokumin; minzoku*
Japanese, 44, 160

national character, 31, 93, 117, 129,
  131–35, 143, 148
  American, 131–33, 135
  Chinese, 135–36, 142, 144
  Indian, 130–31, 144
  Japanese, 77, 144, 150
  Korean, 31
national expression, 109
national religion, 212n53
national socialism, 217n48
nationalism, 17, 43–44, 69, 91, 156, 163
  American, 157
  cultural, 65, 72, 110, 114, 196n14
  ethnic, 91, 196n16
  monoethnic, 204n25
  multiethnic, 91, 108, 115, 204n25
nationality, 26, 50, 52, 77, 91
nation-state, 38, 69, 71, 92, 94, 129, 140,
  142, 166, 181
Nazism, 68, 140
negativity, 93, 102, 174, 189, 202n11,
  203n13, 210n37
Neo-Confucianism, 69
nihon bunka no jûsôsei (multilayered nature
  of Japanese culture), 112
nihonjin-ron, 110, 112, 115, 129, 144, 163.
  See also discourse on Japanese uniqueness
ningen, 76, 78, 82, 84–85, 142. *See also*
  being-between; human being
Nishi, Amane, 48
Nishida, Kitarô, 195n14, 196n16, 197n4,
  198n10, 204n29, 206n9, 207n14,
  208n21, 213n5, 216n22
Nishitani, Keiji, 76, 219n19
non-West, 48–49, 128, 130, 147–48, 150,
  154–55, 158, 163–64, 171, 174. *See also*
  East; Orient

objectivism, 131
observation, 123–24, 129–31, 136, 138
observational stance. *See kansatsu-teki
  tachiba*
observer, 118, 135, 139, 142, 146
Ogyû, Sorai, 23, 28, 65–67, 69, 71,
  204n29
Okada, John, 200n28
ontico-ontological, 81, 120

organic solidarity, 103
organic totality, 144
organicity, 144, 212n53
Orient, 172–73
other
    narcissistic, self-consolidating, 129,
        134
    otherness of the, 71, 97, 191

Palestinians, 140
particularism, 19–20, 114, 127, 149,
    155–58, 163, 165, 169, 170, 192,
    207n18
    Japanese, 115, 160–61
passion, 72, 105
passivity, 73, 105
patriotism, 190
performative, 45
perlocution, 27–28
person, 13, 65, 67–69, 81, 85, 88, 92, 94,
    138, 208n23
personality
    indeterminacy of, 8, 13, 14
    oscillation of, 8, 13, 14
    transcendental, 81–83, 208n23
phatic acts, 27
phenomenology, 207n14
phonocentrism, 2, 20
Plato, 21, 45
Poe, Edgar Allan, 194n3
poetry
    postwar, 177–85, 189, 190, 192
    wartime, 181, 187, 190
poiesis, 13, 39, 56, 68, 120, 147, 195n14,
    198n10
Poincaré, Henri, 49
Pollack, David, 158–63
position, subjective, 47, 85, 113, 183
positionality, enunciative, 45, 46–47, 67,
    118, 120, 128, 156, 182–83, 187
postmodern, 153, 156, 158, 163, 166
Pound, Ezra, 91
Pratt, Mary Louise, 123, 147
praxis, 78, 198n10
    philosophy of, 78
predicativism, 197n4

premodern, 153–56, 174
pronoun, 53, 186, 188, 190

Quine, Willard V. O., 196n17

race, 93, 153, 164, 166, 209n31
racism, 111–12, 131, 134–35, 151–52,
    163, 210n34
Rancière, Jacques, 7, 193n2
rationalization, 158
reduction
    phenomenological, 97
    transcendental, 57
relation
    epistemic, 118–19, 124, 126, 145–46,
        149
    practical, 119, 121–27, 130–31, 136,
        138, 140–41, 145–46, 149–50, 213n5
relationality of subjective positions,
    84–89, 93–97, 100, 113, 138,
    142, 146, 208n23, 213n7. See also
    aidagara
relationality, practical, 79, 97, 137
repetition, 5, 14
    originary, 121
resistance, 172, 174–76
resoluteness, 83, 95, 100–101, 115
responsibility, 104
restoration, 90–91
return, 88–91, 93–94, 96, 98, 100–101,
    124. See also Rückkehr
    to the East, 91
    to the West, 91, 124, 210n33
rewording, 10. See also translation, intra-
    lingual
rhetic acts, 27
Romantics, Japanese, 211n40
Rorty, Richard, 220n4
Rückkehr, 90. See also return

sacrifice, 211n45
Said, Edward, 172
Sakabe, Megumi, 85, 207n15, 208n21
Sakai, Naoki, 193n1, 195nn11, 12;
    198n6, 199n22, 204n18, 205n31
Sartre, Jean-Paul, 49, 119

Scheler, Max, 88
schema, 19, 21–22, 32, 54, 56, 58, 60, 69, 71, 199n24
    arborescent schemata of the species and the genus, 14, 203n13
schematism, 15, 21, 83, 199n24, 202n11, 203n12, 207nn11, 16
    international, 1
    in translation, 11
    of cofiguration, 3, 15–17, 37, 49, 51–52, 54, 58–68, 144
schema-world, 32, 199n24, 202n11, 204n29, 207n11
Schmitt, Carl, 99
Searle, John R., 29–30
Sedgwick, Eve Kosofsky, 216n26
Sein, 86
self-awareness, 43, 206n9, 213n5. *See also jikaku*
    Japanese national, 50
    ontology of, 80. *See also jikaku sonzai-ron*
self-determination, 167
self-pity, 75
sentimentality, 75, 109, 114, 190
Shiki group, 180
Shôtoku, Prince, 46
Shôwa emperor, 75. *See also* Hirohito
shu no ronri, 202n11. *See also Logic of Species; species*, logic of
shukan, 24, 80–83, 119–22, 124, 128, 138, 142, 145–46, 148, 150, 198n25. *See also* subject, epistemic
shutai, 24, 30, 78–81, 83–86, 90, 96, 98, 105, 119–20, 122, 124, 128, 134, 142, 145–46, 148, 150, 167, 198n10, 199n22, 201n5, 206n6, 212n53, 213n5, 216n22. *See also* subject, practical
shutai-teki (subjective), 24, 78, 81, 86
shutai-teki gijutsu, 24–25. *See also* technology, subjective
Simmel, George, 206n8
simultaneity, 211n38, 213n4
singularity, 71, 149, 213n5, 215n8
sinophobia, 141, 143
Snead, James, 18
sonzai, 86

space, 90, 204n29, 209n30
species, 16
    logic of, 202n11. *See also Logic of Species; shu no ronri*
speech acts, 27, 29
Spencer, Herbert, 206n8
spirit, 43, 90, 112
state, 166–67
    as a work of art, 212n53
stillbirth of Japanese, 2–3, 15
subject, 1, 11, 12, 21, 24, 73, 79–80, 85, 88, 90, 97–98, 119–20, 135, 142, 166–67, 170, 173–74, 179–81, 184–85, 190, 201n5, 211n43, 213n5, 216n35
    as a nation, 68, 147
    epistemic (*shukan*), 119, 120, 124, 128, 138, 148, 213n5
    ethnic, 14–15
    in transit, 11, 13, 36
    of the emperor (*shinmin*), 103, 119
    of the enunciated, 12–13, 180, 188–89, 191
    of enunciation, 12–13, 121, 180, 188–89, 191
    of translation, 11
    practical, 78, 85, 122, 124, 195n14
    propositional (*shugo*), 51, 113, 198n4
    thematic (*shudai*), 1, 80, 119
    transcendental, 81–84
subjectivity
    modern, 68, 175, 189
    national, 14–15, 17, 44, 126, 167, 201n5
subjectivism, 197n4, 207n14
substratum, 29–30, 64, 166, 198n10, 201n5, 202n11. *See also kitai*
sunyata, 88, 92
surplus in the social, 96, 98
Suzuki, Akira, 23–24, 38
Suzuki, Shigetaka, 219n19
symbol of national unity, 103–4
sympathy, 74–75, 113–14, 147, 184–85, 190, 213n7
    society of, 146–47
syncronicity, 57, 119, 121, 124, 128, 131, 145, 149, 150, 213n4, 216n22

systematic unity, 56–57, 59
systematicity, 57, 85–87, 94, 97
  syncronic, 191, 213n7

Takahashi, Tetsuya, 93
Takamura, Kôtarô, 210n34
Takeuchi, Yoshimi, 170–76
Tamura, Ryûichi, 183, 186–90
Tanabe, Hajime, 64–65, 76, 196n16,
  199n24, 201n5, 202n11, 203n13,
  204n29, 207nn11, 16; 210n37
technê, 67, 212n53
technology, subjective, 24–25, 35, 37, 63,
  68, 147. *See also shutai-teki gijutsu*
tegen-teki sekaishi, 35, 166–69, 197n2. *See
  also* world history, pluralistic
testamentary executor, 182, 184, 189
theory, 117–20, 124–25, 127–28, 148,
  162
thing-in-itself, 178
thought
  Japanese, 40–43, 45–46, 50–52, 60,
    62–64
  Oriental, 62
  Western, 49–50, 60–62
Toda, T., 206n8
Tokieda, Motoki, 118
Tonoki, Kei'ichi, 218n56
Tosaka, Jun, 44
totality, 66, 87–93, 96–98, 101–4, 106,
  110–13, 115, 122, 138, 142, 158, 162,
  169, 191
  national, 76, 112
transculutration, 147
translation, 1–3, 5, 7–8, 10, 26, 52–54,
  58, 119
  interlingual, 3, 10, 16
  intersemiotic, 10
  intralingual, 10, 16
  regime of, 2, 16–17, 22, 51–52, 54, 58,
    61, 66, 71
  representation of, 2, 6–7, 9, 14–16,
    54–55
  work of, 14
translator
  oscillation or indeterminacy of posi-
    tionality of, 14, 66

place for, 8
position of, 8–11, 13, 52, 66
transmutation, 10
trust, 97
Tsuda, Sôkichi, 50, 202nn8, 10
Tsurumi, Shunsuke, 212n53

ultranationalism, 68
unconscious, the, 94
universalism, 20, 69, 93, 127, 149,
  155–58, 163, 165, 169
  American, 115
  colonialist, 71
  missionary-style, 69
  theological, 68–69
unrepresentability, 54
untranslatability, 5, 54
unwork, 36, 38, 200n27. *See also désœuvrement*

Valéry, Paul, 91, 209n32
virtue, 24
Volk, 209n31. *See also Minzoku;* nation
volonté générale, 104. *See also* general will

wake, wakatte (to articulate), 86, 97,
  208n24
wakun (Japanese way of reading Chinese),
  66
war, total, 99
"Waste Land, The." *See* "Arechi"
Watanabe, Morio, 218n59
Watsuji, Tetsurô, 43–44, 50, 63, 75–106,
  109–15, 129–52, 201n5, 206n8,
  207n16, 209nn27, 29; 213nn5, 7;
  216n26
Way of the Sages, 65–67
Weber, Max, 156
wen, 28
West, 48–52, 61, 63, 66, 68–71, 77, 79,
  90–91, 95, 124, 127–28, 131, 134,
  139–40, 144–51, 154–57, 162–63,
  169–74
  narcissism of the, 63, 70–71, 126–29
Westernization, 164
Wittgenstein, Ludwig, 53
Wolferen, Karel van, 144

work, 25, 28, 36
  aesthetic, 75
world history, 101, 132, 164–68, 170
  philosophy of, 19, 164, 166, 168, 170
  pluralistic, 35, 166–69, 197n2

Yokomitsu, Riichi, 136–37, 139, 218nn52, 60
Yonetani, Masafumi, 217n48

yoshi (good), 89, 102
Yoshimoto, Takaaki, 180
Young, Robert, 70, 126, 204n20
yû (or *u*) (being), 82
yû-teki fuhen (or *u-teki fuhen*) (ontological universals), 166

Zizek, Salvoj, 140–41, 143

NAOKI SAKAI was born and lived in Japan until he finished a B.A. in European philosophy at Tokyo University. After college Dr. Sakai worked in Europe and Japan for about ten years. He gave up a business career in 1979, joined the University of Chicago for graduate study, and received an M.A. in 1980 and a Ph.D. in 1983. His dissertation was published as *Voices of the Past: The Status of Language in Eighteenth-Century Japanese Discourse* by Cornell University Press. He is associate professor of Japanese literature and history at Cornell University. Dr. Sakai has written for intellectual and academic journals in both English and Japanese, and is on the editorial board for *Hihyo Kukan* (*Critical Space*) and *Positions East Asia Culture Critique*.

MEAGHAN MORRIS is Australian Research Council Senior Fellow in the Faculty of Humanities and Social Sciences at the University of Technology, Sydney. Her books include *The Pirate's Fiancée: Feminism, Reading, Postmodernism, Ecstasy and Economics*, and *Australian Cultural Studies: A Reader*, coedited with John Frow.